HOW TO CAMP IN THE WOODS

HOW TO CAMP IN THE WOODS

A Complete Guide to Finding, Outfitting, and Enjoying Your Adventure in the Great Outdoors

DEVON FREDERICKSEN

BLACK DOG
& LEVENTHAL
PUBLISHERS
NEW YORK

Black Dog & Leventhal Publishers
Hachette Book Group
1290 Avenue of the Americas
New York, NY 10104

www.hachettebookgroup.com
www.blackdogandleventhal.com

First Edition: May 2019

Produced by Girl Friday Productions

Black Dog & Leventhal Publishers is an imprint of Hachette Books, a division of Hachette Book Group. The Black Dog & Leventhal Publishers name and logo are trademarks of Hachette Book Group, Inc.

The publisher is not responsible for websites (or their content) that are not owned by the publisher.

The Hachette Speakers Bureau provides a wide range of authors for speaking events. To find out more, go to www.HachetteSpeakersBureau.com or call (866) 376-6591.

Illustrations by Peter Pearsall
Interior design by Paul Barrett

Information about relieving a choking person (page 277) and performing CPR (page 281) courtesy of American Red Cross. All rights reserved in all countries; Constellation information on pages 211–217 courtesy of Astronomy Magazine/Kalmbach Media; Recipes on pages 166, 176, 180, 186 courtesy of Fresh Off the Grid.

Library of Congress Control Number: 2018961629

ISBNs: 978-0-316-42081-5 (paper over board); 978-0-316-42080-8 (ebook)
Printed in the United States

LSC-W
10 9 8 7 6 5 4 3 2 1

INTRODUCTION

Chapter 1 GEAR GUIDE

Chapter 2 TRIP PLANNING AND PREPARATION

Chapter 3 FINDING AND SETTING UP CAMP

Chapter 4 CAMPING BASICS

Chapter 5 CAMP COOKING

Chapter 6 CAMP ACTIVITIES

Chapter 7 **CAMPING ETIQUETTE**

Chapter 8   CAMPING WITH KIDS

Chapter 9   CAMPING WITH PETS

Chapter 10 CAMP SAFETY

Chapter 11 RETURNING HOME

Thousands of tired, nerve-shaken, over-civilized people are beginning to find out that going to the mountains is going home; that wildness is a necessity . . .

—John Muir, *Our National Parks*, 1901

There are no words that can tell the hidden spirit of the wilderness, that can reveal its mystery, its melancholy and its charm.

—Theodore Roosevelt, 1910

Introduction

CAMPING FOR RECREATION IS NOTHING NEW, having become a popular pastime as early as the 1860s. As a way to experience the outdoors, camping has continued to grow and evolve over the past 100-plus years. In the United States, shortly after the first guide to recreational camping was published in 1908, the Boy Scouts and Girl Scouts organizations were founded. Around that same time, vacations to explore national parks soared in popularity. In an increasingly industrialized society, the scouting programs and national parks offered paths for children and their parents to reconnect to the natural world—and they still do today.

In 1856, Henry Hopkins Sibley, an officer in the US Army, patented his canvas bell-style conical tent modeled after the traditional tepee structure used by native Plains and Great Plains peoples. Eventually, the functional design allowed campers to quickly set up and take down temporary outdoor shelters—a convenience that made camping more appealing and accessible. During the Great Depression, camping got a boost when the Civilian Conservation Corps (CCC) was developed as part of President Roosevelt's New Deal program. The goal of the CCC was to lower the unemployment rate by hiring laborers to work on conservation and natural resource projects. One of the by-products of this program was the creation of more than 800 state parks, which made the outdoors more accessible to many.

After World War II, as a result of increased wealth and leisure time, a surge of campers flocked to wilderness areas across North

America, embracing time-tested nomadic traditions and designs that certain Native American tribes had been employing for thousands of years. Summer camps gained popularity, teaching games and rituals adopted from various North American tribes. In the 1960s and '70s, the cultural shift toward conservation and environmental protection sparked a growing interest in outdoor recreation. Now, with the advent of social media and instant photo sharing—a phenomenon that allows thousands of people to learn the exact GPS coordinates of a picturesque campsite—the popularity of camping has reached an all-time high. With this growing trend comes an ever-increasing urgency to link camping with environmental stewardship.

As people camp in the wilderness in greater numbers, fragile natural areas can suffer the consequences—a threat that necessitates extra care be taken to limit the environmental impact of camping. The Leave No Trace Seven Principles outlined in this book are not just codes of conduct for proper camping etiquette—they are rules that should be closely followed to preserve our wild spaces for generations to come.

Advancements in manufacturing have made camping more approachable for many. However, it can still seem out of reach for more marginalized groups in society, where cultural norms or the amount of leisure time or money can be limiting factors. Steps have been taken in the outdoor gear industry and the national parks system to help groups that are typically underrepresented in the outdoors world feel more welcome, but there is still a long way to go. One of the goals of this book is to present information about camping in a way that makes it more accessible to everyone. Camping doesn't require investing in the most expensive gear or learning hard-core wilderness survival skills. It simply requires a bit of know-how, enough gear to stay safe in the elements, and the right temperament to revel in the joys that camping can inspire.

How to Camp in the Woods is a comprehensive guide to enjoying the great outdoors, covering trip planning, gear selection, basic skills, etiquette, cooking tips, activities, and safety protocols. If you are new to camping, you will find all the information needed to confidently plan and execute a safe and enjoyable trip. If you are an experienced camper, you will learn new tips and tricks to make your forays more streamlined, enjoyable, and sustainable.

WHY CAMP?

For some, camping is about exploration or testing the human limits of endurance. For others, it's about leisure and quality time spent with family and friends. The common thread behind the myriad reasons for camping is usually the desire to connect with nature. Away from population-dense city centers, a starlit night sky is no longer obscured by light pollution. The stars shine with more definition, and in the most remote places on a clear night you can observe the sparkling expanse of the Milky Way. A chorus of birdsong accompanies each sunrise. Water filtered from a cold stream is the most refreshing reward at the end of a day spent in the wilderness, and when you're camping, food simply tastes better. As the sun sets, frogs begin to croak in chorus, marking the time to gather around a campfire and share stories. When the moon is full, it casts so much light across the landscape that you can see your shadow. This time spent in nature can realign your sense of self. Even an overnight camping trip can feel restorative.

Camping in the traditional sense means finding the right balance between comforts and basic human needs for shelter, food, and water in the wilderness. However, it doesn't need to feel like roughing it. Precautions can be taken and gear can be packed that will limit your exposure to uncomfortable or harmful situations. However, traditional camping isn't typically luxurious. Luxuries like electronics, lavish living quarters, or modern amenities such as refrigeration, air-conditioning, or central heating aren't considered part of the classic camping experience, so they won't be covered in this book.

A number of situations have the potential to reduce your enjoyment of the great outdoors. A swarm of mosquitoes can convince even the most seasoned camper to retreat into the confines of a tent. Relentless rain can dampen high spirits. A poorly insulated jacket or sleeping bag, an unstable tent flapping in the wind, or a stiff sleeping pad positioned over a tree root can make sleep impossible. Yet with the right tools and know-how detailed in this book, you can take measures to minimize discomfort by packing and preparing for all possible variables. When you're wearing the appropriate layers, and your tent is holding steady in the wind, and you're cozy inside a warm sleeping bag and lying on a comfortable sleeping pad, you can then relax and listen to the breeze rustling through the trees.

Once any discomfort or safety issues have been addressed, the joy of engaging with nature can commence. There are many ways to interact with and enjoy the outdoors while camping. Many people relish the relief from the distractions and stress of work, technology, and household chores. Some look forward to the social aspect of gathering around a campfire and singing songs. Children delight in the opportunity to roast marshmallows and explore all the wonders of a forest. Intrepid campers like to test their outdoor skills and endurance by carrying minimal gear along a trail for days on end. Regardless of your motivation, the experience of spending time in the outdoors creates memories that bond people to each other and to the natural world in ways that can last a lifetime.

FRONTCOUNTRY VS. BACKCOUNTRY CAMPING

Just as there are many ways to appreciate the outdoors, there are many ways to camp. The choices range from amenity-packed recreational vehicle (RV) camping to an ultralight ramble with just a tarp and some cord to rig a makeshift shelter. The more luxurious the camping setup you require, the more money you'll spend on gear and the less time you'll spend in direct contact with nature's elements. Choose the style of camping best suited to your disposition, budget, and fitness level.

FRONTCOUNTRY

Defined as the style of camping where you can drive right up to the campground or campsite, frontcountry camping lends itself to packing a lot more gear than you would for backcountry camping. Frontcountry camping includes RVing, glamping, car camping, van camping, and walk-in camping. When frontcountry camping, the size of your vehicle determines the amount of gear you can pack. Many frontcountry campgrounds include wheelchair-accessible paths and toilet facilities, running water, food-storage boxes, fire rings, picnic tables, and sometimes even showers.

Car camping

Car camping is most commonly used as an umbrella term for frontcountry camping. But in its truest form, car camping refers to parking right next to your campsite. This makes unloading gear incredibly convenient. Some car-camping campgrounds provide outhouses or composting toilets, while others are outfitted with amenities such as restrooms, a campground store, and sometimes even a swimming pool.

RV camping

Camper vans and RVs are permitted only in select campgrounds, so you should check ahead to make sure you can camp at your destination in a motor home. RV camping is appealing to people who want the comfort of certain amenities to make it easier to sleep, cook, and use the bathroom, while also enjoying easy access to the outdoors. Some RV-friendly campgrounds provide hookups for electricity, and sometimes even a dump station for disposing of human waste from RV toilets. It's possible to park RVs in some campgrounds that don't offer hookups. This is called *dry camping*, when no electricity, water, or sewer connections are supplied. RVs and camper vans are also well suited for roadside camping on long road trips in areas where campgrounds are few and far between.

Glamping

A term used to describe a luxurious camping style, glamping can be very high-end and almost resort-like, depending on the destination. Certain home-rental and camping reservation websites now advertise yurts, platform cabin tents, and bare-bones structures that come with amenities that make the camping experience feel downright deluxe, while still allowing for easy access to scenic areas. This type of camping is not covered in this book, but it's easy to find online.

Walk-in camping

Many campgrounds include both car-camping and walk-in campsites. While you can park your car right next to car-camping sites, walk-in sites require you to park in a designated parking area and then haul your gear on foot to a campsite located away from the car. Some campgrounds provide wagons to help transport gear. Although walk-in sites require some extra work to unload the car and set up camp, they are often much quieter and farther removed from other campers. This is a good option when you want the ease of car camping but choose to avoid the potential downsides of nearby neighbors.

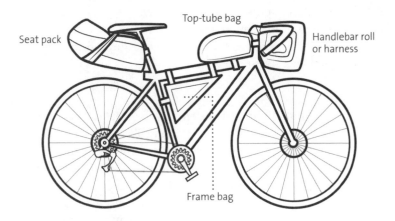

Seat pack

Top-tube bag

Handlebar roll or harness

Frame bag

Bike touring and bikepacking

Bike touring is similar to backpacking but instead of traveling on foot, you travel on a touring bike to get to each new destination. Panniers are typically used for carrying gear, as they securely attach to racks on the front and back of a bike. Some panniers are waterproof so gear doesn't get soaked in wet weather. Bikepacking is different from bike touring in that a mountain bike is used to travel on trails and rougher terrain. The trick to bike touring and bikepacking is to pack as light as possible. The amount of gear that you would pack on a bike is about equal to the amount you would carry while backpacking. A bike that isn't loaded down with a lot of heavy gear is also much easier to ride uphill and for long distances.

Van camping

It's becoming increasingly popular to outfit a van with a built-in bed and sometimes even a kitchen unit. Van camping provides a comfortable place to sleep, even on the side of the road, and

Roof-rack tent

protection from the elements. Vans also usually get better gas mileage than RVs or camper vans, so they are a more affordable option when extra amenities are your style.

In the past few years, manufacturers have begun making tents designed to sit on a rigid platform secured to the top of a vehicle roof rack. These rooftop tents come in a variety of styles and sizes. Some have vestibules and ladders and can accommodate a queen-size inflatable mattress. With a roof tent, you gain elevated sleeping space. Some roof-rack tents are made to fasten to the top of sedans. A similar type of tent can be set up in the bed of a truck.

BACKCOUNTRY

Backcountry camping encompasses the kinds of trips that require carrying gear into the wilderness via human-powered modes of transportation, such as backpacking, kayaking, mountain biking, canoeing, snowshoeing, or skiing. Backcountry camping often requires being much more weight- and space-conscious than frontcountry camping, because all gear must be hauled by you and packed into the limited confines of backpacks, dry bags, or panniers. Still, certain kinds of backcountry camping allow for a surprising amount of gear. For example, more gear can be packed into a canoe than, say, a backpack or kayak, but a canoe can hold only so much. If you overload a canoe, you risk gear falling overboard or weighing the canoe down so much that it becomes difficult to maneuver.

If you choose to pursue backcountry camping, be sure to read the rules and regulations that apply to the specific place where you plan to camp to learn about food-storage protocols, fire restrictions, and any safety updates.

Backpacking

Backpacking involves hiking on foot from a trailhead to a wilderness camping area. It requires owning a backpack fitted to your size and height and a selection of specialized gear and clothing.

The rule of thumb is that the pack, when loaded, shouldn't weigh more than 20 percent of your body weight. So a 150-pound person should aim to carry a backpack no heavier than 30 pounds. A loaded backpack can be weighed at home by standing on a scale without the backpack and recording your weight, then stepping back onto the scale while wearing the backpack and subtracting the difference to determine the backpack's stand-alone weight.

Some backpackers prefer to hike to a backcountry campsite destination and then stay at that site for a few days, day hiking from the home base. Others choose to backpack to a new campsite each day, which requires packing up the tent on travel days and setting it up again at each new destination.

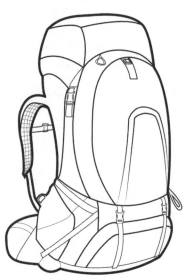

Backpacking backpack

Minimalist camping

Considered to be one of the original minimalist campers, naturalist and author John Muir would carry little more than bread, sugar, a tin cup, and a couple of blankets on some of his expeditions. Today, minimalist camping is less extreme. Also referred to as *ultralight* backpacking, minimalist camping requires investing in featherlight gear, which is often more expensive. There are ultralight options for all sorts of gear, including stoves, backpacks, sleeping bags, sleeping pads, cooking utensils, and clothing. The goal of the minimalist camper is to strip down the number of items packed to only the bare essentials, with each item weighing as little as possible.

Thru-hiking

A term coined to refer to extended backpacking trips along one of the three longest trails in the US, *thru-hiking* requires an incredible amount of planning, preparation, and endurance. Thru-hikers typically backpack along the Pacific Crest Trail, Appalachian Trail, or Continental Divide Trail, which range in length from 2,100 to 3,100 miles and usually take several months and many resupply stops to complete. Many thru-hikers opt to pack ultralight gear given the sheer number of miles that must be traveled daily.

Winter camping

Some forms of winter camping require snowshoeing or skiing to your destination with a pack on your back. Rustic basic huts or cabins are sometimes located at the end point for these trips into the backcountry, which allows winter campers to leave their tents behind. Some people backpack in the winter or late fall, when snow blankets the ground. For this type of camping, a four-season tent is the optimal choice and an extra-warm sleeping bag and clothing are absolute essentials. Depending on the destination, taking an avalanche safety course may be necessary.

Camping with pack animals

Certain backcountry trails permit bringing pack animals with you. This means you can either bring your own pack animal or pay for a pack animal as part of a backcountry trip with a tour company that offers this service. Typically, the animals will carry your gear while you hike. Depending on the pack animal service, you can sometimes even ride the pack animal into the backcountry instead of hiking. This is a good option for people who still want to enjoy the backcountry but who aren't physically capable of traveling the whole way while also carrying gear.

Water touring

Kayaks, canoes, and inflatable rafts allow you to pack more gear than you would think, and the speed and mobility of a watercraft can help you travel to remote backwater campsites located on ocean islands or along the shorelines of rivers and lakes. Various sizes of dry bags or tightly tied garbage bags are used to keep your gear dry.

Certain models of kayaks are built for sea kayaking versus lake or river kayaking. Similarly, certain models of canoes are better suited for camping trips and weigh less for easier portaging. Various types of rafts are used for camping trips along rivers. Framed rafts offer good stability for going over rapids without the risk of gear falling out. Lightweight pack rafts can be folded to fit into a backpack. This allows more mobility and the freedom to hike to a river put-in where there is no road access.

WHERE TO CAMP

Camping destinations abound if you know where to find them. The trick is determining where you are allowed to camp safely and legally. The other requirement is to strictly follow the Leave No Trace Seven Principles wherever you stop, especially in locations without designated campsites. To limit the traffic to fragile ecosystems, it's always best practice to camp in designated campgrounds and campsites whenever possible.

NATIONAL PARKS

The US and its territories are home to more than 400 National Park Service sites, which are areas of scenic, historical, or scientific value that have been set aside for protection and outdoor recreation. Yellowstone National Park was established in 1872, after Congress signed an act designating it as a protected public park. This then set a precedent worldwide for preserving important scenic areas for generations to come. The National Park Service, created in 1916 by President Woodrow Wilson, was given authority to manage and conserve these preserved areas. It was also given the responsibility of limiting human impact on these natural and historic spaces, while allowing people enough freedom to recreate.

The 84 million acres set aside as national parks feature dramatic landscapes, unique geology, and seemingly endless opportunities for exploration. Consequently, some of the more popular camping destinations are national parks. They feature established campgrounds and campsites that are available for car camping, RV camping, and van camping, as well as designated campsites in the backcountry areas that are ideal for backpacking and getting away from the bustle. To reduce the human impact on fragile ecosystems, some of the most popular hiking trails enforce a reservation lottery system that limits the number of people camping along the trails each night. However, national parks reserve a small percentage of permits for walk-ins, either the day of or before your planned trip. Just be sure to get to the park office early to get in line. Whether you're frontcountry or backcountry camping, check in advance of your trip to find out whether a campsite can be reserved.

> The National Park Service website has a "Find a Campground" page (www.nps.gov/subjects/camping/campground.htm), where you can type in your destination location and find the national park campgrounds in that specific area.

FREE CAMPING

Free camping is also referred to as bandit camping, dispersed camping, boondocking, or wild camping. The essential idea is to locate a camping spot in an area where no fee is required to stay there. In some countries you can camp on privately owned property. Investigate applicable laws and ask for permission before pitching a tent. It's inadvisable to camp right next to a main road or walking path. Instead, find a location hidden from view and near a water source, if possible. If you see any litter from previous visitors, pack it out.

You can sometimes purchase a book or find online sites that provide information about free campsites in your specific destination area. Free camping is a somewhat controversial form of camping because it creates the potential for irresponsible campers to damage wild areas. The benefit of paying an overnight camping fee is that the money helps pay for upkeep and maintenance of the campground and its facilities. These fees are especially important for government-managed park and forest systems that rely on a combination of user fees and tax dollars for maintenance and preservation.

NATIONAL FORESTS

Most designated national forests and grasslands in the US allow people to camp for free. Before you head for one of these areas, be sure to find out what rules apply to the specific area and whether camping is prohibited due to safety issues or environmental protection. Nightly fees might apply when staying in established campsites or campgrounds. Camping in a national forest or grassland is a good option for backpacking, car camping, bike-packing, van camping, and RV camping. Although the camping is free outside of designated campgrounds, the time that you're allowed to stay in any one location is typically 14 days. For tent camping, you will want to pull off along a forest service road and then haul gear on foot from your car to a level spot to pitch a tent, at least 200 feet from any water source. For van camping or RV camping, you will want to find a spacious pullout on a forest service road and set up camp there. National forest and grassland camping usually does not provide easy access to amenities, so you will need to bring your own water, unless you know where to find a nearby body of water.

When camping in national forests or where there are no established campsites and campgrounds, be sure you camp responsibly. Before building a campfire, you should check in with a ranger station to see whether you need to secure a fire permit and whether any fire regulations apply to your specific camping area.

Pick up all trash, even if it isn't yours. Dispose of waste properly (see page 32), and after you disassemble fire rings, scatter or bury all ashes.

STATE PARKS AND FORESTS

Similar to national parks, state parks and forests are areas that have been protected by state governments. They are managed by each state, not the federal government. Check the state-specific regulations for the park or forest you plan to visit, as rules and restrictions can vary. Many state parks provide established campgrounds and campsites with amenities, along with trails that lead to more remote campsites ideal for backcountry camping trips.

In some state forests, free camping is permitted outside designated campgrounds and recreation areas. The restrictions that apply to any specific state forest usually depend on the laws of that state, so advance research is necessary before camping anywhere you like in a state forest. Developed campgrounds can be found in many state forests, so you can find places to camp that provide amenities and established campsites.

BLM LAND

Many of the western states in the US include regions of land that are publicly owned and managed by the Bureau of Land Management (BLM). Although these areas do not provide developed campgrounds, campsites, or amenities, you do not need to pay a fee to camp on the land. However, you'll need to research the area where you want to camp to make sure it isn't in the middle of cattle grazing land or a mining operation, since ranchers and miners can lease BLM land for these purposes. If you can find a spot away from these uses, camping on BLM land is a good option for car camping, van camping, bikepacking, and RV camping. In most areas you can set up camp in pullouts or carry your gear from a road to a more secluded area and camp there for a maximum of 14 days. A van or RV can be parked on the side of the road as long as the vehicle is situated completely off the road.

As with camping in national forests, you should camp at least 200 feet from any water source, pick up any trash, dispose of human waste responsibly, and remove any evidence of a firepit. You should also check in with a BLM field office to identify any fire restrictions, and to see whether obtaining a campfire permit is required.

WILDERNESS ETHICS

The only way beautiful, pristine areas will remain accessible to the record number of people who want an outdoor experience is to take steps to reduce recreational impact on the environment. This is a matter of taking personal responsibility for your own actions. The following guidelines should not be considered optional. They are critically important for ensuring the enjoyment of all campers and preserving our last remaining wild spaces.

When camping is an entirely new endeavor, easing into it will help ensure a pleasant experience that may lead to future—more adventurous—campouts.

Beginner-friendly camping options include:

- A rustic cabin with running water
- A campground near your home so that you can easily pack up and find comfort if necessary
- An overnight stay in a large tent furnished with cots, which can be found on a number of glamping websites like tentrr. com and hipcamp.com
- A true glamping experience, complete with running water, electricity, and furnished accommodations, located in a picturesque setting where you can still hear the sounds of nature

LEAVE NO TRACE SEVEN PRINCIPLES

Wilderness ethics have evolved in response to the environmental impact of increasing numbers of people participating in outdoor recreation. Camping is no longer the exclusive domain of rugged survivalists. Over the last century, inventions like sleeping bags, gas stoves, and synthetic tents have opened camping to people from all walks of life. After World War II, a surge of campers visited the national parks to enjoy the outdoors in a new, more comfortable way. By the 1960s, in order to help mitigate the effect of this influx of campers, the United States Forest Service, the Bureau of Land Management, and the National Park Service began teaching wilderness ethics to public land visitors. In 1987 these three government agencies collaborated to create a pamphlet titled "Leave No Trace Land Ethics." These guidelines have since been nicknamed Leave No Trace. The principles were developed as a framework for making low-impact decisions in the backcountry, but can also be applied to the frontcountry, or campgrounds closer to civilization. A summary of the principles is listed below. More detailed explanations of some of the principles appear as side notations throughout the chapters of this book. They have been reprinted from the official website of the Leave No Trace Center for Outdoor Ethics.

1. *Plan ahead and prepare:* When properly prepared, a camper is less likely to resort to high-impact strategies to resolve a dangerous situation that could put themselves or others at risk. When a camper plans ahead, it's easier to think clearly and problem-solve, thereby reducing harm to the environment or to the campers involved.

2. *Travel and camp on durable surfaces:* Degradation to soil, vegetation, or communities of organisms is caused by veering off trail or camping outside of designated campgrounds. Over-trampling leads to erosion, exposed soil, and harm to plant and animal life.

3. *Dispose of waste properly:* All litter and human or dog waste should be carried out unless trash receptacles are available for this specific type of waste. Otherwise, leftover trash and waste will detract from the natural beauty of an area, and has the potential to cause environmental damage to soil and waterways.

4. *Leave what you find:* While it can be tempting to alter a campsite by permanently clearing an area of rocks or debris, or to take home a souvenir like an animal bone or feather, this can disrupt an ecosystem or leave a campsite beyond repair. Campers should avoid making alterations like digging tent trenches, hammering nails into tree trunks, or cutting live tree branches.

5. *Minimize campfire impacts:* Because wildfires are so easy to start, it's important to practice low-impact fire techniques or use alternatives to campfires when appropriate or required.

6. *Respect wildlife:* Do not follow, feed, or motivate animals to flee, as this can impact animal survival. Give animals the space they need to find water, to feel unthreatened, and to care for their young.

7. *Be considerate to other visitors:* The golden rule applies to camping. *Do unto other campers as you would have them do unto you* is a good principle to follow to ensure that every camper has an opportunity to enjoy the outdoors.

It is one of the blessings of wilderness life that it shows us how few things we need in order to be perfectly happy.

—Horace Kephart, *Camping and Woodcraft*, 1919

Chapter 1

Gear Guide

WHETHER YOU'RE PREPARING FOR A multi-day adventure in the backcountry or getting ready for a low-key overnight trip to an outfitted campground, the first rule of camping is to plan ahead. Having a plan increases the likelihood of a safe and enjoyable outdoor excursion. Prepare for sudden changes in weather conditions, unexpected injuries, and scenarios that necessitate camping for more days than you originally scheduled. Nature can be unpredictable, so it's critical to prepare for the worst. You want to avoid getting stuck in a snowstorm wearing only a cotton sweatshirt and jeans, or enduring an especially bug-ridden area without insect repellent, or waking up in a soggy down sleeping bag drenched by rain from a leaky tent. While sleeping under the stars without a roof over your head is something every camper should try, weather can shift quickly and it's also hard to get a good night's sleep with a mosquito buzzing in your ear. Invest in the right gear for the outdoor activities you're most likely to undertake, and pack the essential items necessary to keep you comfortable, in high spirits, and most importantly—safe.

WHAT TO BRING

When car camping, it's tempting to pack too much, while every backpacker struggles to eliminate items to lighten the load they must carry. The trick is to pack the right things for the type of camping you plan to pursue. And there are certain items that you just don't want to leave home without. For example, once you're out in the wilderness, there's no simple substitute for a lighter or matches. That's why it's critically important to remember to bring—at the bare minimum—the 10 Essentials, listed below. Minimalist campers will bring little else. For a more comfortable outing and added safety, an expanded packing list is also included. The expanded list will help you make tasty camp cuisine and dress appropriately for the elements, and it will also remind you to bring the coffee filter.

To the novice camper, gear can seem to come in endless variations, so a more thorough explanation of the types and technologies is featured later in this chapter.

THE 10 ESSENTIALS

The original 10 Essentials list first appeared in 1974 in *Mountaineering: The Freedom of the Hills*, which was written by 40 outdoor experts. Over the years, the list has evolved to adapt to gear trends and new modes of camping. The original list is now referred to as the "classic" essentials, and is recommended for the bare minimum gear to take, whether camping in the backcountry or in an established campground. The classic essentials follow:

1. Map
2. Compass
3. Sunglasses and sunscreen
4. Extra clothing
5. Headlamp (or flashlight)
6. First-aid kit
7. Fire starter
8. Matches
9. Knife
10. Extra food

Headlamp

The new and improved 10 Essentials list has been updated with a more functional, systems-based approach to include the following:

1. Navigation
Map, compass, and GPS system (optional)
Navigation tools are used for trip and route planning, as well as for orienting to your map and surroundings. Before leaving home, learn how to use a compass (and GPS unit if you have one), in addition to being able to read a topographical or relief map.

2. Sun protection
Sunglasses, sunscreen, and hat
Sun protection includes items that are essential for shielding your skin and eyes against damaging UV rays. To prevent sunburns and minimize skin cancer risk, be sure to take and use sunscreen with an SPF of at least 30. Protect your ears and face and other areas with an SPF 50 lotion if you have sensitive skin. Covering your skin with sun-protection clothing, like long-sleeve shirts, lightweight pants, and hats, will help reduce your exposure. Wear sunglasses in sunny weather, especially near water or snow, where the reflective glare can hurt your eyes.

3. Insulation
Jacket, warm hat, gloves, rain jacket, and thermal underwear
Anticipate sudden changes in weather by bringing appropriate clothing for all types of conditions, and pack extra layers.

4. Illumination
Flashlight, lanterns, and headlamp
Artificial lighting is essential for safety at night. It's best not to leave it behind. The only substitute for artificial lighting is a fire, which is difficult to control as a light source. Headlamps can be more convenient than flashlights, because they're hands-free. Lanterns are best for illuminating a larger circumference. It's always a good idea to bring a backup light and extra batteries.

5. First-aid supplies
First-aid kit, insect repellent, and prescription medications
Pack first-aid supplies and a guide for how to handle medical emergencies. You can purchase a premade kit and modify it by adding items specific to your trip and your medical needs, such as an EpiPen or inhaler. Be sure to replace any expired supplies before you head out. See page 252 for a more detailed list of first-aid supplies and emergency procedures.

6. Fire

Matches, lighter, and fire starters

In addition to using fire as a heat source for staying warm and cooking, it can be used as an emergency signal. Cover your bases by packing waterproof matches, a lighter, and fire starters.

7. Repair kit and tools

Knives, scissors, screwdriver, pliers, multi-tool, trowel/shovel, duct tape, cable ties

Pack a kit that includes all the tools necessary to repair your gear. A multi-tool is handy because it includes several useful tools like a knife, can opener, and screwdriver. Don't forget to pack tools specific to your trip or activity, like a bike pump and tire patch kit if you plan to go mountain biking or bikepacking.

8. Nutrition

Meals for every day of the trip and extra food for one additional day

Bring enough food to cover every meal of every day of your trip, plus at least one extra day as a precaution. No-cook items such as dehydrated foods are lightweight and compact, and just require adding water. Salty and high-energy snacks like nuts, trail mix, and granola bars are ideal for sustained outdoor activity.

Based on the specifics of your planned trip, research whether you should pack any other items not included in the 10 Essentials list that might be necessary for your health and safety. Some examples include a life jacket, radio, or personal locator beacon. Various lists are available from different outdoor organizations, some of which are specific to local conditions and camping areas.

9. Hydration

Water and water purification supplies

Pack water treatment supplies and enough water to cook with and drink. Dehydration is a greater risk during physical activity because your body loses water and salts at a higher rate. To prevent dehydration, drink one-half liter to a full liter every hour if you're participating in an outdoor activity like running, swimming, biking, or hiking. One liter equals approximately four cups, or two standard 16.9-ounce water bottles. If you're well hydrated, your urine should be a pale color. Calculate how much water you should pack if you're planning to camp in an area without a nearby water source. If you're camping in a place where you will need to purify the water yourself, locate the water sources you plan to use on a map ahead of time. Be sure to prepare the water and drink it before getting thirsty. Pack an extra two liters of water for one additional day, to be used in case of emergency.

10. Emergency shelter
Tent, space blanket, tarp, and bivy
While it can be memorable to sleep under the stars without a roof over your head, shelter will protect you from harsh conditions and exposure to the elements in an emergency situation. Pack a tent at the very least, and bring a tarp, bivy sack (personal-sized waterproof shelter), or emergency Mylar space blanket as backup.

FRONTCOUNTRY CHECKLIST

Car camping allows the flexibility to pack more and bring heavier items. Everything in the backcountry gear checklist should be packed when frontcountry camping, along with the items listed below.

CAMPSITE GEAR
◊ Tarp (doesn't need to be lightweight)
◊ Extra blankets
◊ Lantern and lantern fuel

KITCHEN GEAR
◊ Stove (can be a larger propane camp stove)
◊ Propane tank (if applicable)
◊ Cutting knives
◊ Pots and pans (can be heavier)
◊ Food-storage containers and bags
◊ Paper towels or reusable cloths
◊ Ice
◊ Cooler
◊ Multi-gallon water container
◊ Spatula
◊ Ladle
◊ Cutting board
◊ Tongs
◊ Dish towel or cloth

OTHER OPTIONAL ITEMS
◊ Small shovel
◊ Board games
◊ Dutch oven
◊ Corkscrew
◊ Measuring cups and spoons
◊ Ax
◊ Folding table
◊ Camp chair(s) or stool(s)

BACKCOUNTRY CHECKLIST

Some backcountry campers enjoy packing a few luxury items from the above frontcountry checklist, such as lightweight chairs or lanterns. This list should be considered the bare minimum required gear when camping in the backcountry, with additional items added only when space and weight permit.

CAMPSITE GEAR

◊ Tent
◊ Tent poles
◊ Tent rainfly
◊ Tent footprint
◊ Tent guylines
◊ Tent stakes, plus extra stakes
◊ Sleeping bag with stuff sack
◊ Sleeping bag liner (optional)
◊ Sleeping pad
◊ Pillow (optional)
◊ Lightweight tarp (optional)
◊ Headlamp and/or flashlight
◊ Extra batteries
◊ Fire starter
◊ Rope or cord (nylon or parachute)
◊ Insect netting

KITCHEN GEAR

◊ Stove
◊ Stove fuel
◊ Matches and lighter
◊ Cutting knife
◊ Fork
◊ Spoon
◊ Plate
◊ Bowl
◊ Cup
◊ Lightweight pots and pans
◊ Ziplock bags
◊ Large trash bags
◊ Water bottle
◊ Spatula (optional)
◊ Ladle (optional)
◊ Foil
◊ Biodegradable soap
◊ Sponge

CLOTHES

◊ Sun-protection clothes, like long pants and long-sleeve shirt
◊ Rain jacket and rain pants
◊ Sleepwear
◊ Extra pair of socks
◊ Underwear
◊ Thermal underwear
◊ Gloves
◊ Hats (cold-weather hat and sun hat)
◊ Appropriate footwear for conditions, activities, and terrain (e.g., hiking boots, tennis shoes, sandals, down booties)
◊ Warm base layers (shirt and pants)
◊ Warm jacket (down or synthetic down)

FIRST-AID SUPPLIES AND TOILETRIES

◊ Sunscreen (for lips and face)
◊ Insect repellent
◊ Biodegradable soap
◊ Toothbrush
◊ Toothpaste
◊ Prescription medications
◊ Toilet paper
◊ Face cloth/hand towel or bandanna
◊ Feminine products

OTHER ESSENTIALS

◊ Maps, area information, stored in a resealable plastic bag
◊ Pet supplies and food
◊ Compass and GPS (optional)
◊ Whistle
◊ Multi-tool
◊ Trowel
◊ Duct tape

OTHER OPTIONAL ITEMS

◊ Camera
◊ Cards
◊ Book(s)
◊ Swimsuit
◊ Journal and pen/pencil
◊ Binoculars
◊ French press or portable drip coffee cone and filters
◊ Can/bottle opener

HOW TO SELECT THE RIGHT GEAR

Today's wide range of outdoor gear choices can be overwhelming. Down or synthetic? Ultralight or a few extra ounces? Zero-degree or 20-degree? Learning how to read the specifications on labels will help you confidently select the right type of gear for your purposes. Before heading to the store, make a list of all your requirements for each item of gear. What is your budget? What kind of camping will you be doing? What will the average size of your group be? The following list covers the important factors to consider when choosing the most expensive items of camping gear, but it does not recommend specific brands as new gear comes out daily. Read product reviews to narrow down your options. Any outdoor gear store or online retailer sells products from quality brands like Patagonia, Mountain Safety Research (MSR), The North Face, Outdoor Research (OR), Marmot, Cascade Designs, Cotopaxi, and Mountain Hardwear. Some national retailers include Recreational Equipment, Inc. (REI), Cabela's, Backcountry.com, CampSaver.com, Sierra Trading Post, and Moosejaw.

TENT

Mode of camping

Before buying any piece of gear, you'll need to consider what type of camping you plan to do most of the time. Do you need a featherweight tent you can carry for miles into the backcountry, or would a heavier, roomier tent make more sense for all the car camping you plan to do with your family? Consider renting a tent before buying, so you can figure out what features and amenities best meet your camping needs. Many brick-and-mortar outdoor retailers offer gear rentals. A quick internet search for gear rental outfitters in your area will usually lead you to the right place.

If you only have the budget to buy one tent, but plan to do all kinds of camping, it's best to opt for a lightweight backpacking tent. You might be sacrificing space and certain amenities, but your back will thank you for sacrificing those extra pounds of material on your backcountry trips. Ideally, a two-person back-packing tent should weigh no more than six pounds, including the rainfly and footprint. Often, the lighter the tent, the more expensive it is, and the less durable it may be in rough weather conditions or over its useful life.

If you plan only to car camp, or won't do more than one backpacking trip per year, it might be worth buying a more spacious tent. Larger tents offer convenient amenities like extra vestibules for storing gear or additional entries. If you end up needing to pack it on backcountry trips, splitting up the weight between several people in your party can help lighten a single backpacker's load. For example, one person can pack the rainfly and stakes, and another person can carry the tent body and poles.

Sleeping capacity

On average, how many people will be sleeping in your tent? Do you prefer to have extra room to store some gear inside your tent or would you prefer to use an exterior vestibule for storage? Do you have a dog that will also be sharing the sleeping quarters? You should assume that the fit will be snug. For example, in a two-person tent, two adults of average size will be sleeping shoulder to shoulder. There are a number of reasons why you might buy a larger, three-person tent for two people: if you tend to get claustrophobic, if you want the room to accommodate more gear, if you need space for a dog or a child, if your tent partner is a larger person, or if you would simply like to have more elbow room. A tent's shape can make it feel roomier. For example, you can stand up in some domed tents with high ceilings. But a bigger size means more—and often heavier—material, which isn't ideal for backpacking. A taller tent is also often less wind- and snow-resistant.

Seasonality

Consider climate and conditions. You'll be thankful for more ventilation materials like mesh when camping in hot or humid weather. During temperate months a three-season tent will provide the weather resistance to keep you dry, but may fall short when it comes to withstanding a sustained storm or harsh winds. Three- to four-season tents offer a better balance of ventilation, warmth retention, and durability. They're a bit sturdier and warmer, because most come with one or two extra poles and less mesh. For snow camping, or any camping in extreme cold conditions, a four-season tent is optimal, as it will provide that extra resistance to cold, wind, and snow. Four-season tents are often made of more durable fabrics, and are therefore heavier to carry and can feel warmer and stuffier in mild weather. But if you encounter extremely inhospitable conditions, like fierce wind and snowstorms, you'll welcome the extra warmth and won't mind packing a few extra ounces.

Ease of use

Not all tents are created equal when it comes to how easy they are to set up or pack away. Always read the instructions before setting up a tent, and follow the diagrams. If the retailer allows for it, set the tent up a couple of times in the store. Some tents come with all sorts of poles, hooks, pockets, and sleeves, and it can be telling if you still struggle to set up the tent the second time you try. For example, it's often easier to attach a pole to a hook than it is to slide a pole through a long sleeve of tent fabric. A large tent can be difficult to fold back up and pack away, so take note of how it was packed by the manufacturer before you start setting it up for the first time. Once you get caught in a rainstorm while setting up or putting away a tent, you'll truly appreciate having chosen a model that has an intuitive design.

Key features

Peak height: If you want to be able to stand up in your tent, opt for a dome-style or cabin-style structure, which will be listed in the tent specifications on the tag. Dome-style tents are good for withstanding wind, but have a sloping ceiling that reduces the interior space. Cabin-style tents are engineered with vertical walls that create more livable space, but can be less stable in the wind. Keep in mind that taller tents are often heavier, and therefore not optimal for carrying into the backcountry.

Dome-style tent

Floor length: Taller people should pay close attention to the floor length measurement listed in the tent specifications. If you're over six feet tall, opt for a tent that is 90 inches in length. Make sure there will still be a few extra inches between the ends of the tent and your head and feet.

Poles: Fewer poles often make for a faster tent setup. Also, check whether the tent poles create a freestanding shape. A freestanding tent doesn't need to be staked down to maintain its own shape. Once set up, it can be conveniently picked up and placed in

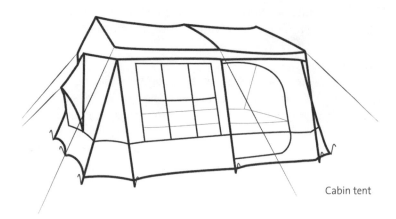

Cabin tent

a different location. When packing up, you can also hold a free-standing tent upside down to shake out any debris.

Doors: Decide how many tent openings are necessary by taking convenience, ventilation, and material weight into consideration. Certain lightweight one- or two-person tents have only one opening at the head of the tent, which can make getting in and out more challenging. An opening on only one side of the tent may mean you will be crawling over your tent partner to get out to go to the bathroom in the middle of the night. Be sure to also test zipper noise. Does it make a lot of noise to zip and unzip the door? Check the make of the zipper. YKK zippers are manufactured to be more durable and snag less.

Rainfly: A rainfly is a separate piece of material that acts as a waterproof barrier between you and the elements. Rain-only rainflies offer reasonable rain protection, let more light in, and increase outside visibility and views from inside the tent. Cover the tent with the rainfly for added warmth, or whenever dew or wet weather is a possibility.

Manufacturing: Is the tent's fabric high-denier or low-denier? High-denier fabrics are more durable, thick, and sturdy than low-denier materials. However, the higher thread count in high-denier fabrics usually means the material will weigh more—a consideration for minimalist and ultralight backpackers. Also make sure the seams joining the tent floor to the walls of the tent are elevated a few inches off the ground and taped, or use high-denier fabric, rather than stitching. This reduces unwanted leakage during wet weather.

Amenities: Tents come with an array of additions and upgrades that can help with organization and comfort. How many ventilation panels are included in the design? Larger mesh panels are good for hot, humid climates, and can improve views from inside the tent. A panel on either side of the tent helps with cross-ventilation. Check whether you like the style and placement of interior pockets and loops. Some tents come with a center loop in the ceiling where a battery-powered lantern can be hung. Also note the number and size of any vestibules. Are they big enough to store your gear and does the rainfly come down far enough to protect stored items from getting wet? Finally, check that there are enough loops (guyouts) on the tent's exterior to hold the structure down in high winds. You can string guylines to guyout loops to prevent a tent from flapping and shaking too much in stormy weather.

Footprint: Most tents don't come with a ground cloth known as a footprint, but it is an essential item during wet weather. A footprint is an extra piece of fabric spread over the ground under the tent, which is pitched on top of it. It provides an additional layer of protection between the tent's floor and any dampness, twigs, rocks, or dirt that can damage the tent's fabric. When buying a footprint, make sure it has the same dimensions as the surface area of the bottom of the tent. Some are designed for specific tents and fit the tent floor shape perfectly, preventing any water from pooling around the edges of the ground cloth. If you use a tarp larger than the surface area of the bottom of the tent, tuck the edges of the tarp underneath the tent to prevent condensation or rainwater from pooling.

Accessories: Extra accessories that you may want to pack are tent stakes, anchors, and utility cord for fashioning guylines. Other options include a repair kit, seam sealer, and an inside or outside floor mat to reduce the amount of debris tracked into the tent.

BACKCOUNTRY BACKPACK

Used to haul gear on backpacking, thru-hiking, and minimalist backcountry trips, a backpack can make or break a camping trip. When a backpack has the appropriate holding capacity for the length of your camping trip and fits your body well, it can be a back-saving asset. But when a backpack isn't the right size for your gear or it rubs or causes strain on your body, it can cause extreme discomfort, and in some cases may even be a safety liability. To find the right backpack, you'll need to take four elements into consideration: style, features, fit, and capacity.

Style

Before choosing a style of backpack, consider what kind of backpacking you plan to do most, how much gear you plan to bring, and how much your gear weighs.

External-frame backpacks: The classic style of backpack, an external-frame pack often comes with many pockets, compartments, and straps to help organize gear. However, it is often the heaviest pack option, meaning that you will be carrying the extra weight of the pack in addition to your gear. External-frame packs are best designed for hauling especially heavy loads.

Internal-frame backpacks: The style of choice for most backpackers, an internal-frame pack is somewhere in the middle between an external frame and a frameless in terms of weight and organizational features. An internal frame usually has one main compartment to store gear, whereas an external-frame pack has more pockets and compartments, making organizing gear a little easier. Some people prefer an internal-frame pack for its load-supporting design that allows the hips to hold up most of the weight, rather than the back.

Frameless backpacks: Also composed of a single main compartment, frameless packs are designed for minimalist and ultralight backpackers. However, frameless packs don't come with as many load-supporting design technologies, so it's important to pack as light as possible, since the weight isn't transferred onto your hips as much as it is with a framed pack.

Features

Backpacks come with an array of added features, pockets, straps, and compartments—some of which you may find to be necessities for organization and comfort, while others may not feel as crucial. When selecting a backpack, take time to explore all the features and consider how they might come in handy or whether, for your purposes, they are just adding unnecessary weight to the pack's design.

Lid/brain: The lid, or brain, of a backpack often comes with pocket compartments to store lightweight gear. Some backpack designs also allow you to remove the brain and wear it as a makeshift fanny pack or shoulder bag—a useful feature for day hikes or if you just want to save weight and remove it entirely from the backpack on shorter overnight trips.

Padding: Frameless packs are often designed with minimal padding around the hip belt and lumbar area. If you're someone who needs extra support around those areas to reduce soreness, consider opting for a backpack design with more padding.

Ventilation: Some packs come with ventilation features like a mesh panel that provides a breathable barrier between your back and your backpack.

Compartments and pockets: Compartments and pockets provide options for organization, so it's prudent to observe where pockets are located and to consider how you might use them to your advantage. Top-loading backpacks are the most common style of pack, where a main compartment stores larger items like your sleeping bag, clothes, and cookware. Panel pockets come with some packs, which allow access to the interior of the main compartment to avoid having to blindly dig down to the bottom of the pack or pull everything out to get to the bottom. Packs with wider hip belts sometimes come with hip-belt pockets, which are convenient for storing small items that you want to keep handy, such as lip balm, bug spray, or a phone.

Hydration reservoir: Only useful if you plan to use a hydration bladder to hydrate, a built-in reservoir is used to store a bladder inside a backpack. A hydration bladder is used in place of a water bottle for convenience, since a bladder comes with a sipping hose that eliminates the hassle of pulling a water bottle out of a pack and unscrewing the lid. Packs that include hydration reservoirs come with holes and loops through which you can run the hydration bladder's hose so that it hangs just over one shoulder in such a way that you can easily sip water while hiking.

Rain cover and day pack: Some backpacks come with a custom-fitting rain cover—used to keep the contents of your pack dry. A rain cover can be purchased separately when the pack does not include one. Small, minimalist day packs are also sometimes included in the larger backpack, which can be used for day hikes out from a backcountry base camp.

Fit

Even the most state-of-the-art backpack with all the bells and whistles won't be well suited for your needs if it doesn't fit you right. A backpack fitting is recommended for anyone trying on new packs. Expert staff at outdoor gear stores are often trained to do these fittings. They'll take your measurements and then select a backpack sized for your dimensions. They'll also help you adjust all the straps so that the pack hugs your hips and rests on your shoulders correctly and safely. Packs can also sometimes come with an adjustable suspension system so that the pack can be lengthened or shortened if your dimensions put you between sizes.

Eighty percent or more of the weight should rest on your hips, not your shoulders. So be sure to move and walk around the store to make sure that your shoulders don't get sore and that the pack isn't rubbing in an uncomfortable way. Some stores have return policies that will even let you try out a backpack in the backcountry before deciding whether it's the one for you.

Capacity

The amount of gear that a backpack can hold is a top consideration. A backpack with too little capacity makes it difficult to store all your gear, or it forces you to invest in potentially expensive ultralight gear. A backpack with too much capacity can mean that you pack more gear than necessary (because you can fit it) and then, once packed, your backpack becomes too heavy for comfort.

- *30–50 liters:* One to three nights
- *50–80 liters:* Three to five nights
- *70+ liters:* Five nights or more, trips with kids, and winter trips

STOVE

When fires aren't an option for heating water or cooking food, it's important to have a camp stove or backpacking stove handy. Even when fires are permitted, a stove should always be packed as backup. Choosing the right model of stove for your purposes can be the tricky part. Follow some simple guidelines and you'll be able to find a stove that meets your needs.

Backpacking vs. camping stove

If you only have the budget to purchase one stove, and you plan to do any backpacking, a lightweight backpacking stove is the best option. However, choosing the right model of backpacking stove requires considering some simple guidelines. Backpacking stoves are lightweight, fuel-efficient, and often quite small. Some are tiny enough to fit into a pocket. Some backpacking stoves are designed to only boil water, such as a Jetboil; whereas others can accommodate smaller pots and pans.

If you plan to car camp, the benefit of a camp stove is it can handle larger pots and pans, and it's more stable. Backpacking stoves tend to be top-heavy and can tip over easily.

Types of backpacking stoves

Integrated canister systems: While a standard canister stove typically features a burner device that screws onto the top of a fuel canister, an integrated canister system comes with a built-in windscreen and insulated cooking pot with a lid. Designed to boil quickly, an integrated canister system is not ideal for cooking food or simmering water. However, certain models come with an alternative vessel that can be used as a pot for cooking food or as a bowl for eating food. And some models are made with a built-in pressure regulator that is handy for maintaining a consistent outflow of fuel, even at higher elevations or lower temperatures. Tall in stature, integrated canister stoves should be placed on a level surface when in use to prevent them from tipping over.

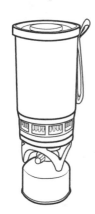

Integrated canister systems are best used for boiling water

Remote canister systems: Unlike top-heavy integrated canister systems, remote canister stoves feature a burner device that sits directly on the ground rather than atop a canister. A fuel hose connects the burner device to a canister. The benefits of this setup include being able to use a windscreen around the stove and to support a larger pot on the wider stove base.

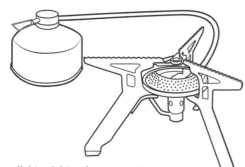

Remote canister systems are lightweight and can support a pot or a pan

Wood-burning stoves: A lightweight option for longer treks into the backcountry, wood-burning backpacking stoves allow you to leave fuel canisters behind. The stove produces a flame by burning collected leaves and twigs. Certain models come with an optional grill attachment or even produce enough electricity while burning to charge electronic devices like a GPS unit or mobile phone. The only downside to wood-burning stoves is encountering a situation where a burn ban prevents burning wood or wet weather prevents collecting dry fuel.

Denatured alcohol stoves: An ultralight option for minimalist or thru-hikers, denatured alcohol stoves only weigh an ounce or two and require minimal maintenance. The only fuel required is a bottle filled with enough denatured alcohol (inexpensive and easily sourced within the US) to last the duration of your trip. Another desirable feature is that the fuel burns silently. The only downsides are that denatured alcohol can be difficult to source outside the US, a windscreen is often necessary, and it can take longer to boil water than other types of stoves.

Solid-fuel tablet stoves: An inexpensive option for ultralight campers, these stoves are so compact they can fit into a pocket. Like denatured alcohol stoves, solid-fuel tablet stoves can take a while to bring water to a boil, and the tablets used to keep the stove burning can leave a greasy residue on the bottom of a pot.

Considerations

Group size: How big of a group will you be routinely cooking for? Backpacking stoves can only accommodate one pot or pan at a time, so if you'll be camping and cooking with a larger group, plan to ask other members of the group to bring stoves as well. It's best to bring at least one backpacking stove for every two people. There are generally two styles of camp stoves: two-burner and freestanding. Groups of four or less can make do with a single two-burner stove, while larger groups should either bring a two-burner and a smaller backpacking stove as backup, or a three-burner freestanding stove with legs.

BTUs: A British thermal unit (BTU) is the amount of energy it takes to heat or cool one pound of water one degree Fahrenheit. Generally speaking, the more BTUs a stove lists, the more power-ful it is. A compact, wind-resistant stove design can be more heat-efficient, and therefore may have more heating power than a stove without those features. So before making a stove purchase, be sure to look at the burn time and boil time listed in the specs.

Fuel type: Most backpacking and camping stoves require propane fuel, while others use liquid fuel (white gas).

Fuel type comparison		
	Propane	**Liquid**
Cost	Less expensive (though the cost of canisters can add up)	Can cost more, but you don't need to buy a new canister each time
Ease of use	• Less messy, since it usually just requires screwing a propane canister or tank onto the stove • Lights quickly	• Must be pumped to build up enough pressure to emit fuel • You can look inside the canister and see what the liquid-fuel level is, so you know when it's getting close to empty
Maintenance	Occasional maintenance is required, but many propane canister stoves can be used for years without requiring maintenance	Often requires regular maintenance like replacing the O-rings or cleaning the fuel hose
Boil time	The stove becomes less efficient in cold elements and when the canister gets close to empty	Often boils faster than propane
Waste	Backpacking-sized propane canisters create more waste than liquid-fuel canisters, since each propane canister must be thrown away after each use	Liquid-fuel canisters can be reused and refilled

When choosing the type of fuel that will work best for you, consider whether you plan to do any international camping. A stove that uses liquid fuel is often the safer bet, as liquid fuel is usually easier to find. However, it's best to avoid fuel pumped at a gas station because the gasoline additives can clog up your stove.

Wind resistance: Some stove models come with windscreens to help keep the stove burning in a steady, even flame. Windscreens can also be bought separately. Alternatively, you can create a makeshift windscreen by stacking rocks and placing the stove on the lee side, out of the wind, or by simply placing the stove in a protected area behind a natural barrier in the campsite. Just make sure the protective barrier isn't a flammable material like the side of a tent.

Simmering ability: Many backpacking stoves boil water fast, and if that's all you need a stove for, then simmering ability doesn't need to be a consideration. If you plan to do any cooking beyond adding hot water to dehydrated or freeze-dried food, then it's important to have a stove with the capacity to simmer food. Single-flame stoves don't distribute the heat evenly, so food can easily burn to the bottom of a pot or pan. If you want a simmering-capable stove, read product reviews to find models that can be set to a low flame without going out.

> Caution: If setting up a wind-shield for a propane canister stove, do not wrap a windscreen around the full circumference of the canister. Simply place the wind barrier on one side of the stove. Encircling a canister stove can trap so much heat that it might cause the canister to explode.

Weight: If car camping, stove weight shouldn't be a concern. But if backpacking, a lightweight stove is essential. Often, the lighter the stove model, the higher the price tag.

Piezo-igniter: Often built into an integrated canister system, a piezo-igniter lights a stove via a push button that produces a spark. This can be a convenient feature if you've misplaced your lighter or matches. However, lighter and matches should always be brought as a backup.

Stabilizers: Sold separately, stabilizers help support the top-heavy design of some canister stoves by attaching to the bottom of the fuel canister.

SLEEPING BAG

Temperature rating

The temperature rating listed on the tag is the lowest temperature at which the sleeping bag will keep an average person warm. For example, a 20-degree bag will keep most sleepers comfortably warm until the temperature drops below 20 degrees. Keep in mind that the temperature ratings listed assume that a person is wearing thermal underwear and is lying on an insulated sleeping pad. Temperature ratings are also not an exact science, so pay attention to your own internal thermostat. If you are colder than most or hotter than most, buy accordingly.

Shape

The shape of a sleeping bag affects how warm the bag will keep you. When lying inside your sleeping bag, noncirculating air is held in the space between your skin and the walls of the bag. Your body heat warms this air. The less space between you and the bag, the faster you'll warm up. For this reason, consider what shape of sleeping bag would be best for your use. Lightweight backpacking sleeping bags are often a tighter fit, but will heat up faster and keep you warm longer, whereas roomier sleeping bags may feel more comfortable, but may not be as heat-efficient. Before you leave the store, be sure to get inside the sleeping bag and test out its fit and comfort.

Some sleeping bag models are manufactured specifically for women and kids. Shaped to fit an average-size woman's contours

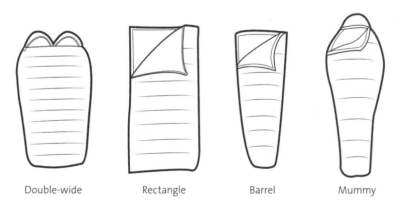

Double-wide   Rectangle   Barrel   Mummy

(narrower at the shoulder and wider at the hips), women-specific models provide added comfort without sacrificing warmth. Sleeping bags for kids are smaller in size, and sometimes come with added features like a pillow pocket for a comfortable headrest, or a sleeve at the bottom of the bag that fits over a sleeping pad to hold the sleeping bag in place.

Rectangle: A rectangular sleeping bag is often a comfortable shape, as it allows more space for your feet to move around. Rectangular sleeping bags are also often the easiest to zip together to make a more spacious sleeping bag for two people.

Semi-rectangle/barrel: A semi-rectangular bag or barrel-shaped bag has a more tapered shape than a standard rectangular sleeping bag. The narrower end increases the bag's insulating effect, while still providing a comfortable, roomy shape.

Mummy: Mummy-shaped sleeping bags offer a snug fit for maximum warmth. However, they are also the most restrictive in terms of comfort, due to narrower shoulder and hip widths.

Double-wide: The most spacious camp-sleeping option, a double-wide bag accommodates two average-size people comfortably. The bags are usually manufactured to be able to zip apart to create two separate single sleeping bags.

Insulation

Depending on the climate and typical seasonal weather patterns for the areas where you'll camp most often, a sleeping bag's insulation can be a crucial consideration. A down sleeping bag will function well in cold, dry climates, whereas a bag with synthetic fill is the safest—and warmest—choice in wet conditions.

Synthetic: Depending on the quality, synthetic sleeping-bag fill may not provide as much warmth as goose-down fill, may weigh more, and may not compress down as small. However, synthetic sleeping bags are hypoallergenic (i.e., not likely to trigger allergic reactions) and are usually less expensive than goose down. Synthetic fill is appealing because it is quick-drying and will continue to insulate even if it gets wet.

Goose down: Though easier to pack into a small size, and often weighing less than synthetic fill, goose down loses its loft when it gets wet, meaning it loses its ability to insulate. Be sure to leave your head exposed while you sleep, because the moisture from breathing into the bag can dampen the down insulation and cool you down. If wet conditions are a regular possibility for the seasons in which you plan to camp, synthetic bags are a safer bet for more comfortable—and warmer—nights.

Water-resistant down: Almost like a hybrid of down and synthetic, water-resistant down bags provide the compressibility of goose down along with the weather protection of synthetic-fill bags. To create the water-resistant effect, the goose down is coated with a water protectant. Though a marriage of two desirable features, water-resistant down is currently a new technology with a high price tag, and the longevity of the water resistance has not been thoroughly tested.

Features
Shell and lining: Check whether a sleeping bag's outer shell fabric is treated with a durable water repellent (DWR) finish, which forces any exterior water to bead up instead of soaking through the fabric. To test whether a sleeping bag shell is treated with DWR, wipe a wet cloth across the surface. If it is treated with DWR, it will bead up. Sleeping bag interiors are not treated with DWR and are instead manufactured to aid in the dispersal of body moisture (like sweat) throughout the bag's interior.

Pillow pocket: Some sleeping bags come with a pillow pocket that can be stuffed with a rolled-up jacket, clothes, or a travel pillow to serve as a comfortable headrest.

Sleeping pad sleeve: To keep you from rolling off your pad in the middle of the night, some bags come with a built-in sleeve to hold the pad and bag together as a single unit.

Stash pocket: Certain sleeping bag models include small stash pockets to store small items like a headlamp, watch, glasses, or wallet.

Head hood: If camping in cold conditions, invest in a sleeping bag with a hood for your head. Since you lose a lot of body heat through your head, it's important to keep it covered. A sleeping bag hood often comes with a built-in drawstring that can be cinched around your head to help retain warmth.

Accessories

Stuff sack: Usually, sleeping bags come with a stuff sack (compression sack) for portability. Stuff sack tags will often list the volume of the sack in liters, as well as the length and width dimensions. Some stuff sacks are manufactured with straps that cinch down to compress the sleeping bag into a smaller and more packable size.

Storage sack: To lengthen the life of your sleeping bag, store it in a large cotton sack. Sometimes the cotton storage sack is sold with the sleeping bag. Storing the sleeping bag loosely in a large bag prevents any permanent compression of the fill, which can reduce its insulating power.

Liner: Typically sold separately, a sleeping bag liner is a soft sack that reduces wear and tear on the inside of a sleeping bag, and also keeps it clean. Liners can also add 8–15 degrees Fahrenheit of warmth.

SLEEPING PAD

A sleeping pad is not just for comfort; it also serves as an important insulator between you and the ground. As with most gear, a variety of sleeping pads exist, so it's a good idea to decide what type of pad suits your outdoor needs. Be sure to test out your sleeping pad of choice before you leave the store. Inflate it (if it's inflatable) and lie down on it the way you normally do when you sleep.

Styles

Air pads: Ideal for backpacking due to their lightweight design, most air pads are usually the most compact style of sleeping pad when folded up. However, the lightweight material means they are also more prone to abrasion than other heavier models, and can be punctured by something as small as a pine needle. Gear manufacturers have engineered a way to preserve an air pad's lightweight design without compromising warmth. These days, most air pads are produced with an insulating material that helps keep you warm at night, but the material sometimes produces a crinkly sound, which can be a nuisance. Air pads require manual inflation, usually with your breath, a built-in hand pump, or an external pump (often sold separately). The firmness of the pad depends on how much you inflate it. The firmness of the mattress can fluctuate depending on the outside temperature, so it's a good idea to inflate it to your desired firmness right before bed. One final consideration is that lighter and smaller air pads are usually more expensive.

Air pad

Closed-cell foam pads:
Closed-cell foam pads are an inexpensive alternative to air pads. They are also often as lightweight as air pads and much more durable because they can't be punctured. The downside is they are less compact than air pads when folded or rolled up. Because of the extra bulk, a foam pad will usually need to be strapped to the outside of a backpack when hiking. The other downside is a foam pad can be less insulating. They're also much firmer than air pads, which can feel less comfortable to some sleepers, especially people with hip or back issues.

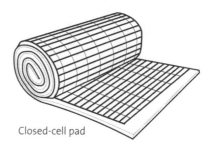

Closed-cell pad

Self-inflating pads: A hybrid of open-cell foam insulation and inflation technology, a self-inflating pad is a lightweight, often inexpensive, and durable option. When opened, the mattress's valve self-inflates the air chambers. Some models are built to be folded lengthwise and then rolled up into a small shape to fit inside a backpack, while other less compact car-camping designs can be rolled up without folding. While they can still be ripped or punctured, self-inflating pads are often made of heavier material, which can easily be patched in the field. Because of their durability, they can be strapped to the outside of a backpack without fear of irreparable damage. On the other hand, they are a bit heavier than air pads and their firm structure often makes them less comfortable.

Insulation and R-value

A pad needs to insulate you from the ground, even in mild weather. The majority of air and self-inflating pads are now made with a built-in layer of synthetic insulation, and some are even designed with down insulation for added warmth.

R-value is a term used to indicate the insulating strength of a sleeping pad. It measures the pad's ability to resist heat flow. The higher the pad's listed R-value, the warmer you can expect to be while sleeping. R-values range from 1.0 (least insulated) to 9.5 (most insulated). Unlike sleeping bags, selecting a higher insulation rating for a sleeping pad shouldn't cause you to overheat.

Weight and dimensions

Weight: Certain sleeping pad models come in tapered shapes to reduce the weight of the pad for backcountry purposes. Choosing a shorter, three-quarter-length foam pad is an option for shaving ounces. Two-person sleeping pads are a third option for partner camping, and can be lighter than two separate sleeping pads.

Length: Lie down on the pad before purchasing it to make sure that your feet don't hang off the end (unless you're opting for a shorter pad to save weight). If the pad is too short, your legs and feet will not benefit from the pad's insulation. Pads listed as "regular" in length typically measure 72 inches, and "long" pads generally measure 78 inches (and are often wider).

Width: Make sure that both your shoulders and hips fit squarely within the width of the pad. The standard width measures 20 inches. Other designs measure 25–30 inches and can accommodate a larger person or someone who tosses and turns while sleeping. Be sure to measure the interior width of your tent to make sure it can accommodate your sleeping pad's measurements.

Other features and considerations

Construction: Some sleeping pads are made with extra features for added comfort, such as rails to keep you from rolling off the pad (good for children) or a built-in pillow for your head.

Inflation: Sleeping pad inflation levels differ between models. Valve design also varies. Some air pads come with a high-volume inflation valve and a deflation valve, which can assist in quickly inflating or deflating the pad. Other air pads are designed with air valve neck openings that allow for faster inflation using just your breath. Certain pads are built with separate air chambers or layers, so if one chamber gets punctured, the rest of the pad will remain inflated.

Surface design: Some sleeping pads are textured to add a bit of friction to keep restless sleepers from sliding off.

Sleep systems: Check to see whether your sleeping bag has a built-in sleeve to hold a sleeping pad, and measure its width. This setup helps keep the two together as a single unit while you sleep.

Patch kits: For peace of mind, pack a patch kit to be used in the event that your inflatable sleeping pad springs a leak.

Hand pumps: Certain pads come with built-in hand pumps. You can also purchase a separate bag-style lightweight hand pump that rolls up into a small, packable size.

Best style for camping type

Before investing in a sleeping pad, consider what type of camping you plan to do most often. Depending on the activity, a lighter, more compact pad might be ideal, or a heavier yet more luxuriously comfortable air mattress might be what you need to sleep through the night.

Car camping: A heavier, wider, and thicker air pad is often ideal if you plan to car camp exclusively. Double-wide inflatable air mattresses are also an option, and can accommodate a double-wide sleeping bag or bedsheets and blankets. These larger air mattresses are not usually constructed with built-in insulation for staying warm in cold temperatures, so they're best used in mild weather conditions only. Bulkier and heavier, this type of mattress is not at all ideal for backcountry camping, and a separate hand pump is usually required to inflate the mattress.

Backpacking: For optimum comfort and carrying the least amount of weight, a self-inflating air pad is ideal for backcountry camping. Self-inflating mattresses come in a variety of thicknesses, insulation qualities, durable materials, and prices, so it's likely you can find a design well suited for your needs and budget. For added luxury, you can invest in a chair kit, which allows you to transform your air pad into a comfortable seat.

Minimalist backpacking: Ideal for camping excursions that require packing the least amount of weight, an ultralight air pad is a good investment.

Thru-hiking: To strike the right balance between durability and low weight for lengthy trips, consider a closed-cell foam pad. To shave off more ounces, you can opt for a shorter, three-quarter-length foam pad to provide a barrier between just your torso and the ground, and then place extra clothing under your legs for a bit of extra comfort and insulation.

Winter camping: For snow camping, extra insulation is crucial, so sleeping on two pads is often necessary. A closed-cell foam pad can be used as the bottom layer, and then an insulated, high-R-value pad or self-inflating pad can be used as the top layer. The combo provides sufficient insulation against the cold, and added insurance against puncturing the inflatable top layer.

HAMMOCKS AND COTS

Certain terrain can warrant sleeping in an elevated fashion, plus sometimes it just feels better to sleep off the ground. When the ground is especially rocky or there aren't established campsites, a hammock provides a comfortable and low-impact place to sleep. Cots are another option for elevating a sleeping bag above rocky ground, and for providing a higher bed for people who have difficulty getting up and off the ground.

Hammocks

Hammocks can be a simple, compact, and comfortable option for sleeping (or just relaxing) off the ground. Before you invest in a hammock or bring nothing but a hammock for sleeping in while camping, consider a few factors.

Use: How do you plan to use a hammock? Will you sleep in the hammock or just lounge in one during the day? While some people are perfectly comfortable sleeping in a hammock through-out the night, others find the confines of a hammock unpleasant over a longer period of time. The U-shape position can cause discomfort and back pain, so it might be worthwhile to bring a backup sleeping option if you're trying out a hammock for the first time.

Another factor to consider is the number of people who will be in the hammock at the same time. Certain hammocks are manufactured to bear the weight of two people, while others can only support the weight of one person.

A final consideration is whether you plan to use a hammock while car camping or backcountry camping, since hammock models vary by weight and size.

Weight: Some hammocks are made with lightweight materials, while other models are simply too heavy to haul into the backcountry. Check the weight listed on the product specifications. The hammock body and the hammock suspension ropes are sometimes sold separately, in which case, you must add the two weights together and consider the total weight you will be carrying.

Size: Certain hammock models are built to compress down to a compact size. Some even come with their own compression sacks. If you plan to use a hammock exclusively for car camping, size is less of a concern.

Suspension options: Some car-camping hammocks come with their own freestanding suspension support and do not require trees for hanging. Backcountry hammocks will require two sturdy tree trunks to suspend the ropes, so it's necessary to factor in whether trees will be sparse or plentiful where you plan to camp. Bringing a backup sleeping system is always a good idea.

Added accessories: A number of hammock-specific accessories can be purchased for added comfort, including mosquito netting, rain tarps, string lights, and insulation padding. Many hammocks don't provide sufficient insulation to keep you warm, even when inside a sleeping bag, so extra insulation can be a good idea if you plan to use a hammock as a sleep system.

Cots

A comfortable sleeping option in the outdoors, cots are often not a practical option in the backcountry, due to their size and weight. A couple of factors should be considered before investing in a cot.

Cot style: Check the fabric type when shopping for cots. Polyester fabrics will retain their shape the longest, but aren't as insulating. Cotton and canvas cots typically provide more warmth than other styles, but they are also more prone to stretching and are not as water-resistant.

Size: Some tents are not wide or tall enough to house a cot. If a cot is a necessity for a good night's sleep, then a tent upgrade might be necessary. You should also test a cot in the store to make sure it's wide enough and long enough for your body.

CLOTHING GUIDE

For comfort and safety, it's important to pack clothes that are appropriate for the type of activity you'll be doing. Part of the process of choosing what clothes to pack includes paying attention to the materials used to make the clothing. Before leaving on a trip, consider where you'll be going, what kind of weather might be possible, the specific activities you'll be doing, and how long you'll be camping. This clothing guide will help you consider all these factors and choose the right clothing, made from the right materials, for your trip.

CLOTHING AS A SYSTEM

Modern outdoor clothing is designed to be worn in layers that can be put on or taken off as weather conditions shift. This is why it's advisable to invest in a cold-weather jacket, a rain jacket, rain pants, midlayers, and base layers. Below you'll find examples of the garment types and materials that should be included in a layering system to keep you warm and dry.

◊ Cold-weather jacket (down or synthetic insulation)
◊ Waterproof shell jacket
◊ Fleece jacket
◊ Synthetic or wool long-sleeve shirt
◊ Synthetic pants
◊ Fleece pants
◊ Waterproof pants
◊ Synthetic underwear
◊ Thermal underwear (pants and long-sleeve shirt)
◊ Wool socks
◊ Warm hat (wool or warm synthetic material)

◊   Gloves (fleece, wool, or insulated)
◊   Hiking boots or sturdy shoes
◊   Down booties for lounging around camp (optional)

Below you'll find examples of the garment types and materials that can be used to keep you cool when camping in hot conditions. However, items from the above list (warm jacket, warm base layer, waterproof shells) should also be packed as backup in case the weather turns cold or wet.

◊   Cold-weather jacket (as backup)
◊   Waterproof shell jacket
◊   Cotton long-sleeve shirt (optional, for sun protection)
◊   Synthetic long-sleeve shirt (as backup)
◊   Synthetic or cotton shorts
◊   Synthetic or lightweight cotton pants (for sun and bug protection)
◊   Brimmed hat (for sun protection)
◊   Cotton or synthetic underwear
◊   Cotton or wool socks
◊   Bandanna (for wiping off sweat)
◊   Sandals
◊   Hiking boots or sturdy shoes

FABRIC OPTIONS

Cotton: Cotton is hydrophilic, meaning it absorbs water easily and dries slowly. That's why it's inadvisable to wear cotton clothes during strenuous activity where you might sweat, or in cold and wet weather where your body will need to work harder to stay warm. The adage *cotton kills* warns campers and hikers that wearing cotton clothing in cold, harsh conditions can lead to hypothermia, a potentially deadly condition. Cotton clothing usually includes many kinds of T-shirts, jeans, sweatshirts, underwear, and flannel. Check the label of each garment to see what material or fabric it's made of. Some fabrics are a cotton-polyester blend, which feels soft like cotton, but dries faster.

Cotton can be the ideal, breathable fabric you want when you're camping in an area that's dry, hot, and sunny. A long-sleeve cotton shirt will help keep you cool and provide some sun protection without sunscreen. However, if you are sun-sensitive, it is possible to sunburn through lightweight cotton, so a better option might be a sun-blocking fabric.

Even if the weather calls for hot, sunny conditions, it's still always a good idea to bring warm synthetic or wool layers as backup in case the weather changes.

Wool: A breathable, moisture-wicking fiber, wool retains heat even when wet. Unlike synthetic material, wool is odor-resistant due to its natural antimicrobial properties. Wool will not catch fire as easily as synthetic fabrics, and even if it does, it might naturally extinguish itself. The drawback to wool is that some people find the fibers too itchy and uncomfortable. Merino wool is a smoother, non-itchy wool option that keeps you warm in cold weather and cool in hot weather. Although some people—particularly those with more sensitive skin—still find merino wool to be too itchy.

Bamboo: Soft to the touch and breathable, bamboo fabric is a type of rayon that dries faster than cotton. However, it still absorbs plenty of water and therefore isn't the best choice for wet or cold conditions.

Cocona: Soft and comfortable, cocona is fabric enhancer made from the husks of coconuts. Cocona-treated fabrics are usually quick-drying, moisture-wicking, odor-resistant, and protect skin from ultraviolet (UV) rays.

Tencel: Silky and smooth to the touch, Tencel is a wrinkle-resistant material perfect for travel. Tencel-manufacturing techniques are considered to be some of the more sustainable in the clothing industry. Although it's quick-drying, Tencel doesn't wick moisture as well as other synthetic materials like nylon or polyester.

Nylon and polyester: Many outdoor clothing fabrics will feature nylon or polyester, as they are lightweight, breathable, moisture-wicking, and quick-drying materials. They're also abrasion-resistant and tend not to pill.

Sun-protection fabric: Some fabrics are manufactured with an ultraviolet protection factor (UPF) rating that blocks both UVA and UVB rays, a feature that doesn't wear out even when a UPF garment is washed. The UPF rating system ranges from 15 (good) to 50+ (excellent). All fabrics protect skin from ultraviolet radiation to varying degrees, but if you want to be sure your skin is protected from all types of sun damage, it might be worth investing in some clothing made from specialized UPF sun-protection fabric.

Bug-protection fabric: Permethrin-treated clothes do a decent job of deterring bugs, which is important not only for enjoying the outdoors but also for protecting against disease. Permethrin, a fabric-specific insecticide, acts as a barrier between your skin and biting insects like ticks and mosquitoes. With repeated washing, permethrin will lose its effectiveness over time. Some brands guarantee protection to last up to 70 wash cycles. You can reapply permethrin with a spray bottle, or apply it to any clothing item for bug protection that should last through five or six wash cycles.

JACKETS

When investing in a jacket, it's important to assess four different attributes: durability, weight, warmth, and water resistance. You should also consider which jacket features you'll need for the type of activity you'll be doing most. Are you looking for a featherweight shell that compresses down to nothing, or a more durable exterior layer that can weather years of wear and tear? Do you need waterproof fabric along with exceptional breathability? Research your options to make sure you buy the right jacket for your needs.

Fleece

A fleece jacket is best used in cold weather, or as a midlayer. A fleece jacket should never be used as a replacement for a waterproof rain jacket. Although fleece serves as an optimal warming layer, it is often bulkier and less compressible than its down and synthetic down cousins. When choosing the right fleece for you, try it on; the fleece should be soft—not itchy—against the skin. While some fleece is made of a blend including sheep's wool, most models these days are made from synthetic materials like soda bottles. Since synthetic fleece is made from petroleum products, it's inherently hydrophobic, meaning it doesn't absorb water. So even if a fleece jacket gets wet, it should still keep you relatively warm. However, if drenched, the fleece will lose most of its insulating power. The downside of its hydrophobic qualities is the tendency for fleece to trap sweat, but recent manufacturing techniques are improving the breathability of most fleece jackets.

For added ventilation, look for side and underarm panels made of stretchy, breathable fabric for added ventilation. For increased weather protection, some fleece jackets are DWR-treated. When it comes to the right thickness and degree of weather protection of fleece, there are typically four levels to choose from:

Lightweight: For the most strenuous or technical outdoor activities, a lightweight fleece is optimal for performance. Made for optimistic forecasts since a lightweight fleece provides less warmth, this weight is more breathable, streamlined, and slim fitting.

Midweight: Best used as a midlayer in cold weather, a midweight fleece will keep you warm in milder temperatures as a stand-alone layer, and can be used for both technical pursuits and general use.

Heavyweight: Most functional when hanging around camp, a heavyweight fleece is the warmest—but bulkiest and heaviest—level of fleece.

3-in-1: A 3-in-1 jacket combines fleece with a waterproof or insulated shell. The fleece component usually zips up underneath the outer shell. If the pieces don't separate into two layers, it's usually best to buy both an individual fleece and an individual outer shell for layering capability.

Synthetic vs. down

Like sleeping bags, goose down is also often the warmer alternative for jacket fill. Down also compresses into a smaller size, often weighs less, and is more breathable. Down jackets are perfect for staying warm in cold, dry climates. If you get a down jacket wet, it will lose its ability to insulate. By contrast, synthetic jackets are good for cold, wet climates. They will keep you warm even if the synthetic fill gets wet. They are also usually less expensive than down jackets. However, synthetic jackets weigh more, are a bit bulkier, and less durable. On average, a synthetic jacket will retain its warmth for about six years, whereas a down jacket will lose its warmth after 10–20 years. A down jacket will also better preserve its shape over time, and regains its shape more quickly after being compressed. When it comes to abrasion, a synthetic jacket will often outlive a down jacket. A hole in a synthetic jacket is usually easy to patch, whereas even the smallest hole in a down jacket will leak feathers. A final consideration for down versus synthetic is that a synthetic jacket is sometimes the more humane option, depending on where the down has been sourced. More companies are using responsibly sourced down as the insulation fill for jackets, but it is up to the consumer to check.

Traceable or certified down

Down is found between a goose's skin and its outer feathers; it is the protective layer that keeps the goose warm in cold temperatures. Bioengineering has yet to perfectly replicate goose down's natural insulating properties, so the real stuff must be plucked directly from geese. To assure consumers that responsible practices were used to harvest the down—meaning the feathers weren't plucked from live geese—an increasing number of companies are using "traceable down" or "certified responsibly sourced down." Consumers can check the jacket tag for these certifications. Companies that trace their down disclose where the down was sourced and what harvesting methods were used. Often, geese are sourced from farmers in the food industry, who verify that the geese were treated well during their lives. Ultimately, it's up to the consumer to research which companies maintain humane practices, and to purchase accordingly.

Hydrophobic vs. regular down

Since down loses its insulating properties when wet, some jacket models are filled with hydrophobic down, or down that has been treated with a durable water repellent (DWR) coating. This helps prevent water from rendering the down ineffective. DWR treatments will eventually wear off, so it's not yet clear how long you can expect a DWR-coated down jacket to retain its repellent quality.

Down fill power

Fill power and fill quantity are two determining factors for down warmth. Fill power is often labeled on the tag in 50-unit increments, such as 650, 700, and 850. These numbers reflect the quality of the down and the volume, measured in the number of cubic inches one ounce of down fills. Consequently, the higher the number, the higher the quality of down. However, a jacket with a lower fill power of 650 that has 10 ounces of down might feel as warm as a jacket with a higher fill power, but may contain fewer ounces of down. So when trying to evaluate the warmth-to-weight ratio for any jacket, it's best to look at both the fill power and how much the jacket weighs.

Materials and design

The lighter and thinner the outer shell material of a jacket, the more vulnerable it will be to getting snagged or ripped. A more durable fabric may extend the life of a jacket, but it will also likely be heavier. It's prudent to consider the types of activities you'll be doing and the weather you may encounter. Will you spend most of your time sitting by a campfire or going on long hikes? Does the jacket need to have armpit vents, allowing for more breathability? Is the outer shell treated with DWR to make it more waterproof? Before making a purchase, thoroughly read the specs listed on the tag to get a sense of the jacket's warmth-to-weight ratio, durability, water-repellency, and breathability.

Other features

Hood: A hood adds bulk and weight to a jacket, but it also increases the warming effect considerably. Since you lose a lot of heat through your head, protecting it from the elements will keep you much warmer in cold, wet, and windy conditions. If buying a jacket to function as a midlayer, it is easier to add layers over the jacket if you forgo the hood. Jacket hoods vary in shape and size to accommodate various activities. For example, certain hoods are large enough for a climbing helmet to be worn underneath. Some hoods have a tighter, more streamlined fit, to add weather protection without the bulk while running or hiking, or to be worn under a helmet.

Hem draw cords: Play around with the hem draw cords around the waist. Some draw cords are located inside warm hand pockets, to reduce the chance of a cord getting caught on something.

Hood draw cords: Hood draw cords tighten the fabric of a hood around your face and head for added protection against the elements. Some draw cords are found at the back of a hood, while others are situated on either side of the hood near your chin.

Pockets: Some jacket pockets are lined with fleece or other soft fabric for added warmth. Internal and external chest pockets are a welcome feature for stashing small valuables. Internal pockets usually offer more insulation, which is beneficial for keeping a phone battery charged in cold weather. A few jackets come with large inside pockets, which are ideal for storing bigger items like hats and gloves. Check that waist pockets are low enough for a backpack strap to ride above them.

Stuff sack and clip: Many compressible down and synthetic jackets come with a stuff sack. Some stuff sacks even come with a small carabiner for clipping the stuffed jacket onto a backpack or climbing harness. Before making a purchase, it's a good idea to pack a jacket into its stuff sack to see how small it compresses.

RAINWEAR

Waterproof vs. water-resistant
Jackets with a waterproof coating should keep you dry, even if you get caught in a torrential downpour. A waterproof/breathable jacket is made to keep water off your skin, while allowing enough ventilation to keep you from getting drenched in sweat underneath the jacket. A waterproof/non-breathable jacket is often the least expensive option, and often resembles a rain slicker or emergency poncho. Usually neither stylish nor windproof, a waterproof/non-breathable jacket is best used to simply keep the rain off while sitting around. Water-resistant rain jackets are still breathable, but likely won't keep you dry in the event of sustained rainstorm.

Windproof vs. wind-resistant
A waterproof jacket should also be windproof, meaning that it will prevent a draft from getting through the fabric to your skin. Similarly, a water-resistant jacket should be wind-resistant. This means that it should offer enough protection in light winds, but won't be an adequate safeguard against high winds or storms.

Shell types
A shell is a jacket worn in combination with other layers, typically as the outer layer.

Hard: Usually made of a stiffer fabric, a hard-shell rain jacket is built for optimum weather protection. However, it often will not include insulation, so a warm base or midlayer will sometimes need to be worn underneath.

Soft: A combination of both a water-resistant shell and an insulating layer, a soft-shell jacket offers top performance for high-exertion activities when perspiration might be a factor. The downside is a soft shell offers less protection from the elements.

Hybrid: A hybrid design incorporates both the waterproof/windproof fabrics of a hard shell and the breathable, flexible fabrics of a soft shell (often sewn into the sides, back, and undersides of sleeves).

Insulated: Since many down or synthetic down jackets are designed to be water-resistant, they can also serve as a protective shell. However, the seams need to be sealed to be fully waterproof, and even then, the jacket might not withstand a steady rainstorm.

Layers
Three construction designs are used in manufacturing rainwear.

2-layer: The quietest (least swishy) of the rainwear designs, 2-layer construction is best for urban wear and travel, and is often moderately priced.

2.5-layer: The lightest design, a 2.5-layer jacket is usually not as breathable or durable as other constructions, but it is also the most affordable.

3-layer: Built for the most extreme wet conditions, a 3-layer jacket is the most durable and breathable. But that means it is also the most expensive.

Features
You'll want to check a rain jacket's design features, such as armpit vents, hood and waist draw cords, and packability. Certain added features like waterproof zippers or extra pockets will sometimes add to the cost and weight of the jacket.

GEAR CARE, REPAIR, AND CLEANING GUIDE

Buying camping gear is an investment, so extend the life of your gear by storing it correctly, cleaning it regularly, and repairing and restoring it as necessary.

TENT

Let it dry out: If your tent is wet, covered in dew or rainwater, let it dry out completely before packing it up. Otherwise, the tent fabric will mildew between uses.

Waterproof the seams: Apply a waterproofing sealant to the seams of your tent (even tents with taped seams) at least once a year.

Use a ground cloth or footprint: To protect the bottom of your tent from wear and tear, place a footprint on the ground and your tent on top of it.

Stuff, don't fold: Repeatedly folding a tent along the same creases will cause those folds to wear down over time. Instead, stuff your tent into its stuff sack every time you pack it away.

Stake it down: Use tent stakes and guylines to secure your tent and rainfly to the ground. Windy conditions can cause tents that are not securely fastened down to roll away, which can bend tent poles or rip fabric.

RAINWEAR

You'll find care instructions on the tag of your waterproof garment and these should serve as the default cleaning method to prolong the life of your rainwear. The fabric care tips provided below should be followed only if instructions are not stitched into your waterproof garments.

Wash regularly: Although counterintuitive, washing rainwear regularly will help preserve its waterproof properties. Smoke and dirt can reduce rainwear's performance over time.

Use rainwear-specific detergents: Only specialized cleaning products should be used to wash rain gear. Mass-market detergents contain additives that can leave behind residues, which reduce the effectiveness of waterproof fabric. Prewash stain removers are usually OK to use, but check the care instructions for the garment first.

Rinse thoroughly: Be sure to rinse the item well to remove all soap residue. Sometimes two rinse cycles are necessary.

Hand-wash or front-load: Rain gear should only be hand-washed or run through a front-loading washing machine. Fabric can snag on the agitator in a top-loading washing machine.

Batten down the hatches: Turn rainwear inside out before washing. Empty and close pockets and fasten hook-and-loop closures to prevent snagging or abrasion during a wash cycle.

What to avoid: Never dry-clean a waterproof garment or use bleach, fabric softener, or dryer sheets. Open flames or high heat should also be avoided since rain-gear fabric is usually flammable.

DOWN OR SYNTHETIC DOWN JACKET

Dirt and regular use can wear out a cold-weather jacket's insulating properties and any DWR coating applied. With proper care, you should be able to extend the life of a jacket by several years.

Regular washing: Like washing rain gear, it can be counterintuitive to wash a down jacket, considering what water can do to down feathers. However, if a down jacket is worn as often as every week, it can be beneficial to wash it as much as once a month. The same washing schedule applies to a synthetic down jacket that is worn regularly.

Spot-clean: Prior to washing the whole jacket, spot-clean any stains, dark patches, or high-wear areas like wrists and elbows. Pull the outer fabric away from the insulation material so you can avoid getting the insulation fill wet. Apply a small amount of mild soap (the same used for washing the entire jacket) to a toothbrush, and rub the bristles gently over the stain. Rinse the area thoroughly with a wet sponge.

Washing protocol: Read the care instructions printed on the jacket's label for proper washing technique. Some manufacturers recommend sending down garments to a professional down cleaner, but careful home care should also be sufficient. Use only a front-loading washing machine, as top-loaders can damage down feathers or synthetic fibers. Wash the jacket on a cold-water cycle using a detergent made for the specific type of insulation in the jacket. For example, mass-market detergents will strip the natural oils from the feathers, causing them to lose their insulating properties. As with rain gear, be sure to give the jacket a thorough rinse to remove all soap residue from the fabric.

Dryer technique: Dry the jacket on a low heat in a tumble dryer. Running two dryer cycles may be necessary to dry the jacket completely. Adding a tennis ball or two to the dryer will help restore the jacket's shape.

What to avoid: Do not use bleach, fabric softeners, mass-market detergents, or an iron when cleaning cold-weather jackets. Avoid open flame or high heat, which can melt the flammable fabric. If there is a hot spot in your dryer on the low heat setting, place any jacket made from nylon or synthetic materials in a large cotton drawstring bag before putting it in the dryer.

DOWN OR SYNTHETIC DOWN SLEEPING BAG

Whether a sleeping bag has down or synthetic down fill, simple maintenance steps can be taken to prolong the bag's performance and restore its loft. Body oils and dirt can build up over time and reduce a sleeping bag's effectiveness in cold temperatures.

Wash annually: A sleeping bag shouldn't be washed after every trip, but annual laundering is beneficial if the bag is used regularly. Late fall is a good time to wash the bag, or at the end of your usual camping season.

Spot-clean: Sometimes you can avoid cleaning the whole sleeping bag by spot-cleaning those areas of the bag that are most prone to getting dirty, such as the head and foot of the bag. It's necessary to spot-clean stains before washing the entire sleeping bag, since detergent can build up in those areas and break down insulation. Spot-clean a sleeping bag using the same techniques recommended for clothing made with the same fill material. Pull the outer shell fabric out to avoid getting the insulation wet. Apply a small amount of mild soap (the same used for washing the entire sleeping bag) to a toothbrush, and rub the bristles gently over the spot that needs extra cleaning. Rinse the area thoroughly with a wet sponge or cloth.

Washing protocol: Check the bag's tag for proper care instructions to make sure they align with this information. Sending the bag to a professional sleeping bag cleaner is also an option. If you decide to DIY, turn the sleeping bag inside out, loosen any drawstrings, close all zippers, and fasten any hook-and-loop or Velcro connectors together. Wash the bag by hand in warm water (or cold, depending on the care instructions) in a bathtub or on a gentle cycle in a front-loading washing machine. Make sure to use a detergent that is specifically manufactured for the fabric and insulation you will be washing. If washing by hand, soak the bag in the bathtub for up to one hour before draining the tub and gently pressing out any excess water. Fill the tub again with cool or warm water to rinse the bag. Gently work out the soap, and let the bag soak for another 15 minutes. Drain the water, and repeat the rinse step as many times as necessary to remove all the soap. If using a washing machine, two rinse cycles should be sufficient. When the bag is thoroughly rinsed, whether hand-washing or machine-washing, gently press out any remaining water, scoop up the entire bag (rather than lifting one end), and place it carefully in the dryer.

Dryer technique: Place the sleeping bag in a dryer with a couple of tennis balls, and dry on low heat. Tennis balls aren't necessary for restoring a synthetic bag's loft, but they help fluff the down fill. The drying compartment should be big enough that the bag doesn't need to stay balled up to fit inside. If your home dryer isn't big enough, you may need to take your sleeping bag to a laundromat. A down bag will take several hours to dry, while a synthetic bag will take about an hour. Check the bag at intervals to make sure the fabric doesn't overheat. Alternatively, a sleeping bag can be air-dried by hanging it up or laying it flat on a clean surface in a place that's out of direct sunlight and with low humidity. It might be necessary to gently break up clumps of insulation with your hands as the bag dries. When the bag is nearly dry, hang it up to let it dry even more thoroughly overnight. A large cotton drawstring bag can also be used to protect a sleeping bag from coming into contact with hot spots in a commercial dryer.

What to avoid: Never dry-clean a sleeping bag or use bleach or fabric softener. Don't wash a bag in a top-loading washing machine because the agitator can rip the seams. If your sleeping bag gets damp during the night, avoid packing it into its stuff sack before the bag has fully air-dried in the morning. Also avoid leaving it in direct sunlight for too long, as the UV rays will compromise the fabric.

Repair and maintenance: Air out your sleeping pad every morning of your camping trip by turning it inside out when it's not in use. Keep the inside of your sleeping bag clean by only wearing clean clothes when you go to bed or investing in a sleeping bag liner. You can keep the outside of your bag clean and abrasion-free by keeping it off the ground with a sleeping pad. When a down sleeping bag is leaking feathers, gently work them back into the bag. After every camping trip, scan your sleeping bag for any larger holes or tears, and repair them with some sleeping-bag-specific repair tape or sticky fabric. If your sleeping bag is water-protected with a DWR coating, you can opt to occasionally reapply a waterproofing spray. When the bag is still relatively new, a dryer's heat is usually enough to reactivate the DWR waterproofing agent. When packing up your waterproofed shell, turn the sleeping bag inside out, as this will make it easier to compress into a stuff sack. Store your sleeping bag in a larger storage sack to help the bag maintain its loft.

HYDRATION BLADDER

After returning home from a camping trip, cleaning a hydration bladder is an oft-neglected task, since the parts that you need to clean are oddly shaped and not easy to access. If you neglect to clean a hydration bladder for too long, bacteria and mold will start to make themselves at home. Ideally, a hydration bladder should be cleaned after you get home from every camping trip, and the cleaning process is fairly simple as long as you have the right supplies: cleaning solutions and tools, and a drying aid.

Cleaning solutions: In addition to mild dish soap, you'll need to have one of the following cleaning solutions handy:

◊ Reservoir-cleaning tablets (available for purchase at an outdoor gear store): One tablet per cleaning will do the job
◊ Baking soda: ¼ cup in ¾ cup of water (prep enough to fill the reservoir)
◊ Household bleach: 2–5 drops per liter of water (can be combined with baking soda to kill bacteria, viruses, and odors)
◊ Lemon juice: ¼ cup per liter of water (can be combined with bleach or baking soda to kill bacteria, viruses, and odors)

◇ Denture-cleaning tablets: One tablet per cleaning should do the trick

Cleaning tools: To thoroughly clean the various parts of a hydration bladder, you'll want to invest in a hydration-bladder brush made specifically for cleaning the reservoir and drinking tube. Lacking this kind of brush, you can also pull a knotted cord through the drinking tube, provided the cord is longer than the tube and the knot is large enough to scrape the inner walls of the tube as it is pulled through. A kitchen scrub brush or pad will work to clean the inside of the hydration reservoir.

Drying aids: To dry the inside of the reservoir and tube completely, air must circulate around and through them. Hang the bladder upside down, and use a reservoir hanger (most are made to fit any bladder), clothespins, or a kitchen whisk pushed inside the reservoir to hold it open.

Cleaning process

To clean the bladder, first fill it with warm water and add one of the above cleaning agents. Seal it up and shake it thoroughly. Hold the reservoir up so that the drinking tube is hanging down toward the sink, then pinch the bite valve open, letting some water out and ensuring the cleaning solution reaches the inside of the drinking tube. Let the hydration bladder sit for 20 minutes (reservoir-cleaning tablets can take just 5 minutes), then drain the reservoir through the drinking tube.

Next, fill the bladder and tube with warm water mixed with mild dish soap. Scrub the interior walls of the reservoir and the inside of the tube with one of the cleaning tools. You can usually remove the bite valve to make this step easier. When finished, thoroughly rinse the system, disassemble it (tube, reservoir, and bite valve), hang the reservoir and tube up to dry so that water drips out, and set the bite valve aside. Be sure to hang the hydration bladder somewhere out of the way so it can dry completely. Reassembling it with any water left inside will encourage bacteria or mold to regrow.

TARP

Before your trip, run your Tyvek tarp through the washing machine and hang it up to dry. The washing machine agitator will soften the material and make it easier to hang and store.

DIY GEAR TIPS AND TRICKS

For size and cost economy, it's smart to pack gear that serves more than one purpose or that can be made at home. Below are some ideas for troubleshooting problems in a pinch or DIY camping preparation before you leave for a trip.

DUCT TAPE

Wrap a roll of duct tape around a water bottle so you always have it handy. Duct tape can be used in a pinch to fix many camping conundrums, including those listed below.

Duct tape wrapped around a water bottle for easy accessibility

Repairing shelter:

◊   Reinforce a broken tent pole by wrapping duct tape around the two broken pole ends.

◊   Patch a torn tent by ripping off two pieces of duct tape the length of the tear and adhering the tape to the inside and outside of the tent.

◊   Create guylines to protect a tent during high winds. Twist several lengths of duct tape together to make a cord, then tie one end of the cord to a side of the tent, and tie the other end of the cord to a large rock or tree, maintaining enough tension in the line to keep the tent rigid. Continue crafting and tying cords to the tent until it's held securely in place.

Make guylines out of twisted duct tape to help keep a tent from flying away during high winds

Patching, reinforcing, and protecting:

◊   Patch a leak in a water bottle or hydration bladder by securing a piece of duct tape over the hole.

◊   Protect blister-prone areas by covering them with duct tape as a preventive measure.

◊ Stabilize a damaged shoe or boot by wrapping duct tape around the boot or patching a hole.

◊ Waterproof boots or shoes by covering them entirely with duct tape.

◊ To keep snow, rocks, or dirt out of your shoes, create gaiters that cover your instep and run above your ankle by wrapping duct tape loosely around the bottom of each pant leg.

Gaiters made out of duct tape

TRASH BAGS

Shelter

Packing a tent or tarp for shelter is ideal. But when there are no other alternatives, a makeshift shelter can be made by using trash bags. See page 83 for instructions.

Waterproofing

Trash bags can be used to keep yourself and your gear dry. They can also be wrapped and taped around boots or ankles to protect your feet from getting wet.

To create a makeshift rain jacket, rip or cut a hole in the center of the bottom seam of a trash bag. The diameter should be slightly less than the width of the top of your head. Create two other holes, just below the bottom seam, on either side of the trash bag. Poke your head through the hole at the bottom of the bag and your arms through the two other holes. The poncho can be worn with your head all the way through the hole, or with the edge of the top hole stretched over your head like a hood.

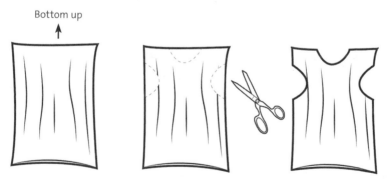

If you get caught in the rain without a rain jacket, make one out of a trash bag and keep your torso dry

Bug proofing

Fashion a bug screen by hanging one or two trash bags over the opening of the tent on the outside, and cut several slits up to within a few inches of the top of the bag.

Warmth

Space blankets are ideal for emergency situations, but trash bags can be used in a pinch to warm up. Simply use the bags like blankets.

Shade

Hang trash bags from a tree to provide makeshift temporary shade in hot weather conditions. Be sure to remove any trash bag pieces that might get snagged in branches when removing the bags.

LINT AS A FIRE STARTER

Collect lint from your dryer, and store it in a small baggie or container. When starting a fire, pull out a wad of the collected lint and ignite it as a fire starter. In a pinch, small pieces of torn-up duct tape also work as fire starters. See page 123 for fire-building instructions.

DIY TRAVEL-SIZE CONTAINERS

This trick is especially handy while backcountry camping, when paring down weight is a necessity. Rather than buying expensive travel-size toiletries or packing large or heavy containers, economize by making some single-use tubes before you leave home. Cut a wide plastic drinking straw into four-inch lengths. Seal one end of each tube by pinching the end with pliers and carefully melting the edge closed with a lighter. Next, squeeze toothpaste, antibiotic cream, cooking spices, or any other toiletry or medicine of choice into the open end of the tube. To make the pouring easier, squeeze the substance into the corner of a plastic baggie,

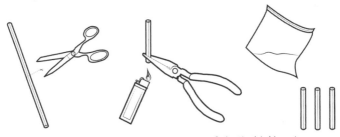

Make your own travel-size containers out of plastic drinking straws

make a small cut in the corner, and pipe the contents into the tube with more precision. To seal the straw, pinch the end with pliers and melt the plastic straw closed. Don't forget to write content labels on the straws. To open a straw packet while camping, simply pinch one end like a honey stick or cut the tip off with a knife or scissors.

TIC TAC SPICE BOXES

If you happen to like eating Tic Tacs or have a family member who does, the leftover boxes can be used as travel-size containers for storing spices while camping. Be sure to add a spice label to each container.

BAREBONES TENT TRICK

Certain freestanding tents can be set up without the body of the tent, using only the rainfly as the shelter. During hot weather, this can be a good way to cool down at night. Just be sure to take the body of the tent with you on your trip in case the weather turns.

WATER JUG ICE PACKS

Before leaving home, clean and fill used milk jugs or other containers with water and freeze them. Use the frozen jugs in place of ice packs in a cooler. When they melt, you'll have extra drinking water ready.

SACRED SOCKS

Store an extra pair of clean, dry socks in the bottom of your sleeping bag. Change into them at night and you'll be a happy camper. Remember to stuff them back into your sleeping bag in the morning so you can use them again at night.

BREAD TAG CLOTHESPINS

Save used plastic bread tags and you'll have clothespins at the ready when you go camping. Simply string a cord between two trees and use the bread tags to clip clothes to the line.

ZIPPER PROTECTANT

It's frustrating when a zipper gets stuck or catches on itself, especially when trying to keep the elements out of a tent or rain jacket. Between camping trips, rub an unlit candle along the zippers of tents and jackets. The wax will preserve the zippiness of the zippers over a longer period of time.

DOUBLE-WIDE SLEEPING BAG

For a more intimate—and often warmer—night with your tent partner, zip two sleeping bags together. To do this, zippers must be the same style, size, and approximately the same length.

FORGOTTEN GEAR

It's easy to forget gear at home. Even the most experienced camper sometimes fails to pack items needed for a trip. Using a gear list when you pack may reduce the chances of leaving something important at home. But if you do, there are ways to improvise common sense solutions using what you have on hand.

TENT

A makeshift bivy shelter can be made by stringing a cord (made of duct tape, if necessary—see page 79 for guyline instructions) between two trees. The trees should be far enough apart that you can lie down lengthwise between them. Tape two trash bags together and then hang them over the cord so that they drape evenly on either side; both sides of the shelter should rest on the ground. Place rocks on the ground on either side of the shelter so that the shelter stays structurally stable in wind.

If you need shelter and forgot your tent, make a bivy shelter out of trash bags strung between two trees

MATCHES OR LIGHTER

Forgetting matches or a lighter doesn't necessarily mean you'll need to channel your inner caveperson to start a fire. While practicing your survivalist skills can be a fun challenge, when it comes time to actually cook dinner and your group is getting hungry, keep it simple.

Some camp stoves are built to be self-igniting by spitting out a spark to light the fuel. If you forgot matches or a lighter but remembered to bring a self-igniting camp stove (like a Jetboil), you can use the stove's flames to light a twig as a substitute for a match.

Packing a flint and steel is always a good idea—it's an easy, lightweight backup for starting fires.

HEADLAMP OR FLASHLIGHT

Leaving home without a light source is not ideal, but shouldn't be a cause for panic. If you're car camping, use the car headlights to accomplish technical tasks like setting up a tent. Just be sure the headlights are set on dim and aren't pointing into anyone else's campsite. If headlights seem too intrusive for the camping area, or if you find yourself without a light in the backcountry, don't fret. It takes only a couple of minutes for eyes to adjust to darkness enough to be able to make out shapes. As you let your eyes get used to the dark, the chemical that helps with night vision, called rhodopsin, continues to activate and strengthen. Give yourself from a half hour to an hour, and you might be surprised how much you can see after the sun has set. Also remember to incorporate enough vitamin A into your regular diet, as people with low vitamin A levels will lack enough rhodopsin to see in the dark—a condition called night blindness.

Water bottles can be turned into lanterns by wrapping a headlamp around them, with the light facing the bottle

If you forgot your lantern but remembered to bring your headlamp, you can wrap the headlamp strap twice around a clear or opaque water bottle with the lamp facing the side of the bottle. Turn the lamp on and enjoy the illuminating lantern-like effect.

EATING AND COOKING UTENSILS

Fork

If you forgot eating utensils and can manage chopsticks, it's easy to fashion a set out of a sturdy stick. Cut the stick in half, then slowly shave off the bark with a pocketknife, whittling each stick into a desired, tapered shape. Set each end in boiling water for 10 minutes to kill any bacteria.

Spoon

Most foods eaten with a spoon can be sipped from a cup or a bowl.

Bowl/cup

Use strips of duct tape to make a bowl. Cut eight pieces of duct tape, each 12 inches long. Lay four strips (sticky sides up) over each other to form an eight-pointed star. Make a second four-strip star and lay that star over the first, lining them up slightly off-center, exposing part of the sticky tape on each side of the star. Fold the strips up, using the sticky edges. Adhere any additional tape to the cup/bowl to patch up any holes.

Pot/pan

Most foods heated up in a pot or a pan can be cooked using tinfoil. Just be sure to crimp the edges tightly and fold the foil so the shiny side is facing out and not exposed to the food. You can also roast certain foods like meat or veggies over the fire, using bark-stripped sticks like marshmallow sticks. Dogwood, ash, maple, and elm are safe choices for cooking sticks.

PILLOW

Fill your sleeping bag's stuff sack with dry clothes. Be sure to flip the stuff sack inside out so that any straps or cords aren't on the outside. Alternatively, a pillow can be made by rolling a fleece jacket into a pillow-sized spiral. One other option is to inflate a trash bag or large storage bag and wrap it in a soft garment.

SLEEPING BAG

For the warmest night without a sleeping bag, put on as many base layers as you can comfortably sleep in. Wear a down or synthetic down jacket, and blanket your legs with any extra layers, like a rain jacket, fleece jacket, or even unused garbage bags. If you have an emergency blanket in your first-aid kit, add that too. Don't forget your extremities. Sleeping while wearing a hat, gloves, and socks will keep you much warmer at night.

COFFEE FILTER

Some campers would rather go without a sleeping bag than forget the coffee filter. If this necessity is forgotten, stretch a clean T-shirt over the filter holder and press it down to the bottom. Set the filter cone over a cup, pour ground coffee beans into the T-shirt, and then carefully pour hot water over the grounds. If a filter holder isn't available, pour ground coffee beans into the middle of a T-shirt and have another camper hold the T-shirt over the opening of a cup while you carefully pour water over the grounds. Forget about ever getting the coffee stain out of your T-shirt.

On the off chance that you packed whole coffee beans instead of ground coffee, a makeshift mortar and pestle can save the day. If you packed a ziplock bag, fill the bag a quarter full with coffee beans. Squeeze all the air out of the bag and seal it. On a flat surface, use a full water bottle like a rolling pin and roll the bottle over the beans in the bag. Some vigorous pulses of the bottle will be necessary to crush the beans at the start. Your arms may get sore from this fairly labor-intensive way of pulverizing the beans, but if you keep at it, you'll be rewarded with fresh-brewed coffee in no time.

TOILET PAPER

Some women opt to drip-dry or use a bandanna as a reusable pee rag. You can hang the bandanna by a tree or on the outside of your backpack to dry. Rinse it out when you can.

For bowel movements, smooth rocks or twigs and sticks can be used in place of toilet paper. Leaves can also be used, but make absolutely sure that you can identify the leaves. Rubbing something like poison oak on your nether regions is a mistake you will never forget.

TEST YOUR EQUIPMENT

Before you head out, do a test run on each piece of equipment to make sure it's functional. Shake out your tent, and take inventory of all the parts. Do you have the stakes, guylines, rainfly, poles, and tent body? Do you have the right size footprint? Consider renting gear before buying so you know what you like. Try backyard camping to see how well you sleep in your tent, on your sleeping pad, and in your sleeping bag. Try lighting your stove to make sure it doesn't need to be cleaned. Go on a walk or short hike to make sure of the fit and comfort of items such as back-packs, hiking boots, and jackets. Go on a walk with a fully loaded backpack to see if you can bear the weight. It's better to know before you go that you need to lighten the load or buy different gear than to find out after you get to your camping destination.

One reason we outdoor
people love the woods is
that it develops self-reliance
and increases our self-respect
by increasing our ability to
do things.

—Dan Beard, *The Book of Camp-Lore
and Woodcraft*, 1920

Chapter 2

Trip Planning and Preparation

T O ENSURE A FUN AND SAFE CAMPING TRIP FOR everyone in your party, you'll need to take steps to prepare and plan for the weather, location-specific variables, and the activities you'll be doing. With careful research and a solid trip plan, you can increase the chances that everyone in your group will enjoy their time in the woods and come home safe.

KNOW YOUR LIMITS

PRIOR EXPERIENCE AND PHYSICAL LIMITATIONS

Evaluate your physical limits, along with the physical limits of each person in your group and their prior camping experience. If you're planning an outdoor activity during your camping trip that requires specialized skills such as rafting, mountain climbing, kayaking, et cetera, assess whether it would be worthwhile to hire a guide or guide company. You don't want to unnecessarily push your group past their physical abilities, as this can have dire consequences. It may be worth asking your doctor about your own physical health before attempting a strenuous activity.

GEAR LIMITATIONS

Where will you be camping and what season will it be? A warm, sunny trip to the desert will require different gear than a fall trip into the mountains. What kind of activity will you be doing? A backpacking trip requires being weight-conscious, whereas a canoe trip requires being space-conscious. Each person in your group should know what to pack beforehand, how much room they will have, and how heavy their gear can be. Send everyone a list of essential gear they should pack, along with any group items you'll be bringing. Make sure everyone has the gear they need before you leave on the trip. Before buying a new piece of gear that might only be used once, check to see if a local gear store or guide company rents that specific piece for your trip. If you're prepping for a backpacking trip, tell everyone to pack their backpacks completely and test carrying the weight before leaving home.

When flying to a camping destination, you may have limited space due to the airline's baggage restrictions. Make sure all sharp items (like knives, ice axes, crampons, and multi-tools) are packed in checked luggage. Bear spray and fuel canisters should not be brought on the plane and should instead be purchased after arrival.

TIME LIMITATIONS

Depending on the duration of your trip, you may need to limit where you go or budget how much time you have for activities. For example, it's not a good idea to be paddling your canoe to your campsite after sunset. Find out when the sun rises and sets on the dates you'll be camping. Research how long the drive will take and how long it might take to reach your camping destination by foot or across water. Overestimate the time it will take to account for unexpected delays, physical limitations, or adverse weather conditions.

RESEARCH

A number of variables can influence how much fun everyone has on your camping trip. Group morale might be affected if your group gets caught in a lightning storm because you forgot to check the weather, or if you arrive at a campground without cash to pay the fee. Take some steps before you leave home to make sure you're not caught by surprise.

Plan ahead and prepare

Poor planning often results in miserable campers and damage to natural and cultural resources. Rangers tell stories of campers they have encountered who, because of poor planning and unexpected conditions, degrade backcountry resources and put themselves at risk.

Why is trip planning important?

You may want to create additional answers for this list:

- It helps ensure the safety of groups and individuals.
- It prepares you to Leave No Trace and minimizes resource damage.
- It contributes to accomplishing trip goals safely and enjoyably.
- It increases self-confidence and opportunities for learning more about nature.

Seven steps of trip planning

1. Identify and record the goals (expectations) of your trip.
2. Identify the skill and ability of trip participants.
3. Select destinations that match your goals, skills, and abilities.
4. Gain knowledge of the area you plan to visit from land managers, maps, and literature.
5. Choose equipment and clothing for comfort, safety, and Leave No Trace qualities.
6. Plan trip activities to match your goals, skills, and abilities.
7. Evaluate your trip upon return and note changes you will make next time.

Other elements to consider

- Weather
- Terrain
- Regulations/restrictions
- Private land boundaries
- Average hiking speed of the group and the anticipated food consumption (leftovers create waste, which can leave a trace)
- Group size (Does it meet regulations, trip purpose, and Leave No Trace criteria?)

CHECK THE FORECAST

One week prior to your camping trip, check the weather forecast to anticipate how weather conditions might impact your trip plans or gear. Be prepared to cancel a camping trip if harsh weather conditions may put you or others in an unsafe situation. Continue to check the weather forecast in the days leading up to the trip, as weather predictions can change dramatically over the course of a week. If you have cell service or another way to check the forecast while you're camping, continue to stay informed about any weather changes that could affect your plans. If you

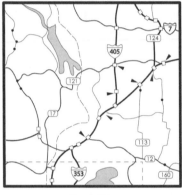 

Road map Topographical map

know you'll be outside of cell range, it might be worth investing in a GPS unit that can track changes in weather, or a radio that you can tune to a station that issues weather updates.

LEARN HOW TO READ A MAP

Understanding how to read a map is vital to navigating, staying on route, and avoiding getting lost. Study your maps thoroughly and learn how to properly navigate before you leave for your trip. The title of a map tells you what location the map depicts. You can look up trail and area maps online and also purchase maps at gear stores, gas stations, visitor centers, and ranger stations. Select your route or area of choice by locating an existing trail or campground on the map. It's always best to use established trails and camp-grounds rather than forging your own path. If you need to fre-quently reference a map while hiking, you can use the "thumbing" trick. Begin by identifying your starting location on the map and then place your thumb over that spot. You can then let the hand holding the map hang down while you hike. When you need to reference the map again, your thumb will mark your last location.

Choose the correct map type

Choose the appropriate type of map (or maps) for your trip, and study the route you will take. You will want to invest in a road map if you might be driving outside of cell service. A topographic map shows detailed information such as elevation, roads, trails, water bodies, and terrain. A road map features main highways, city streets, country roads, and scenic areas like national parks.

Select the right map scale

To be able to read the map's features specific to your trip, you'll want to choose a map that has the right scale ratio of map distance to real distance. The scales used most commonly for short-range trips like hiking and cycling are 1:50,000 or 1:25,000, so you can see the features of the land in more detail. A standard road map has a scale of 1:100,000, which means that 1 unit of distance on the map is equal to 100,000 units in real life. So the higher the second number, the less detail the map will provide. Scales are typically printed on the bottoms or sides of maps.

Learn map features

Every map should have a key or legend that lists the symbols used to indicate features such as roads, trails, water bodies, campgrounds, et cetera. Study these symbols and identify which landscape features you'd like to visit on your trip, such as a lake, a lookout, or a historical site. Read the map in a neutral orientation by locating the compass rose and making sure the north arrow is pointing up, since the top of the map should always reflect north unless otherwise indicated. If you have a compass, you'll be able to orient yourself by

Compass rose

figuring out which direction north is in real life, and then finding which direction north is on the map.

Read contour lines

Contour lines represent changes in elevation and the shape of the terrain. For example, if your map uses a 10-foot contour interval, the space between each contour line represents 10 feet of

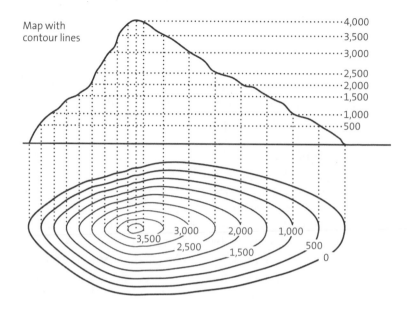

Map with contour lines

elevation. The closer the lines are to each other, the steeper the grade. This information is useful when route planning, so you can avoid traveling along the steepest route across terrain.

Map your route

Chart the most direct, least cumbersome route to get from your starting point to your destination. As you travel, it's a good idea to mark notable landmarks so you can easily find your way back. Many GPS devices allow you to track your route as you move. You can label waypoints along your GPS-recorded route so that you can get back on track should you lose your way.

LEARN HOW TO READ A COMPASS

Use a compass hand in hand with your map to determine where you are and what direction you need to go. Practice using a compass before you're in a situation where you need one. Always keep a compass in your vehicle or gear bag so that you have one available for use. Many smartphones come with a compass app feature that doesn't require the internet to be accurate, but a physical compass should always be packed as emergency backup.

Compass components

A mountaineering compass is a good choice for beginners and experienced campers alike. It is used for orienting or determining

EMERGENCY PLAN

Hope for the best and plan for the worst. Even the best-laid plan can run off course, and you must have a backup plan in place in case the weather shifts, someone gets injured, most of your food gets eaten by critters, or someone in your group goes missing. Will you bring an emergency communication device that doesn't require cell service (e.g., radio, GPS unit, or SPOT device) to be able to signal for help if someone in your party needs a medical evacuation? How many miles will you be from civilization? Acquaint each member of your group with the following emergency-prevention strategies:

- Stay together and use the buddy system.
- Each individual should carry a whistle.
- Agree that if someone gets separated from the group, they will stay put until someone else in the group is able to locate them.
- Review the route with the whole group.
- Avoid taking shortcuts.
- Pack a first-aid kit stocked sufficiently for the size of your group.
- Check the physical and mental status of each member of the group before heading out each day.

Establish which friend or family member will be your emergency contact person. This should be someone who is not going on the trip. Write a comprehensive plan for this person that includes the following information to help first responders assist you in case of emergency:

- The start and end dates and time for your trip
- Full name and contact information for each person in your group
- License plate number, make, and model of each vehicle or boat that will be taken on the trip
- The exact location or locations you'll be camping, and the dates you plan to camp in those specific places
- The activities you've planned for each day
- Your backup plan in case you must camp somewhere else
- A list of the equipment you've packed

Agree on the date and time this person should report you as missing in the event that you don't return on schedule.

Make sure each member of your group knows how to use your emergency devices to call for help. If one of the members of your group goes missing and you do not have a way to call 911, flag down other campers and ask them to alert rangers at the nearest ranger station. When in a situation where no other campers are nearby, split your group up using a buddy system. Send some people back to the closest ranger station to get help. Others should stay behind in case the missing member locates your group. If you are able to call for help using an emergency device, follow the below steps immediately if one of the members of your group gets lost:

1. Call 911.
2. Tell the operator when and where the missing person was last seen.
3. Describe the person: e.g., age, height, what they were wearing and carrying.
4. List any medical conditions they may have.

If your party doesn't come home when scheduled, these steps should be taken by your emergency contact person:

1. Call 911.
2. Tell the operator where the group was camping and when the group was supposed to return.
3. Identify all the members of the group and their vehicles.
4. Describe the last place the group should have been before their return home.
5. Contact the nearest ranger station.

Make sure every member of your party knows what to do in an emergency situation before you head out. Do your research to know what kinds of injuries might occur depending on where you're going, the fitness and experience level of the group, and what activities you'll be doing. Draft a comprehensive plan in case any of those possible scenarios occur.

Familiarize each member of the group with the STOP plan in case anyone gets lost.

Stop: Once you notice you are lost, stop moving. Stay calm and stay put.

Think: Mentally retrace your steps. What landmarks do you remember seeing last? How long ago were you still familiar with your surroundings?

Observe: Pull out your compass and determine where north is. What landmarks can you observe from where you are?

Plan: Make a plan based on your surroundings, the time of day, the gear you have with you, and the information you have. Draft several different plans and think through which option is the safest. When unsure about a route, it's usually best to stay where you are until help finds you. Stay put if it's nighttime, you're injured, or you're exhausted. If your plan is to stay put, you can use a whistle to signal to others where you are. Three short blasts on a whistle is the accepted distress call.

The man who goes afoot,
prepared to camp anywhere
and in any weather, is the most
independent fellow on earth.

—Horace Kephart, "Outfit
for Walking Trips," 1915

Chapter 3
Finding and Setting Up Camp

U PON ARRIVAL AT A CAMPING AREA, SOME campers pick the first campsite they see and leave arrival tasks such as registration, reviewing campground rules, gear organizing, and tent setup for later. Generally it's prudent to take the time to thoroughly walk through all your arrival tasks. Take a look at the layout of the campground, and pick a site that meets your safety and comfort needs. Review the camp rules and regulations with all members of your group so you won't need to be the group's rule enforcer. Organize your gear in predictable ways to help your group locate items without having to ask. By methodically approaching your arrival tasks, you'll face less work for yourself later and likely improve your overall enjoyment of the whole trip.

UPON ARRIVAL

CHECK-IN AND REGISTRATION

Most campgrounds and trailheads have a registration station that you will need to visit upon arrival. Some campgrounds ask that you pay the overnight camping fee when you register. At some trailheads you are required to fill out a registration form so rangers know how many people are in your party and where you plan to camp. Often these trailhead registration forms come with a tear-off permit that you will need to fasten to the outside of your backpack or tent.

Standard drive-up campgrounds label their campsites with a letter or number that you will need to list on your registration form. Some registration stations will list the sites that have already been claimed. Many campgrounds will instruct you to clip a card or piece of paper that lists your checkout date to your campsite post. Have each member of your group memorize the number and location of your campsite. Point out nearby landmarks to help you and members of your group remember the location.

Upon arrival, check in with a camp host or ranger to get an update on any hazards, regulations, or weather predictions that might impact your plans. If the camp host is unavailable, review any campground rules or regulations posted on the registration bulletin board when you check in.

CHOOSING THE RIGHT CAMPSITE

The perfect campsite is open to subjective interpretation, but there are a few factors you can take into consideration when comparing sites.

LOOK UP

How many trees surround your site and how much shade will there be throughout the day? On a hot day, shade might be a saving grace. Inspect trees for dead branches that might suddenly fall to the ground, and be sure not to stake your tent underneath any. Are there any trees or boulders that might serve as a windbreak in stormy conditions? You may want to determine what direction any prevailing wind is coming from and camp on the lee side, or the side behind the windbreak.

EVALUATE YOUR NEEDS

For convenience, do you need to camp close to a bathroom or shower house? Do you require complete darkness in order to sleep well? Do you want sun in the morning and shade in the afternoon? If you're staying in a busy frontcountry campground and prefer camping someplace quiet, you may want to choose a site that's farther away from the bustle. If you require an electrical

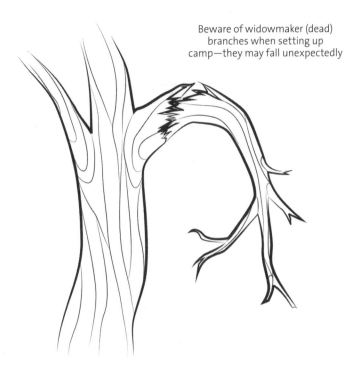

Beware of widowmaker (dead) branches when setting up camp—they may fall unexpectedly

hookup for an RV, you should choose your campsite accordingly. Note where the restroom or outhouse is located so you can avoid camping downwind from it.

Check the rules for the area to determine how far a tent needs to be from natural water sources. In many cases, campsites must be at least 200 feet away from shore. Be sure to also check any rules or regulations for proper food storage and disposal.

Be considerate of other campers, and try not to camp too close to someone else's site, especially in the backcountry. Check first to see if there are other campsite options that put some distance between you and other campers; camp right next to someone if that's the only option.

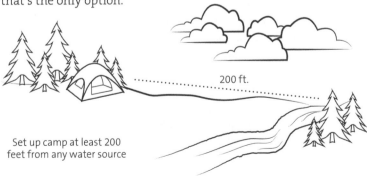

200 ft.

Set up camp at least 200 feet from any water source

LEAVE NO TRACE SEVEN PRINCIPLES

Travel and camp on durable surfaces

Travel damage occurs when surface vegetation or communities of organisms are trampled beyond recovery. The resulting barren area leads to soil erosion and the development of undesirable trails or recreational spaces. Backcountry travel may involve travel over both trails and off-trail areas.

Camp on durable surfaces

Selecting an appropriate campsite is perhaps the most important aspect of low-impact backcountry use. It requires good judgment and often involves making trade-offs between minimizing ecological and social impacts. A decision about where to camp should be based on information about the level and type of use in the area, the fragility of vegetation and soil, the likelihood of wildlife disturbance, an assessment of previous impacts, and your party's potential to make an impact.

Choosing a campsite in high-use areas

Avoid camping close to water and trails, and select a site not visible to others. Even in popular areas the sense of solitude can be enhanced by screening campsites and choosing an out-of-the-way site. Camping away from the water's edge also allows access routes for wildlife. Be sure to obey regulations related to campsite selection. Allow enough time and energy at the end of the day to select an appropriate site. Fatigue, bad weather, and late departure times are not acceptable excuses for choosing fragile campsites.

Generally, it is best to camp on sites that are so highly impacted that further careful use will cause no noticeable impact. In popular areas, these sites are obvious because they have already lost their vegetation cover. Also, it is often possible to find a site that naturally lacks vegetation, such as exposed bedrock or sandy areas.

On high-impact sites, tents, traffic routes, and kitchen areas should be concentrated on already impacted areas. The objective is to confine impact to places that already show use and avoid enlarging the area of disturbance. When leaving camp, make sure that it is clean, attractive, and appealing to other campers who follow.

Camping in undisturbed remote areas

Pristine areas are usually remote, see few visitors, and have no obvious impacts. Visit these special places only if you are committed to, and highly skilled in, Leave No Trace techniques.

In pristine sites it is best to spread out tents, avoid repetitive traffic routes, and when backcountry camping, move camp every night. The objective is to minimize the number of times any part of the site is trampled. In setting up camp, disperse tents and the kitchen on durable sites. Wear soft shoes around camp. Minimize activity around the kitchen and places where packs are stashed. The durable surfaces of large rock slabs make good kitchen sites. Watch where you walk to avoid crushing vegetation, and take alternate paths to water. Minimize the number of trips to water by carrying water containers. Check regulations, but camping 200 feet (about 70 adult steps) from water is a good rule of thumb.

When breaking camp, take time to naturalize the site. Covering scuffed areas with native materials (such as pine needles), brushing out footprints, and raking matted grassy areas with a stick will help the site recover and make it less obvious as a campsite. This extra effort will help hide any indication of where you camped and make it less likely that other backcountry travelers will camp in the same spot. The less often a pristine campsite is used, the better chance it has of remaining pristine.

The most appropriate campsites in arid lands are on durable surfaces, such as rock and gravel, or on sites that have been so highly impacted that further use will cause no additional disturbance. Previously impacted sites are obvious because they have already lost their vegetation cover or rocky soils have been visibly disturbed. If choosing this type of site, make sure your spot is large enough to accommodate your entire group.

A pristine campsite, with no evidence of previous use, is appropriate in arid lands provided it is on a non-vegetated, highly resistant surface. Expanses of rock, gravel, or sand are all excellent choices. It should never be necessary to camp on cryptobiotic soil, islands of vegetation, or within the precious green ribbons of desert creeks or streams. Beware when camping on sandy river bottoms and areas susceptible to flash floods.

Cooking areas, tents, and backpacks should be located on rock, sand, or gravel. Choose durable routes of travel between parts of your camp so that connecting trails do not develop. Vary your routes since the objective is to minimize the amount of trampling and soil compaction on any specific part of the campsite. Limit your stay to no more than two nights.

Never scrape away or clean sites of organic litter like leaves, and always minimize the removal of rocks and gravel. The organic litter will help to cushion trampling forces, limit soil compaction, release plant nutrients, and reduce the erosive forces of rainfall. Disturbing lichen-coated rocks can leave a visible impact for hundreds of years. Once overturned, these rocks are difficult to replace and the lichens will not grow back within our lifetime.

Camping in river corridors

River corridors are narrow strips of land and water with little room to disperse human activities. Campsites are often designated. It is generally best to camp on established sites located on beaches, sandbars, or non-vegetated sites above the high-water line.

FINDING BACKCOUNTRY CAMPSITES

WHAT TO AVOID

In the backcountry, avoid campsites along ledges, or at the top of ridges or peaks where lightning is a potential danger. Never set up camp in a dry riverbed, since flash floods are a deadly hazard. Even when blue sky is overhead, precipitation at higher elevations can cause flash floods downstream.

If possible, avoid camping where the ground is recessed, as these lower-elevation areas can quickly collect water during a rainstorm. This creates the potential for water to pool on the floor inside your tent.

WHAT TO CONSIDER

Even in the backcountry, it's best to protect yourself from the elements by finding an area protected from the wind and rain.

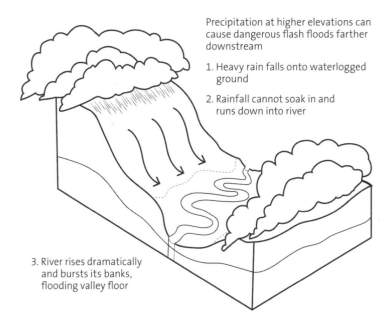

Precipitation at higher elevations can cause dangerous flash floods farther downstream

1. Heavy rain falls onto waterlogged ground

2. Rainfall cannot soak in and runs down into river

3. River rises dramatically and bursts its banks, flooding valley floor

Trees, boulders, hills, and other natural windbreaks and water barriers can help keep your tent from flapping in the wind or leaking rainwater.

Check the ground of any potential site to make sure that it's soft enough for tent stakes, or that there are enough heavy rocks or trees trunks around to be able to secure your tent with guylines.

CHECK THE MAP
Many topo maps include symbols to show where campsites are located. If you're backcountry camping, identify the campsites along your route and set a goal for which one you would like to reach before sunset. Choose a couple of backup campsites that are closer than your goal in case you need to change your plans.

CAMP IN ESTABLISHED SITES
As a rule, you should stick to camping in estab-  lished campsites before choosing to set up in a spot not yet impacted by humans. Building firepits and leveling the ground to create a sleeping area are actions that are counter to the Leave No Trace Seven Principles, as they can damage the landscape and invite other campers to set up camp there in the future.

If camping in an established campsite is not an option, there are a few ways you can limit your impact. Make sure you set up camp at least 200 feet away from the nearest freshwater source. Stake down your tent in an area covered with dirt or pine needles rather than a grassy area where you need to remove rocks or branches to make room for your tent. Avoid damaging plant life by only gathering dead branches and twigs for firewood and by not walking through meadows or other fragile areas.

SETTING UP CAMP

Making the outdoors into a livable space can sometimes require a few adjustments. The trick is to maximize comfort while adhering to the Leave No Trace Seven Principles.

PITCH YOUR TENT

Choose a safe location
To avoid waking up in a couple of inches of water, set up your tent on higher ground, away from slopes, hills, and bodies of water. Do not pitch a tent directly under tree branches that could fall during a storm. Make sure a seemingly dry area is not actually a dry riverbed that could fill with water during a flash flood.

When picking a place to camp, avoid the edges of cliffs or tops of hills or ridges; exposed areas at high elevation are more prone to lightning strikes during a storm.

Clear the site
Remove debris from the tent site that might cause the sleeping area to be bumpy, such as twigs, pine cones, and rocks. Sweep away any sharp objects that could poke a hole in the footprint or the underside of your tent. Do not alter the site irrevocably by removing natural features like roots, stumps, or foliage. Instead, work around these obstacles by situating your tent in such a way that, for example, a bump in the ground will be located between two sleeping pads. Lay the footprint or ground cloth over the area where you want to pitch the tent.

Set up the tent body
Assemble the poles and clip them onto the tent body according to the tent's specific design.

Tent without rainfly   Tent with rainfly

Take note of whether the ground is at a slight incline. You'll want to position the tent so that when you're lying down, your head will be uphill from your feet. Set the tent on top of the footprint or ground cloth, and orient the tent so the smaller side, or the side with the sturdiest poles, is facing the prevailing wind. If the weather is hot, the door should face the wind to optimize ventilation.

Push the corner stakes of the tent into the ground with your hands or feet. If the ground is too hard, you can hammer the heads of the stakes down with the wide side of a rock. Specialized stake hammers are available for sale at most gear stores, along with sand anchors and snow stakes for harsh conditions. If possible, drive the stakes into the ground vertically to secure their holding power. Leave the tops of the stakes exposed so you can tie a cord to them for extra tent stability if necessary.

Secure the rainfly

Orient the rainfly properly. Most tents come with color-coded straps, poles, or loops so you know to align the rainfly with the tent. Velcro strips are located on the underside of some rainflies, which are for wrapping around the tent's poles for extra holding strength.

Cinch the corners of the rainfly evenly until snug. Most rainflies feature buckles or tent pole fasteners that secure the rainfly to the tent body and that can be tightened or loosened for extra support. You'll know if the tension is even on all corners if the seams of the fly line up with the poles and seams of the tent body. Check the tautness before going to bed, as the straps can loosen over the course of a trip and with variations in weather.

If you're trying to pitch your tent in wet weather, cover the tent body with the rainfly before you set it up. You can do this before or after you've attached the tent poles. If before, you can stand underneath the rainfly while you assemble the tent body—an awkward endeavor, but one that will ensure the inside of your tent stays as dry as possible.

Set up guylines

Most tents are made with built-in guyline cords that can be tied to surrounding sturdy objects for added stability and weather protection. Guylines on the bottom edge of the rainfly are used for pulling the rainfly away from the tent body, which helps prevent condensation buildup inside the tent. Even if only a mild breeze is a possibility, it's a good idea to secure the tent down with guylines. Guyout loops are located in strategic places around the rainfly's exterior and can be used to tie extra guylines to anchor the tent. Pack extra cord that can be used to lengthen a guyline and tie it to an object farther away from the tent, if needed. Guyline tensioners can be purchased at most outdoor gear stores and are used to cinch down the line.

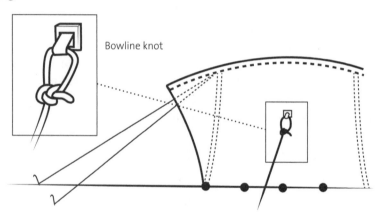

Bowline knot

A guyline can be tied using a bowline knot (see page 132) to attach the line to the guyout loop. A trucker's hitch (see page 134) can be used to pull tension on the line.

It's usually not necessary to attach guylines to all the guyout points on a tent. Loop guylines through the guyout points on the side of the tent facing the wind, and pull enough tension on the tent using guylines until the structure feels stable in the elements.

TIE A RAIN TARP

Setting up a tarp for rain protection might be the difference between a miserable camping trip and a pleasant one. A rain tarp can be suspended over a tent for added rain protection in especially stormy conditions, or it can serve as a separate dry area to gather outside the tent. The best time to hang a tarp is upon arrival at your campsite, and at the very least, before any rain starts falling. With the right technique and knot-tying skills, the setup shouldn't take long.

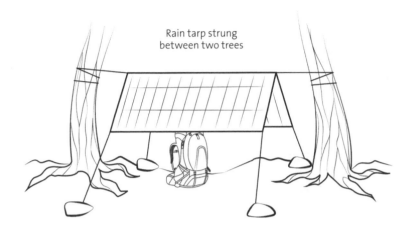

Rain tarp strung between two trees

Choose the right location

Ideally, a tarp should be suspended between two living trees with sturdy trunks that are 10–15 feet apart or more depending on the size of the tarp. The distance between the two trees should be no longer than the length of your tarp. Begin by determining how much rope or cord you need to set, and tie a centerline for the tarp between the trees. Then walk the cord or rope around the tree trunk two or three times, and anchor it by tying the rope to itself, another branch, or a nearby tree. Walk the other end of the rope over to a second tree. Drag the tarp over the rope line, and center it over the rope. Once the tarp is correctly positioned, pull the free end of the rope through an eyelet or loop on each end of the tarp to secure it to the rope. Next, tie a rock onto the free end of the rope and throw it over a branch on the second tree. Lift the tarp overhead by pulling the free end of the rope, and then wrap the cord around the trunk of the tree three times, tying it down as before.

Once the tarp is hanging from the rope, tie separate lines to each corner of the tarp and anchor the free ends to stakes or nearby objects. Continue adding guylines and pulling tension on the lines until the tarp is stretched taut.

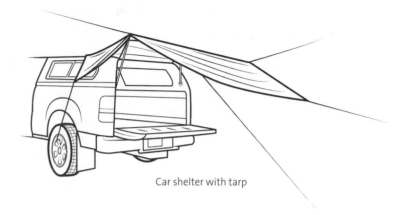

Car shelter with tarp

Other tarp setup options

Car shelter: One option when car camping is to hang the tarp over the back of your car. The ends of the cords tied to one side of the tarp can be tied around the wheels of the car.

Extra vestibule: Hang the tarp on a rope over the door of your tent, and tie the corners down with cords. The space underneath the tarp can be used as an extra vestibule to keep gear dry.

Hammock shelter: A tarp can also be set up over a hammock for some makeshift shade or protection from the elements.

ORGANIZE GEAR

Camping outdoors doesn't necessarily mean you need to rough it. Creating a livable space where you can easily cook, comfortably sleep, and have fun with camp activities is essential to having an enjoyable camping trip. Maintain good organizational and tidying-up habits and you'll always be able to find gear and have a clean place to cook and sleep.

Tag-team tasks

Maximize efficiency by splitting up the camp setup chores. Two people can set up the tent while someone else organizes the kitchen gear and another person hangs or stores food according to the area's regulations.

Keep essentials accessible

All items that you might need in a pinch—like a lighter, head-lamp, bug spray, and rain gear—should be stored in convenient place so you know exactly where to find them when you need them.

Organize intuitively

If you're car camping and bringing more than one cooler, pack beverages in one cooler and food in the other. Since people are taking beverages out of a cooler more frequently, you can limit the number of times the food cooler is opened. Store absorbent items away from the coolers in case the spigots leak water. Place the cooler near the picnic table during the day, but remember to pack it back into a vehicle at night so it won't get opened by a curious raccoon. Set the camp stove on one end of the picnic table, and make sure it sits level.

Store extra clothes or gear underneath a tent vestibule or rain tarp. You can also store clothing inside the tent on one end. Just make sure clothing isn't resting up against the tent walls, as any condensation on the outside of the tent can leak through. If car camping, gear can also be stored in the vehicle. Just don't keep any food or fragrant items (like sunscreen) in the car, as these can tempt animals such as bears to try to break in. Keep your bear spray canister tucked into a shoe or hiking boot outside of your tent for convenience if a bear visits your campsite at night.

Place flip-flops or booties outside your tent door before you go to bed so they are easily accessible for any middle-of-the-night bathroom breaks. Store a flashlight or headlamp in the tent pocket closest to the door.

To make it easier for other members of your group to locate items, store gear in predictable places. For example, all kitchen gear should be placed near or on the picnic table, or designated cooking area. Agree on fixed locations for items like silverware, camp stove fuel, and water. Ask campmates to return items to their designated locations when they are finished using them.

Establish the key-keeper

Designate one person to be the keeper of the car keys (or more than one if there are more than one set of keys). It will be this person's responsibility to keep track of the keys to avoid getting locked out of the car. It's best to store keys in a secure jacket or backpack pocket. Have that person tell every member of the group where the keys are located in case of emergency.

Store food properly

Do not leave food out on picnic tables or in containers that can be easily ripped open by critters. Even leaving a cooler unattended briefly can invite a raccoon to investigate. Conceal odors in airtight containers, and store any food according to the area's food-storage rules and regulations (i.e., in bear boxes or by hanging the food from a tree).

Improvise and add homey touches

Use existing features in the campsite to your benefit. Hang kitchen utensils like a ladle or spatula from an existing nail

LEAVE NO TRACE SEVEN PRINCIPLES

Dispose of waste properly

Proper disposal of human waste is important for avoiding polluting water sources, preventing the negative implications of someone else finding it, limiting the possibility of spreading disease, and maximizing the rate of decomposition in the soil. In most locations, burying human feces in the correct manner is the most effective method for meeting these criteria, unless bathroom facilities or pit toilets are provided. Solid human waste must be packed out from some places, such as narrow river canyons. Land management agencies can advise you of specific rules for the area you plan to visit.

Contrary to popular opinion, research indicates that burying feces actually slows decomposition (at least in the Rocky Mountains). Pathogens have been discovered to survive for a year or more after being buried. However, in light of the other problems associated with feces, it is still generally best to bury them. The slow decomposition rate necessitates choosing the right location—far from water, campsites, and other frequently used places.

Catholes are the most widely accepted method of waste disposal. Locate catholes at least 200 feet from water, trails, and camp. Select an inconspicuous site where other people will be unlikely to walk or camp. With a small trowel, dig a hole 6–8 inches deep and 4–6 inches in diameter. The cathole should be covered and disguised with natural materials when finished. If camping in the area for more than one night, or if camping with a large group, cathole sites should be widely dispersed.

The advantages of catholes are:
- They are easy to dig in most areas.
- They are easy to disguise after use.
- They are private.
- They disperse the waste rather than concentrate it (which enhances decomposition).
- It is usually easy to select an out-of-the-way location where you can be certain no one is going to casually encounter the cathole.

Selecting a cathole site
- Select a cathole site far from water sources—200 feet is the recommended range.
- Select an inconspicuous site untraveled by people. Examples of cathole sites include thick undergrowth, near downed timber, or on gentle hillsides.
- If camping with a group or in the same place for more than one night, disperse the catholes over a wide area; don't go to the same place twice.
- Try to find a site with deep organic soil. This organic matter contains organisms that will help decompose the feces. Organic soil is usually dark and rich in color.
- If possible, choose a location for your cathole that will receive maximum sunlight. The heat from the sun will aid decomposition.
- Choose an elevated site that won't become waterlogged from rainstorm runoff. The idea is to keep feces out of the water. Over time, the decomposing feces will percolate into the soil before reaching water sources.

Latrines
Though catholes are recommended for most situations, there are times when latrines may be more applicable, such as when camping with young children or if staying in one camp for longer than a few nights. Use similar criteria for selecting a latrine location as those used for a cathole. Since this higher concentration of feces will decompose very slowly, location is especially important. A good way to speed decomposition and diminish odors is to toss in a handful of soil after each use. Ask your land manager about latrine-building techniques.

Toilet paper

Use toilet paper sparingly and use only plain white, non-perfumed brands. Toilet paper must be disposed of properly. It should either be thoroughly buried in a cathole or placed in plastic bags and packed out. Natural toilet paper has been used by many campers for years. When done correctly, this method is as sanitary as regular toilet paper, but without the impact problems. Popular types of natural toilet paper include stones, vegetation, and snow. Obviously, some experimentation is necessary to make this practice work for you, but it is worth a try. Burning toilet paper in a cathole is not generally recommended.

Tampons

Proper disposal of tampons requires that they be placed in plastic bags and packed out. Do not bury them, because they don't decompose readily and animals may dig them up. Do not burn them, as it would take a very hot, intense fire to burn them completely.

Urine

Urine has little direct effect on vegetation or soil. In some instances urine may draw wildlife that are attracted to the salts. Animals can defoliate plants and dig up soil. Urinating on rocks, pine needles, and gravel is less likely to attract wildlife. Diluting urine with water from a water bottle can help minimize negative effects.

Special considerations for river canyons: River canyons often present unique Leave No Trace problems. The most common practice is to urinate directly in the river and pack out feces in sealed boxes for later disposal. Check with your land manager for details about specific areas.

sticking out of a tree trunk. Just don't hammer a new nail into a tree yourself. If stumps or rocks have already been moved near the campfire, you can use them as seats—but don't create new ones out of nearby stumps, branches, or rocks, as this is counter to the Leave No Trace Seven Principles.

Place heavy items or rocks on the tablecloth so it doesn't blow off the picnic table in the wind.

Keep the campsite tidy

After every meal, wash dishes and pack the food away. Pick up any litter or food debris from the ground. Occasionally sweep out pine needles or dirt from the inside floor of your tent. Take off your shoes every time you climb into your tent. Routinely tending to small cleanup tasks will keep your campsite feeling more inviting and livable.

Set up a makeshift toilet

If bathroom facilities are not provided, you can easily fashion a makeshift toilet out of a few basic items. Certain fragile wilderness areas require that all human waste be packed out, so in those cases, packing a portable toilet is a must.

To make a simple toilet, purchase a five-gallon bucket and a snap-on toilet lid. Snap-on lids are available at many outdoor gear and sporting goods stores. Line the bucket with a heavy-duty garbage bag, and cover the bottom of the bag with sawdust from a feed store. Pack a bag of sawdust for the trip (the amount will depend on the length of the trip). Situate the bucket about 100 yards downwind of your campsite. After the toilet is used, about a half cup of sawdust should be poured over the waste and the snap-on lid should be closed. An alternative to garbage bags and sawdust is ready-made human waste bags, which are designed to desiccate the waste inside the bag. These can be used to line the bucket, and will also cut down on accumulated weight.

Do not forget that lighting
a fire in hot, dry weather is
child's play, but that it takes
a real camper to perform
the same act in the damp,
soggy woods on a cold,
raw, rainy day.

—Dan Beard, *The Book of Camp-Lore
and Woodcraft*, 1920

Chapter 4
Camping Basics

BEFORE HEADING OFF INTO THE WILDERNESS, spend time learning basic wilderness skills, such as fire building, knots, and first aid. Campfire building is not only a key survival skill in an emergency but also a good way to create a central space for people in your group to gather for meals, storytelling, and simply connecting with each other. Additionally, campfires can be used for cooking meals and for deterring mosquitoes. Practice your campfire-building skills before leaving home to find your favorite technique. That way you won't have to learn under pressure. Knowing how to build and light a campfire is only the first part; you also need to learn how to keep the fire going and how to stay fire-safe to avoid causing a wildfire, since even the smallest spark can cause widespread damage.

Learning how to tie knots might seem like a dated skill set more suited to sailors and survivalists, but knowing some simple knots will help you keep your tent taut, your food out of reach of animals, and your clothesline, hammock, and rain tarp off the ground.

Basic first-aid knowledge and skills may come in handy for keeping you and your fellow campers safe in certain conditions, such as extreme heat or cold. Simple tricks will keep you from becoming hypothermic or suffering from heatstroke. Other skills and camping tips covered in this chapter may help you deal with unexpected challenges during your camping trip, like keeping your food from spoiling and your water from freezing.

CAMPFIRES

CAMPFIRE ETIQUETTE

A campfire is an enjoyable addition to any camping trip. It provides warmth and a heat source for cooking, adds to the general ambience of camping, and simply makes people happy. Practice responsible campfire etiquette every time you build a fire to limit your impact on natural areas.

Rules and regulations

Before building a campfire, check the rules and regulations for the specific area where you're camping. Check whether a fire ban is in place. Even campgrounds that typically allow campfires year-round need to prohibit fires when a fire ban is issued. Check the fire rules each day, because a fire ban can be put into effect suddenly. When camping on land managed by the US Forest Service or the Bureau of Land Management, you may be required to obtain a campfire permit from a local field office.

Location

When camping in alpine areas, do not build campfires. Instead, use a camp stove for cooking. Regions above tree line are especially fragile and susceptible to destructive fire damage.

When camping in areas where campfires are allowed, always use the fire ring provided at your campsite; avoid making your own. If you have to make your own, build it downwind from any camping neighbors if possible, so other campers don't get smoked out. Build the base for your fire on sand or gravel rather than soil. High heat can kill organisms living in the dirt and damage the quality of the soil.

If you do build a fire ring, be sure to dismantle it before you pack up and leave. Once the fire is completely out, carry any large pieces of blackened firewood or charcoal away from the campfire site; break them up into smaller pieces that can be scattered out of sight over a large area or bury them. Campfire ash should also be buried.

Fuel

To avoid spreading invasive organisms and disease, never bring your own firewood to a region located more than 50 miles away from the firewood's source. If available, purchase your firewood from the camp host or from a store near the place where you'll be camping. If allowed, you can also collect firewood from around your campsite, but only in areas where deadwood is abundant. Most national and state parks don't permit you to gather firewood from park land, but if you happen to be camping in a place that allows the collection of deadwood, make sure you only pick up branches and twigs from the forest floor. Do not break or cut branches from living trees.

For a campfire that burns longer, try to collect hardwood rather than softwood. Hardwood trees include maple, oak, cherry, beech, and ash. Softwood trees include fir, hemlock, pine, spruce, cedar, and cypress. If you are unable to identify different trees, you can use the fingernail method to determine how hard or soft the wood is. Simply run your fingernail across the wood; the deeper the scratch, the softer the wood.

Avoid burning forest debris like pine needles and leaves, because this material tends to generate more smoke. Also be sure to give your fire fuel enough breathing room to burn, since the more oxygen available to a fire, the better it will burn. A campfire built with green firewood or firewood placed too close together has more trouble burning, and also creates more smoke.

Never burn plastic. Chemicals from the plastic can leach into the smoke. Also, never put aluminum foil in the fire, as it won't burn. Remove any unburned trash from the fire ring—even if it isn't yours—and take it with you when you head home.

HOW TO BUILD A CAMPFIRE

There are several different ways to build a campfire. The appropriate technique depends on the purpose of the campfire. Does the fire need only to serve as a heat source for people to gather around, or does it need to be functional for cooking? Decide how you plan to use the fire and create the corresponding firewood shape before lighting the fire.

The main tricks for lighting a fire and keeping it going are (1) use dry fuel, (2) give the fire plenty of oxygen, and (3) continue adding fuel that burns slowly.

Necessary elements

In order to light a campfire that stays lit, the fire needs four things: a fire starter (or tinder), kindling, larger pieces of wood, and oxygen. Lacking any one of these elements, a fire may light quickly and burn hot, but then go out. Or it could be too smoky or fail to ignite at all. The right balance of all four elements will help to ensure that the fire lights quickly and stays burning as long as you let it.

Tinder
(paper, lint, wax, etc.)

Kindling (twigs)

Firewood

Fire starter: Tinder must be made of a highly flammable material such as lint, wax, sap, or paper. Before leaving home, pack a baggie of lint from the dryer, or once at the campsite, collect dry pieces of tiny twigs or grass. You need something that will catch fire quickly and produce a large enough flame to ignite the kindling.

Kindling: Twigs and small sticks are used to spread the flames from the fire starter or tinder to the rest of the campfire structure. Once the kindling ignites, these twigs and small sticks can produce enough heat to ignite the larger pieces of firewood. Dry cedar makes very good kindling if it is available.

Firewood: Larger pieces of fuel, like split or chopped firewood, help the fire continue to burn. Softwoods burn fast, while hardwoods burn slower. Hardwoods are also better for cooking, because they form coals that stay hot for a longer period of time.

Oxygen: Without enough oxygen, a fire will go out or become very smoky.

DIY fire starters

Tubes: Stuff toilet paper tubes full of dryer lint.

Baking cups: Lay baking cups in a muffin tin, and fill them each with sawdust. Pour melted wax over the sawdust, and let them dry.

Cotton balls: Dip cotton balls in Vaseline, and store them in a plastic baggie.

Pine cones: Dip pine cones in melted wax, and let them dry. Alternatively, dip cotton pads in melted wax instead.

To melt wax, bring an inch of water in a pot to a boil. Reduce the heat to bring the water to a simmer, set a clean aluminum pan, a glass measuring cup, or a smaller pan in the water, and then place the hard wax inside. Heat the wax until it is melted.

Make sure the fire structure you build has evenly spaced kindling and wood, and that the pieces aren't positioned so close together that they suffocate the initial flame from the fire starter. When adding more wood once the fire is going, place the pieces of wood far enough apart to make sure the fire will get the airflow it needs to continue burning.

Fire structures

Log cabin: A long-lasting fire, the log cabin is built by first laying two large pieces of firewood in the middle of the firepit, parallel to each other. Then two more pieces of firewood are placed across (perpendicular) to the first, laying them parallel to each other as well. The four pieces should form a square shape. Continue placing firewood—of decreasing size—in this pattern until it's not much higher than the walls of the fire ring. Leave enough space between the logs for the fire to get sufficient oxygen. Place the fire starter in the middle of the square, and

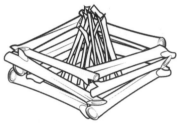

Log cabin

lay the kindling across the first layer of the log cabin, or position the kindling around the fire starter in a teepee shape.

Teepee: If the fire ring in your campsite has a grate, a teepee structure is a good option because it can be built beneath the grate if the grate cannot be removed. It also works well if the grate can be removed, set aside, and then replaced once the fire is burning. The teepee shape lights quickly and burns rapidly, creating a hot fire for cooking. To build a teepee fire, set the fire starter in the middle of the fire ring and rest the kindling and tinder on the fire starter in a teepee shape. Next, rest larger sticks up against the

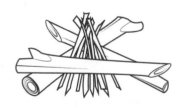

Teepee

small teepee, leaving enough room between the sticks for oxygen to flow, also leaving an opening large enough to light the fire starter. Once the fire is lit and burning, steadily add larger pieces of firewood around the teepee structure.

Lean-to: Another style that works well if the fire ring has a grate for cooking is a lean-to. It is also one of the simplest structures to build. Lay a large piece of firewood on the floor of your firepit, and prop your kindling up against it, perpendicular to the larger piece. Place the fire starter underneath the kindling.

Lean-to

Another setup option is to jam a larger stick into the ground of the firepit's floor at about a 30-degree angle and then rest the kindling along both sides of the large stick, forming a tent-shaped structure, again placing the fire starter underneath the kindling. Once the kindling has ignited and the fire is steadily growing hotter, you can add larger pieces of wood to the flame.

Minimize campfire impacts

Campfires vs. stoves: The use of campfires, once a necessity for cooking and warmth, is steeped in history and tradition. Some people would not think of camping without a campfire. Campfire building is also an important skill for every camper to learn. Yet the natural appearance of many areas has been degraded by the overuse of fires and an increasing demand for firewood. The development of lightweight efficient camp stoves has encouraged a shift away from the traditional campfires. Stoves have become essential equipment for minimum-impact camping. They are fast, flexible, and eliminate firewood availability as a concern in campsite selection. Stoves operate in almost any weather condition, and they Leave No Trace.

Should you build a campfire?

When deciding whether to build a campfire, the most important consideration is to determine the potential amount of damage to the landscape if the fire got out of control.

- What is the fire danger for the time of year and the location you have selected?

- Are there regulations or restrictions from the agency that manages the area?
- Is the firewood abundant so its removal will not be noticeable?
- Does the harshness of alpine growing conditions for trees and shrubs mean that the regeneration of wood sources cannot keep pace with the demand for firewood?
- Do group members possess the skills to build a campfire that will Leave No Trace?

Minimizing the impacts of campfires

Mound fire: Constructing a mound fire is a low-impact way to use a campfire without scarring the ground, and it can be built by using simple tools: a trowel, a large stuff sack, and a ground cloth or plastic garbage bag. To build a mound fire:

- Collect some mineral soil, sand, or gravel from an already disturbed source. The root hole of a toppled tree is one such source.
- Lay a ground cloth on the fire site and then spread the soil into a circular, flat-topped mound at least 3–5 inches thick. The thickness of the mound is critical to insulate the ground below from the heat of the fire. The ground cloth or garbage bag is important only in that it makes cleaning up the fire much easier.
- The circumference of the mound should be larger than the size of the fire to allow for the spreading of coals. The advantage of the mound fire is that it can be built on flat exposed rock or on an organic surface such as litter, duff, or grass.

Fire pans: Use of a fire pan is a good alternative for building a campfire directly on the ground. Metal oil-drain pans and certain backyard barbecue grills make effective and inexpensive fire pans. The pan should have at least three-inch-high sides. It should be elevated on rocks or lined with mineral soil so the heat does not scorch the ground.

CAMPFIRE SAFETY

Adhering to campfire-safety protocol will keep you and others in your group safe, and will protect the surrounding forest from wildfire. The smallest spark can do a lot of damage if the conditions are just right. So practice fire safety every single time you build a campfire, no matter where you're camping or what the posted fire danger level is for the area.

Wear the appropriate clothing

When gathering or handling firewood, it's a good idea to wear gloves to protect your hands from slivers, spiders, and biting ants that might be lurking beneath the wood. It's also a good idea to watch for yellow jackets that nest in and around such material in the woods.

While tending a campfire—or even just sitting near one—avoid wearing flammable clothing, such as fleece or other synthetic fabrics, which might melt or catch on fire if exposed to flames or sparks. Instead, opt for wool layers, since wool is naturally more fire-resistant.

Choose a safe location

Select an open, level piece of ground to make a fire ring. Avoid building campfires near grassy areas or along shorelines, as grass can easily catch fire, and river rocks can burst when exposed to high heat. Make sure you build a campfire a safe distance from your tent so that any drifting sparks won't land on the tent fabric. Build a campfire at least 10 feet away from any stumps, tree roots, logs, or dry vegetation. Any overhanging branches should be at least three times as high as the fire's flames to avoid catching the trees on fire.

Prepare the site

If a campfire ring isn't available, make your own by forming stacked rocks into a ring shape with a diameter no larger than three feet. After making the rock ring, clear away any vegetation such as pine needles, leaves, and sticks from the ring. To avoid being injured by rock shards, do not use river rock to build a fire ring. Air and water trapped in permeable rocks can expand when heated up and can cause rocks to explode.

Light the fire safely

Using a butane lighter or a match, reach under the kindling to light the fire starter. Remove your hand immediately from the

3 ft. wide

Build a 3-foot-wide rock ring for a safe campfire

firepit once the starter ignites. You can also use several fire starters to light the fire from multiple angles. Once the fire starter ignites the tinder, gently blow on the flames in even, slow breaths to help ignite other pieces of wood and spread the flames. Once most of the fuel has been ignited, you can sit back and monitor the fire. When few flames remain, you can add more fuel to the fire, blowing on the coals until new flames form. Only one large piece of wood (no wider than the diameter of an adult's forearm) should be added at a time, while making sure to not reach over any flames or glowing hot coals. As the fire burns, reposition any unburned twigs and sticks over the flames to help keep the fire going and to avoid leaving any charred remnants. The goal is to reduce all the fuel to ash.

While tending the fire
Teach campfire safety to all children and inexperienced campers before lighting a campfire. Demonstrate good fire-safety protocol so that beginners learn by example. Draw a circle around the firepit, about four feet away from the fire, and tell children that they must stay behind the line.

Keep a vessel full of water near the campfire in the event that it gets too big and needs to be put out immediately. To prevent the fire from getting out of control, try to keep it small and manageable by not burning more than about four pieces of firewood at a time. Avoid burning cardboard, because it creates large pieces of glowing ash that can float long distances if caught by the wind to then start grass and forest fires.

Don't burn logs that are longer than the width of the fire ring. If possible, try to break or chop them into smaller pieces.

Never leave a campfire unattended, even for a few minutes. An adult should always be monitoring the campfire and watching for any large sparks that might land on flammable vegetation such as dry grass.

Put the fire out completely

Coals and embers can stay hot for 24 hours if not extinguished properly. To fully put out a campfire, pour water slowly over the burning wood. Carefully scrape off any remaining burning embers from the wood with a stick. Use the stick to stir the wet ashes, then pour more water over the ashes. Keep pouring water over the ashes and mixing them until they feel cool to the touch. Walk around the campsite looking for any hot embers, ash, or burning twigs that may have escaped the fire ring, and douse them with water too.

Wildfire safety

Cancel your trip or change your camping plans if a forest fire is reported in your destination area. Practice good fire safety when managing your own campfire, and say something if you see another camper exhibiting unsafe fire behavior, such as throwing a lit cigarette onto the ground or building a campfire without a protective barrier around it.

If you see fire or smell smoke: Tie a dry (not wet) bandanna or other item of clothing around your face to act as a smoke filter. Retreat quickly from the area where fire is present. If you're on a hill, descend as fast as you can, since fire likes to spread upward. If stranded without a way to safely get back to your car or civilization, seek refuge in bodies of water, areas covered in logs and leafy greens (rather than grassy areas or ground covered in dry pine needles). If neither of those is an option, you can cautiously move to ash-covered areas that have already burned.

KNOTS

It's a good idea to learn a few simple knots before you begin your camping adventure. Some basic knots will help you cinch down tent guylines, pull a rain tarp taut, hang a food bag, or tie two pieces of rope securely together.

If you plan to do other outdoor activities like climbing or fishing that require more technical knots, be sure to practice tying them before leaving home.

SQUARE KNOT

The easiest knot to tie is the square knot. It can be used to tie two pieces of similarly sized rope together to make a longer rope. It is not the best knot to use if you are securing a load that might shift frequently because it can come undone under that kind of stress. One practical use for this knot is to create an arm sling by tying the two ends of the sling together above the injured person's shoulder or behind their back. It can also be used to tie a bundle of sticks gathered

for a fire, to attach gear to a backpack, or to secure a rolled-up sleeping pad.

To make a square knot, hold the ends of the rope and pass the left end over and under the right end, then the right end over and under the left. Then pull the ends taut.

CLOVE HITCH

The clove hitch is a useful knot for tying a rope or cord to a natural anchor, like a tree, stump, or rock. It is also a simple knot to learn. It can be used to secure a tarp to a tree by wrapping the

free end of the rope around the tree and pulling tension, and then tying a quick clove hitch to hold the rope in place. However, the clove hitch can loosen over time, so a more secure knot like the bowline would be better suited to securing a long-term rope or cord guyline.

To tie a clove hitch, make two loops and hold them between your thumbs and forefingers at points A and B. Slide the left loop over the right loop, then slip the double loop over the anchor. Draw the knot tight by pulling each end.

BOWLINE

Since it won't slip, the bowline is a useful knot for tying a tent guyline to an anchor, for tying off a rope or cord when hanging a food bag, and for hanging a rain tarp. You can also use this knot to tie two ropes together, even when the ropes are two different thicknesses. A secure knot that gains strength under an increased load, the bowline is an essential knot to learn for camping.

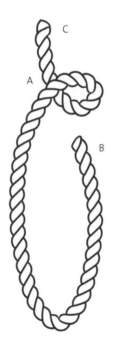

Wrap the rope or cord around the object that you wish to use as an anchor. Make a loop near the end of your rope (A) on the standing side. Hold this with your left hand at A, then with your right hand pass the working end (B) up through the loop, around behind the main part of the rope at C, and down in front of it through the loop again at D. Draw this tight, and you have a knot you can use in a variety of situations.

The bowline is an easy knot to untie. Simply loosen the part of the knot closest to the running end, and then pull the rest of the knot apart.

SLIPKNOT

The slipknot can be used to tie a rope to an anchor. It unties easily, by pulling the free end of the rope. It can also be used in conjunction with other knots, like the trucker's hitch.

To tie a slipknot, make a loop and then pull the standing line through the loop. You can either cinch it down all the way tight and loop it loosely over an anchor, or loop it over the anchor first and then cinch it down tight. To untie it, you need only to pull down on the free end of the rope.

HALF HITCHES

Half hitches can be used to quickly and securely tie off the free end of a rope when using another knot like a trucker's hitch to pull tension.

Pass the end of the rope over and around the standing part between the post and the knot, then under and around the standing part between its own loop and the first loop formed.

Two half hitches

TRUCKER'S HITCH

The trucker's hitch is handy for pulling tension on a line. For example, when stringing up a line to hang a tarp, you can tie one end of the rope or cord to a tree using a bowline knot, wrap the

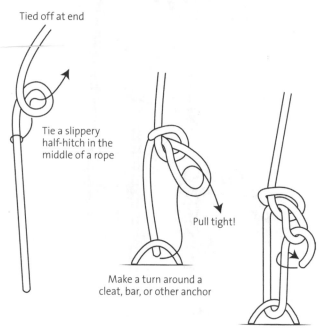

Tied off at end

Tie a slippery half-hitch in the middle of a rope

Pull tight!

Make a turn around a cleat, bar, or other anchor

free end around another tree, pull tension on the rope, and then tie the rope off using a trucker's hitch.

To tie a trucker's hitch, wrap one end of the rope around a tree or whatever anchor you're securing the rope to. Make a slipknot on the standing end of the rope, and cinch it tight. Feed the free end of the rope through the loop in the slipknot, and pull tension on the rope by pulling it back toward your anchor. You can then tie the free end of the rope by tying two half hitches.

CAMPING TIPS FOR ALL SEASONS AND TERRAINS

Extreme conditions warrant changes in the way you camp. Camping in bitter cold makes it more difficult to do simple tasks with numb fingers and toes, and sustained exposure to cold conditions can lead to hypothermia and frostbite. Similarly, camping in hot weather can make outdoor activities like swimming more enjoyable, but can also cause your body to sweat more, which can lead to dehydration—a dangerous condition if not treated quickly. With the right gear and camping techniques, you can reduce dangerous exposure to the elements. Take precautions in hot- and cold-weather extremes to maximize both comfort and safety.

WINTER CONDITIONS

Pack down snow
Tamp down the snow with your boots (or while wearing skis or snowshoes) before you pitch your tent, then wait about a half hour for the snow to harden. This helps slow the rate of snowmelt on a sunny day and prevents your campsite from becoming slushy. It will also help prevent your ripping open the floor of your tent by accidently stepping on a depression of softer snow.

Bury guyline stakes
Since tent stakes can be easily uprooted from the snow, one option is to tie a tent's guylines to rocks and then bury the rocks underneath the snow. This will help stabilize the lines.

Pack hand and foot warmers
Line your pockets or stuff your shoes or the bottom of your sleeping bag with single-use hand warmers. When exposed to air,

these little packets radiate a gentle heat to keep extremities warm. Some warmers generate heat for up to 12 hours. It is best to avoid direct skin contact with the warmers because they can burn sensitive areas.

Boil snow

Water filters can crack or fail in freezing temperatures, so snow is a convenient source for cooking and drinking water in the backcountry. It saves you a trip to the nearest freshwater source, which might be frozen anyway. Simply pack a pot full to the brim with snow, and cover it with a lid. Bring the melted snow to a full, rolling boil and allow it to boil for three minutes to kill any pathogens. Do not eat snow without sterilizing it first, because fresh snow may contain harmful bacteria. If you plan to use boiled snow exclusively as your water source, make sure to bring extra camp stove fuel, because it can take much longer to boil water in cold conditions, especially when you have to melt the snow first.

Sleep with your boots inside your sleeping bag

Avoid letting your boots freeze overnight. If you have boots with removable liners, you can remove the liners and place them at the bottom of your sleeping bag before you go to bed. Alternatively, you can place your boots inside a waterproof stuff sack and place that at the bottom of your sleeping bag to keep the inside of your sleeping bag from getting wet.

Sleep with a vapor barrier liner

Condensation produced by your body overnight can freeze your sleeping bag. Invest in a vapor barrier liner (VBL), and sleep in it as a protective layer to help prevent this from happening. A makeshift VBL can be made using a trash bag or any non-breathable material. VBLs also come in the form of socks, gloves, pants, jackets, shirts, and vests.

Fix a hot meal or beverage

Eating high-calorie foods will help your body stay warm. Prepare a warm meal that only requires adding hot water. Meals that necessitate a lot of prep work are hard on cold fingers. For no-prep calories, pack foods that don't require cooking like nuts, energy bars, and jerky. For quick warmth, heat up some water for a hot beverage such as cocoa, coffee, or tea. Avoid drinking alcohol, as this can actually lower your core body temperature by dilating your blood vessels and cooling your skin down more quickly. Alcohol also reduces your body's ability to shiver, which is one of the body's natural defenses against becoming too cold.

If you plan to snack on high-energy foods like power bars or electrolyte gummies, carry them close to your body during the day so they won't freeze.

Flip your bag and your water

If the weather forecast doesn't call for precipitation, you can turn your sleeping bag inside out and lay it over the top of your tent to dry out during the day. You can also flip it and let it dry out on the inside of your tent if the weather doesn't permit you to keep it outside.

> Sleeping bags with black interior liners dry out faster than other colors because black absorbs more solar rays.

If car camping with a multi-gallon water container, turn it upside down before going to bed. This will keep the spout from freezing overnight. Do the same thing with all water bottles. You can also wrap the container in an insulating layer like a trash bag before turning in for the night.

Waste disposal in snow

When the snow level is deep enough that digging a sufficient hole for human waste is not possible, then you'll need to pack out human waste. Bring resealable plastic bags as the container and smaller plastic bags to serve as gloves for picking up the deposits. You can even pack pieces of standard printer paper or small brown paper bags to use as a target. Then simply fold the paper over the deposit and drop it into the larger plastic bag. You can prep toilet waste kits for your trip beforehand by placing a handful of cat litter (to reduce odor), a piece of target paper, and a smaller plastic bag inside of the larger resealable bag.

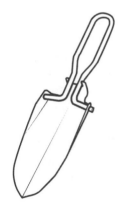

A trowel has many uses while camping, including digging holes to dispose of human waste

Pack lithium batteries

Lithium batteries perform consistently even in freezing temperatures. They're also more lightweight and last three times longer than alkaline or NiMH batteries.

Vaseline as a skin protectant

Cover your lips or any exposed skin with Vaseline (and sunscreen) to protect against the elements. This will help prevent windburn and frostbite.

EXTREME HEAT

Elevate your bed

Sleeping with airflow underneath you will help keep you cool at night. If you know the forecast calls for hot weather, it might be worth investing in a hammock or a cot. Some cots are small and lightweight enough to pack into the backcountry.

Shelter with airflow

Tents that are best for hot-weather camping are ones with plenty of mesh vents and more than one door. Orient the tent so that the door is facing toward the oncoming wind. This will help with airflow and also limit the number of bugs that might get inside your tent when you open the door, because bugs tend to gather on the sides of objects that are protected from the wind. If you know it won't rain overnight, you can set up the tent without the rainfly to allow for maximum airflow. When rain is in the forecast, you can simply hang a tarp over the tent. Setting up a tarp during the day provides shade in a pinch. If the area where you're camping isn't too buggy, you can even opt to sleep under the stars without the cover of a tent.

Clothing

Invest in clothing that provides sun and bug protection (long sleeves and pants are optimal), and is also breathable enough to stay cool. Merino wool and cotton are options. See pages 65–66 for the pros and cons of each.

If you go swimming during the day in either your clothes or a bathing suit, string up a clothesline to hang these items to dry overnight. During the day, you can soak a shirt in a freshwater source and put it back on for the evaporative cooling effect. You can do the same thing with a silk bandanna and tie it around your neck to help cool down the rest of your body.

Food storage

If you're packing a cooler while car camping, there a few tricks you can use to keep your food cold longer. The most effective strategy is to limit the number of times you open the cooler. Freeze meats and other freezable items before packing them into the cooler. Buy a large block of ice rather than a bag of ice cubes, as the block will melt more slowly. Freeze jugs of water and you'll have drinking water available when they melt.

Hydration

You need to not only drink more water in hot weather to stay hydrated but also make sure to replace your body's lost salts with electrolytes. Add an electrolyte tablet or powder to water to reduce your risk of becoming dehydrated. Electrolyte tablets and powders can be purchased at some grocery stores and most outdoor gear stores, and are a lightweight backcountry option when ready-made bottles of electrolyte drinks are impractical to pack. A person should drink an average of two liters of water a day, and when participating in any high-exertion activities, 16–32 ounces of water every hour.

Pets

Monitor your dog's water intake on hot days. When planning hikes or other activities, check the map to make sure there will be freshwater sources along the route where your dog can rehydrate and cool off. Some vets recommend allowing pets to drink only filtered water in the outdoors, but this is up to the owner's discretion.

Evaporative cooling vests can be purchased for dogs at some pet stores. Since dogs don't sweat like humans, this can be a good solution for extremely hot days.

Lightweight sleeping bag

Some sleeping bags are simply too warm for comfortable sleep on a hot night. A fleece blanket is a lightweight and less insulating option than a sleeping bag. Since it's hydrophobic, it will keep you dry even if it gets wet from humidity or sweat. It's a good idea to bring a warmer backup sleeping bag, in case the night temperature dips below 60 degrees Fahrenheit.

Food

Perishable food is much more likely to spoil if not refrigerated, especially if it's left out on a hot day. Be sure to keep the cooler closed while frontcountry camping. If backcountry camping, you can form a makeshift cooler for any perishable items such as cheese or melt-prone items like chocolate by placing them in plastic bags in any fresh water near shore (see page 147).

EXTREME WET WEATHER

Use a ground cloth and footprint

In addition to using a footprint underneath the tent, it might also be worthwhile to place a ground cloth on the floor inside the tent as well. This will keep any moisture off your sleeping pad and sleeping bag.

Don't dig trenches

Most newer tent models shouldn't leak water, so you don't need to dig trenches in the dirt around the tent to redirect rainwater runoff away from your sleeping area. Trenches needlessly disturb the soil and vegetation in the campsite. If the ground is sandy or mostly gravel, then digging trenches is fine as long as you smooth the ground before you leave.

Pack extra

Bring an extra set of waterproof clothes so you have something dry to change into at the end of each day's activity. Pack an extra pair of water-resistant camp shoes that are easy to slip on and off when leaving or entering your tent. Sandals or flip-flops work well for this purpose. Store your boots or hiking shoes in a dry place.

Waterproof your gear

If a tent has seen a lot of use, you can apply a sealer to the seams and then spray a waterproof coating over the whole thing. Before leaving on a trip, you can check for tent holes by spraying the exterior with a hose and looking for leakage inside, or you can hold parts of the tent underwater in a bathtub and look for bubbles where any holes are located.

Waterproof gear like rain jackets can be waterproofed again using a polyurethane spray, which is usually the same kind that can be used on tents.

Bring tent-friendly activities

Pack a deck of cards, a cribbage board, a book, a journal, or other activities to pass the time should you find yourself stuck inside the tent for hours waiting out a rainstorm. Another benefit of setting up a rain tarp is you can cook, eat, and play games with your campmates outside your tent during bad weather. Keep children occupied with coloring books, cards, or games geared to their age, or by telling stories.

Pack synthetic gear

Synthetic gear is ideal when camping in the rain. If wet weather is forecasted, leave the cotton and down at home. Synthetic sleeping bags, insulated jackets, and layering garments are best for keeping you warm and dry when the conditions are cold and wet.

Store gear in waterproof bags

Waterproof bags keep gear dry

To keep gear and food dry, pack it in dry bags or plastic bags. Dry bags are made specifically to keep gear dry in wet conditions or when traveling by boat, canoe, or kayak. They come in various sizes, and are closed by folding the top of the bag several times and securing the folds with a clasp. You can store larger items in trash bags or even line the inside of a backpack with a trash bag. Resealable plastic sandwich bags can be used to store smaller items like electronics, lighters, and money. Invest in a waterproof backpack cover that you can slip over your backpack while you hike to keep the interior dry. In a pinch, a large trash bag also works.

Wear rain pants and gaiters

Rain pants and gaiters can help keep your legs, ankles, and feet dry while hiking or moving around camp. Brushing past flora that's covered in dew or walking through tall, wet grass can soak your lower body. Wearing protective layers like rain pants and gaiters can help reduce the amount of moisture absorbed by your pants, socks, and shoes.

Gaiters

Hang clothes to dry

Underneath a rain tarp or tent vestibule, suspend a line of cord between two trees and hang any wet clothes to dry overnight. For faster drying, stuff the bottom of your sleeping bag with wet clothes, as your body will warm them up.

Dry gear before packing up

Air out your tent, sleeping bag, tarp, and sleeping pad before packing them up. If they're still wet when you get home, lay them out or hang them up to dry completely. Never store wet gear. If you do, you will be using gear covered in mildew or mold on your next trip.

Avoid wet weather hazards on the ground

While hiking or moving around camp, tread carefully and avoid muddy patches of ground. Do not trust your feet on mossy areas or wet rocks as they can pose a slipping hazard. Consider using trekking poles if you know you will be hiking on wet, rocky, or uneven trails.

Stay hydrated

Many people forget to drink water during rainy weather. To avoid getting dehydrated on a wet camping trip, make sure you keep a water bottle near you as you wait out the storm. If you collect rainwater in pots or other vessels, be sure to sterilize the water first before drinking it (see page 153).

Keep campfires away from tents and tarps

Though it can be tempting to start a campfire during cold, wet weather, be sure to set up campfires a good distance from flammable objects like tents and tarps. If using a camp stove, make sure the tarp is high above the flames. Never use a camp stove inside a tent, because doing so creates a fire hazard and a risk of carbon monoxide poisoning.

Wear bright colors

Rainy camping trips often happen during hunting season. To avoid being mistaken for wild game, wear bright colors and stay on existing trails.

Be strategic about tent placement

Avoid setting up your tent in a sunken area, as these spots are more likely to flood when it rains. Position your tent in an area that will receive early-morning sun, as this will help dry the rainfly faster if the weather is good the next day. Don't set up your tent underneath trees, as the branches will continue to drip onto the rainfly even after it has stopped raining.

Pack warm foods and beverages

When the weather is cold, we tend to crave hot meals. If the forecast looks dreary, make sure to pack foods and beverages that will provide warmth on a cold day, such as hot cocoa, tea, coffee, chai powder, soups and stews, hot cereal, miso powder, ramen, chili, and pasta.

At almost every camping spot, nature's dining hall was far more attractive than the most beautiful room in any hotel or private residence.

—Dwight and Stella Woolf, *Tramping and Camping*, 1912

Chapter 5
Camp Cooking

WHEN YOU'RE OUTDOORS, THERE'S something special about the smell of bacon sizzling in the skillet, the first sip of coffee in the morning, the satisfaction of a warm meal after a long day of hiking, and the pure comfort of a steaming cup of hot chocolate before crawling into your sleeping bag for the night. Most campers would agree that food just tastes better when you're camping. After a strenuous activity, you feel like you've earned the calories—food feels like a well-deserved reward. Cooking food over a campfire also gives it that added depth of flavor.

Pack food high in calories if you're planning any strenuous activities. Camping food should be nourishing and energizing—and it should taste good. Packing only power bars and jerky might be space-efficient, but you might also quickly get sick of eating them. Bring a variety of complex carbohydrates, proteins, and foods loaded with other nutrients to get the most enjoyment and health benefits from your meals.

Make sure you bring the necessary cooking utensils for the meals you're planning. Before you leave home, write a menu plan and list all the ingredients you need to pick up from the store (or bring from home), along with all the cooking equipment required to make each meal. Consider how you'll be cooking the food—campfire or stove—so that you pack the appropriate equipment and choose meals that will cook well depending on the heat source. Factor in the weight and bulk of each meal, especially if you're backcountry camping. To reduce the amount of bulk, consider repacking boxed food in reusable bags or containers.

FRONTCOUNTRY VS. BACKCOUNTRY COOKING

Frontcountry camping allows for a greater range of foods because weight and size are not limitations. Plus, you can pack a cooler to preserve perishable foods and you can bring along more cooking gear like a bigger stove, a Dutch oven, or cast-iron skillet.

Backcountry camping restricts what food you can pack based on weight and size. It requires careful meal planning so that you pack enough food for the trip (plus extra), while also making sure it's lightweight and small enough to transport. Convenient backcountry meal options consist of packaged freeze-dried or dehydrated foods that are prepared by pouring hot water into the resealable food bag and waiting for the meal to rehydrate. This form of cooking requires little prep work. You simply need to boil water and prepare the meal bag. Some backcountry campers enjoy packing fresh food that can be added to rehydrated meals for more flavor and texture. If you're inclined to eat fresh food that requires more prep, just be weight-conscious as you plan the meals.

MEAL PLANNING

When planning the meals for your trip, consider steps you can take to maximize taste while minimizing the amount of cleanup required after eating. Before leaving on your trip, write up a meal plan for each day of the trip that includes all the ingredients required for each meal. Calculate how much you'll need to multiply the recipes to feed every member of your group. It's sometimes a good idea to lay out all the food you plan to eat each day, to better visualize the meals. Another rule of thumb is to pack approximately 3,000 calories per person per day.

QUANTITY

One of the 10 Essentials is packing at least an extra day's worth of food, to be eaten if your plans change or in case of emergency. A reasonable weight of food per person per day is about 1.5 or 2.5 pounds (approximately 2,500 to 4,500 calories). The right amount will depend on the appetite size of each member of your group, and whether you have any strenuous activities planned during your trip. With each camping trip, you'll get a better idea of the right amount of food to bring. If you are backcountry camping, distribute the food among members of the group so that no one person is carrying the bulk of the food weight.

WEIGHT AND BULK

The weight and bulk of the food are bigger considerations when backcountry camping, and you can save weight by choosing food items that need to be rehydrated, such as powdered soup, dry noodles, beans, and rice. You can also reduce weight by repackaging food in resealable plastic bags, which helps cut down on garbage accumulation during your trip. Label the bags with their contents and cooking instructions.

ODOR

Do not pack any food that has a strong odor. It will attract wildlife to your campsite. Raccoons, squirrels, chipmunks, mice, and rats are likely to catch the scent and rummage through or damage your food and gear. Bears have a powerful sense of smell, too, so avoid bringing odorous foods to bear country at all costs.

PERISHABILITY

Depending on the length of a frontcountry camping trip, you may want to limit the number of perishable items you pack. Ice and ice packs will melt and thaw after a few days in a well-insulated cooler. Plan your meals so that you eat all the perishable food first, saving nonperishable items for meals later in the trip. Backcountry campers should use caution when packing any perishable items. The best way to store perishables in the back-country is to use a nearby cold water source as a cooler. Seal the food in waterproof bags or double-bag the perishable items in resealable bags, and place them in the water near the shore. Keep the food from floating away by either tying the bags to a rock on shore or encircling them in a ring of rocks that stick out above the surface of the water.

TASTE

Don't introduce your taste buds to new food while camping. Stick to foods you like that are easy to cook over a fire or camp stove.

CALORIES AND NUTRITION

Avoid dieting while camping, especially if strenuous activities are planned. And avoid overdoing it with sweets and carbohydrates too. High-calorie treats like candy bars are a good reward after a long hike, but they shouldn't comprise the bulk of your meals. A balance of proteins and complex carbohydrates helps reduce energy dips and spikes, and offers the nutrients your muscles need to perform well and avoid injury.

WATER AVAILABILITY

Be sure to account for what water sources will be available on your trip. If car camping in a location without a water resource, calculate how much water you should bring in multi-gallon containers. For backcountry trips where water will be a scarce resource, pack meals that don't require adding water.

PREPARATION

Car camping affords a wider range of cooking options. Backcountry camping calls for meals that don't require a lot of varied cooking techniques, utensils, or time to prepare. In either case, bring some no-cook meals that can be eaten as backup in case your stove stops working.

FUEL

Estimate how much time foods will need to cook for each meal and pack enough fuel, plus extra, to cook accordingly.

COST

Buying processed or packaged foods is usually more expensive than scratch ingredients. Freeze-dried meals and high-energy snacks like jerky and power bars often have high price tags. Budget for your trip, and expect to pay more for added convenience.

CAMP COOKING TRICKS

REPURPOSE

If you pack food in large resealable plastic bags, you will be able to use them as waste bags after you consume the contents. Make sure they are double-bagged or are sealed well so they don't spill or stink.

PRE-CRACK EGGS

If you'll be able to keep foods cool, you can pre-crack eggs into a water bottle or other leak-proof container. This will reduce the risk of accidentally smashing the eggs during your trip and creating a mess. You can also keep eggs intact by storing them in egg-specific plastic containers.

CONSOLIDATE

One-pot meals are much easier to clean up than meals that require multiple pots and pans. Plan ahead and consider cooking a few or all meals in just one container. That way, you'll also cut down on the amount of cooking gear you need to bring and clean.

COOK OVER THE CAMPFIRE

If campfires are allowed in the area where you'll be camping, plan a few meals that can be cooked over the fire. Wrap food in tinfoil, with the shiny side facing out, folding and crimping the edges together to create a tight seal. One of the benefits of campfire cooking is that it reduces the amount of post-meal dishwashing. However, it does create more waste. Pack a camp stove as backup in case it's difficult to find dry firewood or the fire regulations change during your camping trip.

CUT UNIFORMLY

To cook foods evenly, especially over a campfire, cut food into uniform sizes when chopping and prepping. This will help reduce the chance that some pieces get burned while others remain undercooked.

PRE-CHOP FOODS

Certain food items like apples, carrots, celery, onions, and peppers can be pre-chopped and stored in small baggies to reduce the amount of meal prep or cooking tools necessary while camping.

STANDARD CAMPING FOODS

DRIED FOODS

Freeze-dried foods like backpacker meals or dehydrated foods like dried soup mixes or fruit are lightweight options for backcountry camping. Dry foods like pasta, rice, beans, noodles, and powdered drink mixes are convenient for both backcountry and frontcountry camping.

CANNED FOODS

Canned foods are high in water content and heavy to carry into the backcountry. Smaller canned items such as chicken or tuna are a more manageable weight, and don't take up a lot of space. Just remember to bring a can opener or a multi-tool. Look for chicken and tuna in foil pouches that are lighter than canned versions, which can be found at most grocery stores.

SPICES

If you plan to prepare food from scratch, add some flavor to your meals with a few essential spices like salt, pepper, curry, garlic powder, cayenne, cumin, cinnamon, or whatever your favorite spices happen to be. See pages 81–82 for lightweight ways to pack spices.

TYPICAL CAMPING MEALS

Many meals that can be cooked at home can also be prepared while camping. A Dutch oven can serve as an oven, and a fire grate as a grill. Camp stoves can be used to heat meals or boil water. Food can also be packed that doesn't require cooking. The food list below features typical options for camping meals. Asterisks denote foods that are best for backcountry camping because of ease of preparation, in addition to less weight and bulk.

BREAKFAST

Start the day right with a meal that balances proteins and complex carbohydrates to give you the fuel you need to power through. Some typical camping breakfast foods include:

- Energy or granola bars*
- Pancakes* (just-add-water dry mix if backcountry camping)
- Eggs
- Bacon, sausages, corned beef hash, or SPAM
- Coffee or tea*
- Hot cereal*
- Dry cereal with powdered milk (if backcountry camping)*
- Freeze-dried,* fresh, or dehydrated* fruit

LUNCH

Plan lunches that don't require a lot of prep or cooking tools. Fast and easy fuel is key for outdoor lunches. Try simple items to stay energized, including:

- Tortillas*
- Pita bread (for sandwiches)*
- Canned or foil-packed* meat or fish
- Fresh vegetables that don't spoil quickly, like cucumber, carrots, peppers, avocados, onions, tomatoes
- Bagels*
- Nuts*
- Fruit (fresh or dried*)
- Cheese
- Cream cheese
- Jerky*
- Cured meats, such as dried salami or summer sausage (no refrigeration required)*
- Fresh or dehydrated* hummus

DINNER

Treat dinner like a reward for a day well spent in the outdoors. Plan your activities to leave enough time to prepare a healthy, filling hot meal for dinner. Some popular dinner foods include:

- Tacos (fish, beef, or chicken)
- Spaghetti or other pasta* (with tomato, meat, or other sauces)
- Rice*
- Baked beans
- Chili
- Hotdogs, brats, kielbasa
- Hamburgers
- Grilled chicken, fish, or steak
- Ramen noodles*
- Instant soups*
- Dehydrated mashed potatoes and instant gravy*
- Packaged meals*
- Fresh or dehydrated* vegetables or mushrooms
- Cheese

FOOD HANDLING BASICS

Prevent stomach illnesses by practicing safe food handling. Pathogens can spread if certain precautions are not taken when preparing raw meat, when you eat or prepare food without washing your hands first, when you eat spoiled food, or when you drink water without treating it first.

RAW MEAT SAFETY

Double-bag store-packed raw meat or raw meat you have cut and packaged before leaving home, and place it at the bottom of your cooler so it doesn't leak on any other foods. Do the same with any raw meat packaging or wrappings. This means that if you cut meat with a certain knife on a specific cutting board, you should not use that same knife or cutting board to prepare other foods that will be eaten raw, like fruits or vegetables. If you need to use that same knife or cutting board to prepare something else for the meal, first wash them with soap and hot water, and wash your hands as well.

GENERAL FOOD HANDLING SAFETY

Before handling any food, wash your hands with warm water and soap or hand sanitizer. When snacking, shake food out of the bag into your hand rather than reaching into the bag to take a handful. Wash your hands every time after you go to the bathroom. Never wash your hands in a freshwater supply such as a lake or pond. If you need to dry your hands, use a towel not designated for drying dishes.

AVOIDING SPOILED FOOD

It can be difficult to keep perishable food from spoiling while camping for several days. Even if you are able to pack a cooler, the ice will eventually melt and the temperature inside the cooler might rise above 40 degrees Fahrenheit, at which point food can start to go bad. But there are some ways you can prolong the amount of time your food will stay chilled.

Freeze meat before packing it at the bottom of the cooler. This will extend the time you have to use it up. Organize the contents of the cooler so that any food you plan to eat first is placed at the top, where the temperature is warmest. If you have a large chest freezer at home, you can place the entire cooler inside to prechill the material before you pack it up. Alternatively, you can place ice blocks inside the cooler and let the inside prechill for an hour before you fill it with food. Pack a thermometer so you can periodically check the cooler throughout your trip to make sure the temperature is below 40 degrees Fahrenheit.

WATER SAFETY

Harmful microorganisms and parasites live in bodies of fresh water, even at high elevations where water is sourced from alpine lakes fed by glacial runoff. To avoid contracting a stomach illness, it's always a good practice to filter or treat your water before drinking or cooking with it. Where established campgrounds provide potable running water, filtering isn't necessary.

The best water-filtering protocol is to collect it from running-water sources rather than still-water sources. It's also better to collect water as far upstream as you can, rather than downstream where running water has the opportunity to accumulate more contaminants. An ideal place to collect water is from a river or a stream rather than a lake. And better yet, the optimal place would be from glacial runoff located above an alpine lake. The icy cold water is also exceptionally refreshing. But when glacial runoff isn't available, any body of water will still do if you use a water filter that clears out debris and unwanted microorganisms.

You can choose from a variety of water purification options, depending on convenience, budget, and the natural water sources available where you're camping. Always bring at least one backup water purification device in case your go-to choice fails.

Hand-pump filter

A hand-pump filter offers the ideal way to pump water when the source you intend to use is muddy or filled with sediment and debris that is difficult to strain out. A water bottle becomes a handy tool when using this method, as its shape easily collects the water filtered through the hand-pump system. Some hand-pump filters come with attachments that are best used with widemouthed water bottles, but the attachments for certain models can be removed to work with any water bottle. Check the instructions for your filter model to see if a specific water bottle style is recommended.

To use a hand-pump filter, remove the lid from the water bottle you want to fill up, then secure the bottle adapter cap to the mouth of the water bottle. If the bottle adapter doesn't fit the lid, you can usually just pull the adapter off and place the output hose inside the bottle. Next, drop the input hose into the water source and then pump the handle until the water starts flowing through the filtration system. The purified water will empty into the water bottle. Once the water bottle is full, you can tighten the lid back onto the water bottle and fill up another one. To fill a hydration bladder, it's often easiest to first fill up a water bottle with purified water and then pour the water from the bottle into the bladder.

Once you're finished filtering, pull the input hose out of the water source and pump all excess water out of the system. Most hand-pump filters come with cleaning instructions in case a piece of the system gets clogged. Most models also come with instructions for how to replace the filter cartridge after the hand-pump filter becomes hard to pump.

Hand-pump filters are proven, successful tools for purifying even the murkiest water, so have one available if the area you plan to camp in has questionable water sources. Note that large sediment particles will gum up the filtration cartridge more quickly.

Squeeze filter

A squeeze filter is similar to a hand-pump filter in that it filters water from a filtration system into an open container like a water bottle. This is a good option for backcountry campers where weight is a primary concern, because a squeeze filter weighs much less and is more compact than a hand-pump filter. A squeeze filter is also less expensive.

To use one, remove the cap from the squeeze bag and then fill it with water from a clear water source. Twist the filtration cap onto the squeeze bag and then compress the bag with your hands, squeezing the purified water into the water bottle. Continue emptying out the squeeze bag and refilling it until your container is full. As with hand-pump filters, it's easiest to pour purified water from a water bottle into a hydration bladder.

Straw filter

A straw filter is an especially lightweight and
affordable mechanism for
purifying water. The biggest
downside is it can't filter
larger quantities of water
into a container. In order to
use one, you must place one
end of the straw into a
water source and then suck
through the straw. The
water that comes through

will be potable. A more convenient option than bending over to drink from a stream through a straw is to first fill up a water bottle and then suck the water through the straw filter. Just don't forget to use the straw filter each time you drink water from your water bottle.

Ultraviolet purification

When exposed to UV rays, pathogens lose their ability to multiply. You can buy a device that, when inserted into water, projects UV rays that disable a pathogen's ability to multiply and cause harm. This system purifies the
water but doesn't filter out any
larger debris. You can buy
separate attachments that can
remove any sediment before
purifying the water with the
UV device. Most of the UV
models require lithium
disposable or NiMH rechargeable batteries to operate
consistently. Always bring
extra batteries and a backup
water treatment system when
using a UV device.

A UV water purification
device is one of the more

expensive options, but can be the most convenient to use if the water you want to treat is already clear and free of debris. For example, while traveling, you can fill up water bottles with tap water that might not be potable and then treat the water with the UV device. Or you can dip your water bottle into a pristine alpine stream and then have it ready to drink within a minute or two.

Boiling

Purifying water by boiling it is a simple option that requires nothing but a camp stove and fuel (or fire) and a pot. First, fill the pot up with water, leaving about an inch between the surface of the water and the top of the pot to avoid any water spilling over the sides once the water starts boiling. You can boil water without putting a lid on the pot, but a lid will increase the heating efficiency and decrease the amount of time it takes to begin boiling. Place the pot over medium-high to high heat, and wait until the water comes to a rolling boil or—if using a pot with a lid—you see steam issuing from around the edges of the lid. Let the water boil for three minutes. You can then let the water cool if you plan to drink it, or you can add the water directly to meals that require the addition of boiling water to rehydrate.

The boiling option doesn't work well as a purification method if the water you're sourcing is muddy, or full of debris, since treating these larger sediments requires longer boiling times. In these cases, a water filter is the optimal choice. Boiling water to purify it also requires packing greater quantities of camp stove fuel, or the ability to build a campfire without breaking any fire restrictions. If you plan on boiling all your water, be sure to calculate how much extra fuel you need to bring so you have enough for purifying water and for cooking. Be sure to add on time if you plan to boil melted snow. Remember that a person needs about two liters of water a day, and more if strenuous activities are planned. See page 159 for fuel calculation tips.

Iodine

Although an affordable and lightweight option for water purification, iodine tablets or liquid iodine sometimes are not a first choice due to the metallic flavor that iodine gives the water, and because you have to wait between 30 minutes to an hour before drinking the treated water. Some people are allergic to iodine, in which case, chlorine or another purifying method should be used. Using iodine will also not strain out large debris or dirt from the water.

Read the manufacturer's instructions for proper use, but typically, one or two tablets will purify one liter of water. Fill a water bottle or other container with clear water and then drop the recommended number of tablets into the water and wait the length of time listed in the instructions. The temperature of the water will determine how long you have to wait. When using chemicals like iodine, colder water takes longer to purify, so icy cold water will need to sit with the iodine for about an hour before it's ready to drink. Warmer water takes about a half hour before it's potable. Some people recommend adding about 50 milligrams of vitamin C to iodine-treated water (after waiting for the iodine to do its work) to eliminate the residual flavor of iodine.

Chlorine

Chlorine purification can be performed using chlorine-based tablets or liquid chlorine. Chlorine is a good option for people who want a lightweight and affordable purification system but who are allergic to iodine or don't like the taste.

Liquid household bleach can be used to treat water, as long as it's between 5.25 percent and 8.25 percent chlorine. Just be sure to read the label first to make sure it doesn't contain dyes, perfumes, or other potentially harmful additives. Add about five drops to one liter of water, and mix or shake thoroughly to distribute the bleach. Wait an hour before drinking. Chlorine-based tablets can also be used; the manufacturer's instructions will list the number of tablets per liter of water.

As with iodine, chlorine does not always kill disease-causing organisms that are found in sediment, so you should be sure to find the clearest water you can and strain out the larger pieces of debris before adding the treatment.

Purification tablets

Other purification tablets aside from iodine and chlorine-based are available and also a lightweight and affordable option. Read the instructions for how many tablets must be used per liter of water, and wait the recommended period of time. Bring a backup water treatment option in case the water source available is particularly muddy or full of sediment.

COOKING OVER A GAS BURNER VS. A CAMPFIRE

If campfires are allowed where you're camping, plan meals that you can cook over the fire. Just be sure to have a backup plan in case a fire ban is issued while you're camping. Cooking over a camp stove requires similar skills to cooking at home, but with a few extra precautions. Cooking food over a campfire will give food that authentic, smoky camp-cooked flavor, but necessitates being extra cautious about fire safety and a little more patient about cooking time. Through trial and error, you'll find that cooking over a campfire can yield delicious results.

GAS BURNER COOKING

The power of your camp stove is measured in BTUs, and the higher the BTU number, the faster your food will cook. However, this also means that your stove may centralize its heat source in a way that can also make food burn to the bottom of your pot or pan more quickly. Some camp stoves have a simmer option, but others need to be closely monitored to make sure your food doesn't burn. The larger your camp stove, the bigger the pot or pan you can use. Some camp stoves have multiple burners, which can speed up the cooking process as well.

To cook over a camp stove, place the stove in a wind-protected area if possible, as any breeze can render a camp stove flame less efficient. Check or stir the food frequently, to make sure it's not sticking to the bottom of the pan. When cooking over a camp stove that has a more centralized burner, it may be necessary to rotate the bottom of the pot or pan above the flame to distribute the heat. For example, when frying pancakes over a camp stove, the pancakes in the middle of the pan may cook much faster than the pancakes closer to the edge of the pan. Monitor any camp stove food closely to ensure an even distribution of heat.

CAMPFIRE COOKING

Cooking over a campfire shouldn't be intimidating, but there is a bit of an art to getting it right. The main trick is to be patient. Wait until the fire has burned down to glowing coals, which can sometimes take as long as 40 minutes. Some food, like marshmallows or hot dogs, can be cooked over open flames of the fire but may catch fire and burn. So waiting long enough for the coals to form is the best strategy to cook food

How much fuel should you pack?

The amount of fuel that you should bring on any camping trip depends on the number of days and nights you'll be out, the number of people, how hot your stove burns, and the number of meals and beverages that will require the addition of hot or boiled water. An additional factor will be how you plan to purify your water if you need to collect it while camping. If you plan to boil all your water, you'll need to take that into consideration as well.

To do the math, first count the number of people in your group. Factor in the method you'll be using to purify water. If you plan to boil it all, you'll need to make sure you have enough fuel to boil at least 2–3 liters of drinking water per person per day, in addition to the amount of fuel you'll need for cooking.

Next, count up the number of hot meals and hot beverages you will be making each day of your trip. Don't forget to count those second cups of coffee. Try to estimate how many total liters of water you'll need to heat or boil. You should also approximate the cooking time for any dishes that need to simmer or heat up over the stove, such as pasta sauce or hot cereal. Consider whether you will be using melted snow as your water source, since melting snow over the camp stove will add more fuel-burning time. If the weather forecast predicts high winds or cold temperatures, that might extend the fuel-burning time as well.

Look up how many ounces of fuel your stove uses to boil one liter of water—a number that should be listed in the product's manufacturing specs. Then calculate how many ounces of fuel you'll need based on the total number of liters of water you might use throughout the duration of your trip. You'll then need to pack this many ounces worth of fuel canisters, plus a small amount of extra backup fuel.

evenly. Plan ahead so that you can eat your meal at a reasonable hour. The best strategy is to make a moderately sized fire and tend it as necessary, rather than making a large fire that burns down quickly and creates coals that are not hot enough for cooking. When cooking food over a fire, you may also need to wait longer than you think for the food to cook all the way through. Consider packing a food thermometer so you can check when meat is fully cooked. It's a good idea to take food off the fire just before you think it's done, as it will continue to cook after it's off the coals.

For best cooking results, burn hardwood like oak or maple, which won't burn down to ashes quickly. Any campfire structure (see page 125) can be used for cooking as long as it is given time to develop hot coals.

Before you leave home, decide what foods you will be cooking over the campfire and what method of cooking you'll use so you know what supplies to bring. For example, you can slow-roast some foods by sealing them in aluminum foil. Use two sheets of heavy-duty aluminum foil (shiny side facing out), and place your food in the middle. Bring the two ends of the foil together over the food and fold them down to make a tight seal, then close the remaining two sides by folding and crimping each to seal the foil. When removing the foil pack, use fire-safe tongs and let the pack cool enough so that it's not hot to the touch when you open it. Carefully pull the foil apart, being sure to avoid any burst of steam. Check the food for doneness. If it needs to cook longer, wrap it back up and return it to the coals.

Certain foods cook well over an open flame, such as anything that you might cook over a gas grill. Some firepits come equipped with a metal grate that can be used like a grill grate. You can also bring your own campfire-cooking grate. Just be sure to pack tongs that you can use to flip food from a safe distance. Use caution when cooking foods that can drip oil onto an open flame, such as steak, bacon, or hamburger. Certain open-flame foods can be skewered and roasted on a stick, such as hot dogs, marshmallows, corn, or kebabs.

Cooking food in a Dutch oven is an optimal way to bake foods over a fire. The design of a Dutch oven creates an airtight seal that, in effect, offers similar

Dutch oven

baking results as an oven, just at a smaller scale. Cast-iron Dutch ovens are heavy, so consider investing in an aluminum version for a lightweight option. To create a more oven-like effect, carefully place glowing coals on the lid of the Dutch oven with a pair of fire-safe tongs. This will help to ensure an even distribution of heat around the oven.

Make sure you're using cooking utensils that can withstand the heat without melting, such as enamel or aluminum. Wear heavy-duty fire-resistant gloves and close-toed shoes when cooking over a campfire.

CAMPING RECIPES

With a bit of planning, patience, and prep, meals can taste as good in the wilderness as they do at home. For convenience and easy cleanup, some campers like to bring no-cook meals or quick-cooking meals like peanut butter and jelly sandwiches, cups of dried ramen, and freeze-dried dinners. Other campers prefer to put in a little more effort to create flavorful camping cuisine. Pick your style depending on what kind of camping you'll be doing (backcountry or frontcountry), how much you like to cook, the type of heat source (campfire or stove), and how much time you're willing to spend.

The following recipes are divided into five groups: breakfast, lunch, dinner, dessert, and snacks. For each group, four different meal options are listed. Two meals in each group can be made from the 25 core ingredients listed below, and are flagged with an asterisk. The other two meals are geared toward car camping because they require a Dutch oven and are best cooked over a bed of hot coals on a metal grate. When cooking over a fire, it's best to place the Dutch oven slightly off direct heat to prevent burning the food on the bottom of the pot. It typically takes at least 40 minutes after lighting a campfire to prepare a bed of hot, glowing coals, so be sure to time the meal accordingly.

Certain core ingredients recipes list backpacking, vegetarian, vegan, or gluten-free variations. Look for how many people a recipe serves, and adjust the amount of ingredients you should pack accordingly. Consider bringing measuring cups and spoons if you are frontcountry camping and can spare the room. When backcountry camping, you can generally approximate measure-ments and the recipes will taste just as good. Experiment with recipes by substituting different vegetables, meats, or grains. It is important to note that the first step for each meal cooked over a campfire is to build the fire far enough in advance to have hot coals ready by the time you want to start cooking.

25 CORE INGREDIENTS*

1. Apples
2. Bananas
3. Cinnamon
4. Sugar
5. Butter
6. Chocolate
7. Yogurt
8. Olive oil
9. Tortillas
10. Bacon or vegetarian sausage
11. Potatoes
12. Pasta
13. Beef (tempeh or tofu for vegetarian/vegan options)
14. Onions
15. Eggs
16. Mushrooms
17. Marshmallows
18. Salt
19. Pepper
20. Garlic
21. Cheese (cheddar or Parmesan, depending on the recipe)
22. Canned chicken (canned tuna for pescatarian option)
23. Bell pepper
24. Zucchini
25. Pesto

BREAKFAST

Campfire potatoes, bacon, and eggs*
Gluten-free
Even the most basic breakfasts can be tricky to cook over a campfire, but with the right technique, the finished product will be improved by that classic smoky campfire flavor.
Serves 4–6

Equipment
- Sharp knife
- Cutting board
- Mixing bowl
- Heavy-duty aluminum foil
- Fork
- Fireproof skillet
- Fireproof tongs
- Fireproof spatula
- Pot holder

Ingredients

Potatoes:
- 12 medium potatoes, scrubbed or peeled
- 1 onion, chopped
- 1 bell pepper, chopped
- Olive oil
- Salt
- Pepper

Bacon:
- 12 strips bacon

Eggs:
- A dozen eggs
- Bacon fat or olive oil
- Salt
- Pepper

Potatoes:

1. Cut the potatoes into half-inch cubes. Place all the vegetables in a large mixing bowl, and drizzle them lightly with olive oil. Sprinkle generously with salt and pepper.

2. Tear off four pieces of heavy-duty aluminum foil that measure about two feet each. Place one piece of aluminum foil over a second piece, lining up the edges, with the shiny side facing down on both pieces. Do the same thing to the other two pieces of foil.

3. Divide the vegetables in half, and place each half in the middle of the prepared foil wraps. Fold two opposite sides of the foil over the vegetables, then fold the other two sides over, crimping the edges together to form a tight seal. Do the same to the other foil packet of vegetables.

4. Place each foil packet on a bed of hot coals, and let them roast for about 30 minutes, flipping occasionally.

5. When opening the foil to check the contents, carefully pry apart the crimped edges, being careful to avoid

getting burned by escaping steam. The vegetables are done when the potatoes are soft.

Bacon:

Lay the bacon flat and side by side in a cast-iron skillet, and place the skillet over the fire. Turn the bacon with a pair of fireproof tongs after the facedown side becomes just cooked or crispy, depending on your preference.

Eggs:

Once the bacon has finished cooking, pour most of the bacon grease into a tin can or glass jar. Then cook the eggs in the remaining bacon fat (or use olive oil if you prefer). To make a large scramble, first whisk all the eggs in a mixing bowl, sprinkle with salt and pepper, and then pour the contents into the skillet. Stir with the spatula until done.

Mushroom frittata*
Gluten-free, vegetarian
If you're camping with a mushroom expert, throw a few wild mushrooms into the mix for some added texture and flavor; otherwise, bring mushrooms from home. Do not pick and eat foraged mushrooms unless you are certain they are edible. Pack some fresh thyme, freshly grated nutmeg, and cayenne for a little extra depth of flavor.
Serves 2–4

Equipment
- Mixing bowl
- Sharp knife
- Cutting board
- Measuring spoons
- Fork
- Fireproof skillet
- Cheese grater (optional)
- Aluminum foil or skillet lid
- Fireproof tongs
- Fireproof spatula
- Pot holder

Ingredients
- 6 large eggs
- 2 tablespoons water
- Salt
- Pepper
- 2 tablespoons butter
- 3 medium potatoes, scrubbed or peeled and sliced into ⅛ inch-thick medallions
- ½ onion, thinly sliced
- 10 ounces of a variety of mushrooms, gently brushed or wiped clean, and sliced (use cremini, white button, portabella, or shiitake mushrooms or a combination of these)
- 1 garlic clove, minced
- ½ cup cheddar or Parmesan cheese, grated or thinly sliced

1. Whisk together the eggs, water, ½ teaspoon salt, and a pinch of pepper in a mixing bowl.

2. In a fireproof, cast-iron skillet (or a regular skillet if cooking over a camp stove), melt the butter.

3. Add the potatoes, and sprinkle them with salt and pepper. Cook potatoes for three minutes, or until they start to soften, and stir with spatula about every minute.

4. Add the onions, mushrooms, and garlic, and another pinch of salt and pepper. Continue to cook for about four minutes, or until all the liquid from the mushrooms has evaporated, stirring every so often. Taste and adjust the seasoning.

5. Spread the vegetables evenly, covering the bottom of the pan, and sprinkle the cheese over the top.

6. Pour the egg mixture over the vegetables evenly. Cover the pan with a lid or aluminum foil, and cook for 10–20 minutes, or until the top of the frittata has set. For more even cooking, place some coals on the lid or aluminum covering with fireproof tongs. Once the frittata is firm to the touch, remove from the heat, let it rest for three minutes, cut it into slices, and serve.

Dutch oven enchiladas
Gluten-free, vegetarian, vegan
This recipe makes a tasty savory breakfast—but can also be enjoyed for lunch or dinner. A gluten-free option can be prepared by using gluten-free corn tortillas, and a vegan option can be made by substituting vegan cheese.
Serves 4

Equipment
- Dutch oven
- Can opener
- Fireproof spatula
- Cutting board
- Sharp knife
- Pot holders

Ingredients
- 2 tablespoons oil
- 1 red bell pepper, cut into strips
- ½ red onion, sliced into thin half-moons
- 4 cloves garlic, minced
- 1 tablespoon cumin
- 2 teaspoons salt
- 1 (14-ounce) can enchilada sauce
- 2 cups cheese (sub vegan cheese for vegan option)
- 1 cup cooked black beans
- 4–6 flour (or corn) tortillas
- Handful of cilantro
- Small can of diced jalapeños
- 1 lime

1. Over medium heat, heat the oil in the Dutch oven. Add the peppers and sauté for a few minutes until they start to soften. Add the onions and sauté them until they're soft and translucent and the peppers are soft. Add the garlic, cumin, and salt. Sauté 30 seconds, until fragrant.

2. Add ½ cup enchilada sauce to coat the bottom of the Dutch oven.

3. To build the enchiladas, place onions and peppers in a line in the center of a tortilla. Add a few spoonfuls of

black beans and top with cheese. Roll the tortilla around the fillings, then place the enchilada, seam side down, into the Dutch oven. Repeat with the rest of the tortillas, or until the filling has been used up.

4. Cover the enchiladas with the remaining sauce and cheese. Place the lid on top.

5. Return the Dutch oven to your campfire. Place it over indirect heat, and set 14–16 coals on the lid. Cook about 10 minutes, or until the cheese is melted. Serve topped with jalapeños, cilantro, and a squeeze of lime, and enjoy.

Dutch oven French toast

Gluten-free, vegetarian
A campfire version of a classic breakfast meal, Dutch oven French toast is a crowd-pleasing comfort food on a cold morning in the outdoors—or any morning for that matter. A gluten-free version can be made by using GF bread. This treat is best suited to front-country camping.
Serves 4–6

Equipment
- Dutch oven
- Mixing bowl
- Measuring spoons and cups
- Pot holders

Ingredients
- 3 tablespoons butter
- ½ loaf sourdough bread
- 4 eggs
- 1½ cups milk
- 2 tablespoons sugar
- ½ teaspoon ground cinnamon
- ½ teaspoon salt
- ½ teaspoon vanilla extract
- Maple syrup (optional)

1. Coat the inside of the Dutch oven with one tablespoon of butter.

2. Tear the bread into 1- to 2-inch pieces, and place them in the Dutch oven.

3. In a medium bowl, whisk the eggs and milk together. Add the sugar, cinnamon, salt, and vanilla and mix thoroughly.

4. Pour the mixture evenly over the bread.

5. Sprinkle the remaining two tablespoons of butter over the bread mixture.

6. Bake the French toast uncovered over the fire for about 45 minutes, or until set.

7. Let cool for five minutes, then slice and serve. Drizzle with maple syrup if you want some extra sweetness.

LUNCH

Pesto chicken salad wrap*
Gluten-free, vegetarian, vegan
A fresh-tasting, healthy lunch option, this meal is lightweight enough to carry into the backcountry and tasty enough to eat while sitting around camp. Experiment and add ingredients according to your taste, such as avocado, cucumber, or some fresh-squeezed lemon. You can also substitute canned tuna or hummus for the canned chicken. You can create a gluten-free version by using a GF wrap. You can also make a vegan version by omitting the cheese or using vegan cheese, and using a vegan pesto.
Serves 4

Equipment
- Small bowl
- Sharp knife
- Cutting board
- Fork
- Measuring spoon
- Peeler (optional)
- Can opener

Ingredients
- 2 (12.5 ounce) cans of shredded chicken meat, drained

- 4 tablespoons pesto
- ½ bell pepper
- 1 small zucchini
- 4 tortillas
- 4 slices mozzarella cheese

1. Mix together the shredded chicken and pesto in a bowl.

2. Slice the bell pepper and zucchini lengthwise into thin strips. Alternatively, if you have a peeler, shave off thin slices of zucchini lengthwise.

3. Assemble each wrap by placing a quarter of the chicken-pesto mix in a narrow strip down the middle of the tortilla. Add one slice of cheese, a quarter of the bell pepper, and a quarter of the zucchini and wrap tightly like a burrito.

Bacon-wrapped trout*

Gluten-free

To make this recipe, you will either need to pack store-bought trout, or you will need to fish for your own at your camping destination. Be sure to bring your own fishing equipment, and research the fishing regulations and whether a license or permit is required. Pack thyme, sage, parsley, and lemon for some added flavor.

Serves 6

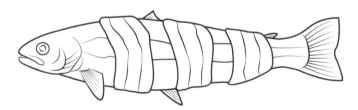

Equipment
- Fireproof tongs
- Sharp knife

Ingredients
- 6 (14-ounce) butterflied rainbow trout fillets, bones removed
- 1½ pounds bacon

1. Wrap each fillet with enough bacon to cover the length of the trout.

2. Grill the trout over the fire on a metal grate, flipping frequently, for 15–20 minutes. The bacon grease dripping into the flames will cause flare-ups, so use caution when turning the fish.

3. Once the bacon is crisp, cut into the middle of the fish with a sharp knife to check that the inside is flaky and done. Remove from the heat, and allow the fish to cool for about five minutes before serving.

Ramen

Gluten-free, vegetarian, vegan

This quick ramen recipe is vegetarian and vegan-friendly, and the lightweight ingredients can be easily carried on a backpacking trip and cooked on a backpacking stove. Frontcountry campers can opt to pack fresh vegetables and cook the ramen in a Dutch oven, since weight is less of a concern. Cooking the ramen in a Dutch oven helps keep the ramen hot for second helpings and concentrates the flavor of the broth. Use gluten-free noodles for a GF version, and use veggie bouillon cubes for a vegetarian/vegan version.

Serves 2

Equipment
- Dutch oven (or lightweight pot if backcountry camping)
- Sharp knife
- Cutting board
- Measuring spoons and cups
- Pot holders

Ingredients
- 1 teaspoon sesame oil
- 1 garlic clove, minced
- 1 teaspoon grated ginger
- 4 cups water
- 2 bouillon cubes
- 6 ounces ramen noodles
- Large handful of shredded, toasted nori

- ½ cup dehydrated corn or mixed vegetables (substitute fresh vegetables such as carrots, corn, and peas if frontcountry camping)
- 2 teaspoons soy sauce
- 2 green onions, thinly sliced
- 1 teaspoon butter (leave out if making a vegan version)
- A pinch of red pepper flakes

1. Heat the oil in the pot or Dutch oven over medium heat, and add the garlic and ginger. Cook for about 30 seconds or until pungent, then add two cups of the water and bring to a boil.

2. Once the water is boiling, add the bouillon cubes, ramen, nori, vegetables, and soy sauce and simmer until the noodles are just cooked.

3. Remove from the heat and add the green onions, butter, and red pepper flakes, then serve.

Dutch oven macaroni and cheese
Gluten-free, vegetarian
An easy-to-make favorite, this popular comfort food takes on a different dimension when baked over the fire. Add herbs like basil, chives, thyme, or oregano for a fresh finish. Use gluten-free noodles to create a GF version. Given the need for a Dutch oven, this recipe is best suited for frontcountry car camping.
Serves 6

Equipment
- Dutch oven
- Measuring spoons and cups
- Wooden spoon
- Cheese grater
- Sharp knife
- Pot holders

Ingredients
- 3 cups milk
- 2½ cups water
- ½ teaspoon fine sea salt
- 1 pound macaroni pasta or pasta shells
- 2 tablespoons butter

- 1 tablespoon Dijon mustard
- ¼ teaspoon garlic powder
- 1½ cups evaporated milk
- 4 cups grated cheddar cheese
- ¼ teaspoon ground black pepper
- Pinch of paprika

1. In a Dutch oven, combine the milk, water, and salt and bring to a boil. Add the pasta shells and gently stir. Partially cover and cook over the fire until the pasta is al dente, about 10 minutes (or the time listed on the package). Do not drain.

2. Move the Dutch oven to a less hot part of the fire and while stirring, add the butter, Dijon, garlic powder, and evaporated milk. Slowly sprinkle in the cheese, and stir until the cheese melts and the sauce thickens.

3. Remove the Dutch oven from the heat and season with pepper and paprika, then serve.

DINNER

Coal-roasted foil packs*
Gluten-free, vegetarian, vegan
For such a tasty reward, this classic camping meal requires very little prep. After chopping the ingredients and assembling the packs, you simply place the food packs in the coals and wait. Experiment by substituting different vegetables such as Brussels sprouts, asparagus, or sweet potatoes. Switch up the meat, or try different seasonings like curry, paprika, or fresh herbs. To make this meal vegetarian or vegan, you can substitute tempeh or tofu in place of meat, or just use vegetables.
Serves 4

Equipment
- Heavy-duty aluminum foil
- Sharp knife
- Cutting board
- Fireproof tongs

How to roast the perfect hot dog

1. Build a campfire, and prepare a bed of coals.
2. With a sharp knife, slice each hot dog lengthwise, down to the middle, making sure not to cut all the way to the other side.
3. Skewer the hot dog all the way through lengthwise (from end to end) with a prepurchased metal stick.
4. Stick the hot dog end into the fire, holding the stick so that the hot dog is about 4–8 inches above the bed of coals. Ideally, you should cook the hot dog in an area of the fire that can roast the dog on all sides, such as over a bed of coals in the middle of a cluster of glowing logs.

5. Rotate the dog slowly and continuously to ensure that the meat cooks evenly. Hot dogs are precooked, so it's not necessary to check the temperature of the meat to make sure it's safe to eat. However, biting into a hot dog that's cold in the middle is not very appetizing. So as a safeguard against this

Ingredients

- 1 pound meat, such as chicken breast, steak, or sausage (tempeh or tofu for vegan/ vegetarian option), cubed
- 1 onion, chopped
- 4 small potatoes, chopped into half-inch cubes
- 1 pound mushrooms, sliced
- 1 small zucchini, chopped
- 1 bell pepper, chopped
- 4 cloves garlic, minced or sliced
- ¼ cup olive oil
- Salt
- Pepper

1. Place one-quarter of each ingredient in the middle of a two-foot-long sheet of aluminum foil, with the shiny side facing down. Season generously with salt and pepper. Drizzle with one-quarter of the olive oil.

2. Place a second two-foot-long sheet of aluminum foil over the first, with the shiny side facing out. Roll the edges and crimp them to create a tight seal. Wrap each pack once more with a

third piece of foil. Crimp the edges down tightly.

3. Place the packs over a bed of hot coals and cook, turning every 10 minutes, until the meat is cooked and the vegetables are tender—or about 40 minutes total.

Chicken pesto pasta*
Gluten-free, vegetarian
A rich and creamy comfort food, you can make this meal vegetarian by substituting vegetables like mushrooms and spinach for chicken. You can also add extra flavor with fresh herbs, sundried tomatoes, lemon, or pine nuts. You can make a gluten-free version by using GF pasta. This meal can be cooked over a backpack stove or a campfire.
Serves 6

unpleasant experience, cook the hot dog for 2–4 minutes, or until the outside layer is evenly browned and bubbling.

6. Meanwhile, toast the bun on a metal grate over the fire's flames. Pull the bun open and lay it facedown on the metal grate. Once the facedown side is lightly toasted, remove the bun with a pair of fireproof tongs.

7. When the hot dog is done, slide it off the stick using a fork or knife and place it inside the prepared bun.

8. Top with your favorite condiments, such as ketchup, relish, mustard, or sauerkraut.

Equipment
- Sharp knife
- Cutting board
- Measuring cups
- Pot or Dutch oven
- Pan or cast-iron skillet
- Pot holders
- Can opener

Ingredients
- 2 quarts water
- Salt
- 1 pound pasta such as bowtie or shell

- 1 teaspoon olive oil
- ¼ cup onion, finely chopped
- 1 small zucchini, chopped
- 2 cloves garlic, minced
- 2 (12.5 ounce) cans shredded chicken
- ½ cup pesto
- ½ cup Parmesan cheese

1. Pour the two quarts of water into a pot or Dutch oven, and add a pinch of salt. Bring the water to a boil.

2. Add the pasta and cook for 8–10 minutes until al dente, or according to the package instructions. Drain the water into a hole dug in the ground, and cover the hole well.

3. Over medium heat, warm the oil and add the onions in a pan or skillet. Cook until the onions start to soften, then add the zucchini and cook until it starts to soften. Next, add the garlic and chicken and cook for about 30 seconds.

4. Add the chicken and vegetables to the pasta, and stir in the pesto. Keep stirring until all the ingredients are well incorporated. Sprinkle with Parmesan cheese and serve.

One-pot beef stroganoff

Gluten-free

A classic camping dish, beef stroganoff can be made over a camp stove, but baking it in a Dutch oven over the fire adds that special smoky flavor. An added perk of this dish is that using only one pot to cook the meal reduces the amount of cleanup. A gluten-free version can be made by using GF noodles.

Serves 4

Equipment
- Dutch oven or pot
- Sharp knife
- Cutting board
- Measuring spoons and cups
- Fireproof spatula
- Pot holders

Ingredients
- ½ pound strip steak

- 1 teaspoon salt
- 2 tablespoons olive oil
- 8 ounces mushrooms, sliced
- 1 small yellow onion, chopped
- 3 cups beef broth
- 1 tablespoon soy sauce
- 1 tablespoon fresh thyme
- ½ pound wide egg noodles
- ½ cup sour cream

1. Salt the steak evenly on both sides. Heat the oil in the pot or Dutch oven over the fire or a camp stove until very hot. Add the steak and turn every couple of minutes until it's browned on all sides and cooked through. Remove the cooked meat from the heat and set aside.

5. Reduce the heat to medium or move the Dutch oven to a less hot part of the fire. Add the mushrooms and sauté for five minutes, then add the onions and sauté for an additional five minutes or until they start to soften.

6. Add the broth, soy sauce, and thyme. Stir the bottom of the pot or Dutch oven, scraping any brown bits stuck to the bottom. Increase the heat to high or move the Dutch oven to a hotter part of the fire. Bring the broth to a boil, then add the noodles, cooking for eight minutes (or as long as instructed on the package), and stirring occasionally.

7. Once the noodles are tender, remove the pot or Dutch oven from the heat. Slice the steak into bite-size pieces. Add the steak and the sour cream to the pot and stir, coating the noodles evenly, then serve.

One-pot vegetarian chili and cornbread

Vegetarian

Two foods that should be eaten together can also be cooked together. To limit the amount of dishes you have to wash after your meal, and to add flavor to your chili and cornbread, try cooking this dish in a Dutch oven over the fire. To simplify the meal prep, measure and mix all the dry ingredients for the cornbread together and transport them in a ziplock bag. Write

the amounts of each wet ingredient needed to complete the recipe on the bag with a permanent marker.
Serves 6

Equipment
- Dutch oven
- Sharp knife
- Cutting board
- Mixing bowl
- Measuring cups and spoons
- Whisk or spoon
- Pot holders
- Can opener

Ingredients
Chili:
- 1 medium onion, diced
- 1 tablespoon oil
- 4 cloves garlic, minced
- 2 teaspoons salt
- 1–2 teaspoons chili powder
- 1 teaspoon ground cumin
- 1 (14.5 ounce) can black beans, drained
- 1 (14.5 ounce) can kidney beans, drained
- 1 (14.5 ounce) can diced tomatoes
- 1 (4 ounce) can diced green chilies
- 2 tablespoons tomato paste
- 1 cup grated cheese (optional, for garnish)

Cornbread:
- 1 cup cornmeal
- ½ cup flour
- 1 tablespoon baking powder
- 1½ teaspoon salt
- 1 cup milk
- 1 egg, lightly beaten
- 2 tablespoons honey

1. In a 10-inch/4-quart Dutch oven over medium heat, sauté the onion in oil until soft and just beginning to turn golden, or about 5 minutes. Add the garlic and spices and sauté for 1 minute. Add the beans, tomatoes, chilies, and

tomato paste, and stir to combine. Simmer for 10 minutes until thickened.

2. In the meantime, prepare the cornbread batter. Mix all the dry ingredients in a medium bowl, and stir to combine. Add the milk, egg, and honey, and mix until the batter forms.

3. Move the Dutch oven over indirect heat to reduce bubbling. Pour the batter over the chili as evenly as possible, then cover the Dutch oven with the lid and shovel embers or coals onto the top. Heat to 400–425 degrees Fahrenheit.

4. Bake until the cornbread has cooked through and is no longer wet in the center, 15–20 minutes.

5. Serve with grated cheese or your favorite chili toppings and enjoy.

DESSERT

Baked apples*
Gluten-free, vegetarian
A sweet treat that's also loaded with fiber, baked apples can be prepared over the campfire, and can be made less sweet or more sweet depending on how much sugar you want to add. You can also add fillings like chopped nuts or raisins for extra flavor and texture.
Serves 6

Equipment
- Sharp paring knife
- Heavy-duty aluminum foil
- Measuring spoons
- Fireproof tongs

Ingredients
- 6 apples
- 6 tablespoons butter
- 6 teaspoons brown sugar
- 3 teaspoons cinnamon

1. Core each apple with a sharp paring knife, cutting from the top of the apple, around the stem and slicing down in a tapered shape so that the bottom of the hole comes to a point and the bottom of the apple stays intact. The core should pull out like a plug. Cut the end of each core plug so that just the top part with the stem remains. Remove all the seeds from the apple and core top. Save each core top and set aside.

2. Fill each apple with 1 tablespoon of butter, 1 teaspoon of brown sugar, and ½ teaspoon of cinnamon. Rest the core tops over the hole of each apple.

3. Wrap each apple in about one foot of aluminum foil, and place it in the coals. Roll each apple to the other side after about 5 minutes of baking. Check the apples after about 10 minutes total, and bake longer if the insides have not softened. Let cool for a few minutes and serve.

Banana boats*
Gluten-free, vegetarian, vegan
Banana boats are a *slightly* healthier take on old-fashioned s'mores, and require much less vigilance to ensure that the marshmallows don't catch fire. This recipe can also be made vegan by substituting vegan marshmallows and vegan chocolate.
Serves 4

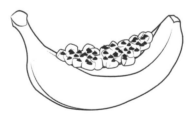

Equipment
- Knife (can be a butter knife)
- Heavy-duty aluminum foil
- Fireproof tongs

Ingredients
- 4 bananas
- ½ cup mini marshmallows
- ½ cup semisweet chocolate chips

1. Leaving the peel on, cut each banana lengthwise, through the peel and the banana, but taking care not to cut through the bottom peel.

2. Pull apart the sides of the banana and fill the opening with one-quarter of the chocolate chips and one-quarter of the marshmallows.

3. Wrap each banana in a foot-long piece of aluminum foil, and crimp the edges down to form a tight seal.

4. Place the bananas on the coals, and roast for about 10 minutes, flipping halfway through, or until the marshmallows and chocolate are gooey. Let cool for five minutes and enjoy.

Dutch oven apple cobbler

Vegetarian

A delicious treat, the topping for this cobbler can be made in advance at home and kept chilled in a cooler or once at camp. The Dutch oven should be kept slightly off of direct heat, to avoid burning the bottom of the cobbler.

Serves 4

Equipment
- Dutch oven
- Measuring spoons and cups
- Mixing bowl
- Fork
- Cutting board
- Resealable bag
- Sharp knife
- Pot holders

Ingredients
Topping:
- ¼ cup almond meal
- ¾ cup all-purpose flour
- 2 tablespoons brown sugar
- 2 teaspoons baking powder
- ¼ teaspoon salt
- ⅓ cup milk
- ⅓ cup butter, chilled

Filling:
- 6–8 medium apples
- ¼ brown sugar
- 1 teaspoon ground cinnamon
- ¼ teaspoon ground nutmeg
- 2 tablespoons bourbon

For the topping (make ahead of time and pack in the cooler, or prepare at camp):

Combine the dry ingredients in a mixing bowl. Using a fork, mix until a crumbly dough forms, then add the milk and cut the butter into the mix to form small pebble-sized balls of butter and dough. Set aside, preferably in your cooler.

For the filling:

1. Core the apples and cut into bite-sized (half-inch) pieces.

2. Heat a Dutch oven over medium heat. Add the apples, brown sugar, cinnamon, nutmeg, and bourbon to the Dutch oven and cook briefly until the sugar has dissolved. Remove from heat.

3. Crumble the topping over the apple filling in an even layer. Set the lid on the Dutch oven.

4. Place the Dutch oven on a ring of 6 coals, then evenly space 18 coals on top of the lid. Bake for about 20 minutes, until the topping is golden brown. Remove from heat and serve.

Dutch oven s'mores cake

Vegetarian

A decadent twist on a classic camping dessert, the s'mores cake is a rich, gooey, and simple sweet treat. Bake an angel food cake beforehand, or buy a ready-made one at a bakery or grocery store.

Serves 6–8

Equipment
- Dutch oven
- Pot holders

Ingredients
- 1 purchased or homemade angel food cake
- 7 ounces (or about 2 packets) graham crackers
- 6 (2-ounce) chocolate bars
- ½ bag large marshmallows

1. Tear apart the angel food cake, and arrange the pieces evenly in the bottom of the Dutch oven.

2. Break apart the graham crackers, and sprinkle them evenly over the angel food cake, pressing some of them into the cake.

3. Break apart the chocolate bars, and lay them evenly over the graham cracker layer.

4. Cover the top with marshmallows.

5. Cover the Dutch oven and set it on top of the

How to roast the perfect marshmallow

1. Build a campfire, and prepare a bed of coals.
2. Use a prepurchased metal roasting stick or whittle the end of a greenwood stick, or a stick not completely dry on the inside. When you cut into the stick past the bark, the inside should still be a greenish color. Don't cut or break off a living stick from a tree. Instead, try to source a greenwood stick that has freshly fallen to the ground. The stick should be about the length of your arm and thick enough around that the stick won't bend when weighed down by a marshmallow on the end.
3. Skewer the marshmallow through its center using the marshmallow stick, then hold the stick so that the marshmallow is 4–8 inches above the hot coals. Any closer and there's a good chance the marshmallow will catch fire and blacken around the outside. Ideally, you want to position the marshmallow in a place over the fire that is surrounded by heat on as many sides as possible. For example, the perfect spot for roasting a marshmallow is often above the coals and underneath

and between a cluster of glowing logs.

4. Rotate the marshmallow stick slowly while balancing the part of the stick that's a few inches away from the marshmallow on a log for added stability.

5. Frequently check the marshmallow for doneness so that it doesn't burn. The marshmallow is ready to eat once the outer layer is a golden-brown color and the inside is gooey. You can test the inner consistency of the marshmallow by giving it a squeeze.

coals, placing a few coals on the lid, and cook until the marshmallows are puffed up. Allow to cool for a couple of minutes, and then serve.

SNACKS

Quesadillas*
Gluten-free, vegetarian, vegan
Simple and quick, quesadillas can be prepared on a skillet over the fire or on a camp stove and then wrapped in aluminum foil for a hiking snack. Add shredded canned chicken for some protein and onion, bell peppers, or mushrooms for some extra flavor and texture. Make a gluten-free version by using GF (or corn) tortillas, and a vegan version by using vegan cheese.
Serves 2

Equipment
- Skillet
- Sharp knife
- Cutting board
- Can opener (if using shredded chicken)
- Spatula
- Pot holder

Ingredients
- 1 teaspoon olive oil
- Chopped vegetables like mushrooms, onions, and bell peppers (optional)
- 1 (12.5 ounce) can shredded chicken (optional)
- 1/2 cup cheese
- 1 large flour tortilla (or 2 smaller tortillas)

1. If adding vegetables, in a skillet sauté the mushrooms in oil until all the moisture has evaporated, then add the onions and cook for another five minutes or until softened. Add the bell peppers and cook until softened. Set the vegetables aside.

2. If adding shredded chicken, open the can and drain the liquid into a resealable bag to store in the cooler.

3. Cut the cheese into thin slices, then lay them evenly over half the tortilla.

4. Spread more olive oil around the bottom of the hot skillet. Place the tortilla on the skillet, and then spread the vegetables and chicken evenly over the half with cheese. Fold the other side of the tortilla over the cheese side, like you would do with an omelet.

5. Flip the tortilla after 3–5 minutes, or until the facedown side becomes golden brown. Cook the other side for 3–5 minutes, and then remove from the heat. Cut in half and allow to cool for a couple of minutes, then serve.

Campfire-baked potatoes*

Gluten-free, vegetarian

Quick carbs are a necessary nutrient, especially if high-exertion activities are on the itinerary. You can eat the potatoes warm, or keep them wrapped in tinfoil for a snack to enjoy later.

Serves 4

Equipment
- Sharp knife
- Heavy-duty aluminum foil
- Fireproof tongs

Ingredients
- 4 potatoes
- ¼ cup butter (plus extra for serving)
- Salt
- Pepper

1. Poke each potato with a sharp knife several times, and then coat the outsides with butter.

2. Wrap each potato in two sheets of foil, and place them on a bed of hot coals or on a fire grate. Cover the potatoes with a few hot coals.

3. Bake the potatoes for 30–60 minutes, or until soft. Serve warm with butter and salt and pepper to taste.

Popcorn

Gluten-free, vegetarian, vegan

Popcorn is an easy, salty snack that can be enjoyed while sitting around the campfire telling stories, or made at camp and then sealed in a plastic baggie for a lightweight bite on the trail. Play around with the seasonings by drizzling on melted butter or olive oil, or by sprinkling on minced garlic, nutritional yeast, brewer's yeast, salt, cayenne, cheese, or fresh herbs.

Serves 4

Equipment
- Dutch oven or large pot with lid
- Measuring spoons and cups
- Pot holders

Ingredients
- 1 tablespoon canola oil
- ½ cup popcorn kernels
- Butter or olive oil
- Seasonings of choice

1. Cover the bottom of a Dutch oven or large pot with oil, then add the popcorn kernels. Cover with the lid and then shake the pot from side to side to coat the kernels with oil.

2. Heat the pot over medium heat, shaking every so often, until the kernels start popping, then shake less frequently. Once the popping slows to one pop every five seconds, remove the Dutch oven or pot from the heat.

3. Drizzle oil or melted butter over the popcorn, and sprinkle on the desired seasonings, then serve.

Dutch oven nachos

Gluten-free, vegetarian, vegan

Campfire nachos are a warmer and more substantial alternative to a chips-and-salsa snack break. Add your favorite toppings like sour cream or salsa, or use vegan cheese as a substitute. You can also sauté vegetables like onions or peppers to add to the mix.
Serves 4

Equipment
- Dutch oven
- Measuring spoons and cups
- Cheese grater
- Sharp knife
- Cutting board
- Can opener
- Pot holders

Ingredients
- 1 tablespoon olive oil
- ½ pound tortilla chips
- 1 (7.75 ounce) can enchilada or hot tomato sauce
- 1 (14.5 ounce) can black beans, drained
- 1 cup grated cheese or vegan cheese substitute
- 1 avocado, cubed
- 4–5 green onions, thinly sliced
- Handful fresh cilantro, stems removed and chopped
- 1 lime, cut into wedges for garnish

1. Cover the bottom of the Dutch oven with the oil.

2. Evenly spread one-third of the chips over the bottom of the Dutch oven, then drizzle one-quarter of the can of hot sauce over the chips. Sprinkle one-quarter of the black beans, one-quarter of the cheese, and one-third of the avocado, green onions, and cilantro. Repeat to form a second layer.

3. For the third layer, add the remainder of the ingredients. Cover with a lid and cook over the campfire for 10 minutes, or until the cheese has melted. Garnish with lime and serve warm.

CAMP COOKING CLEANUP

DIVIDE AND CONQUER

When camping with a group of people, make post-meal cleanups a group activity. While one person washes the dishes, another person can dry them.

Alternatively, designate some people to cook and other people to be on the cleanup crew. You can switch up the meal and cleanup teams according to who likes to cook and who doesn't mind doing the dishes.

Disposable dishes are also an option, but create waste. However, if water is scarce, disposable (or compostable) dishes may be a good idea.

USE BIODEGRADABLE SOAP

Pick up some camping-specific dishwashing soap at a gear store. Though biodegradable camp soap brands are gentler on the environment, they should still only be used in small quantities, and away from freshwater sources. Dispose of soapy dishwater by digging a hole 200 feet from any nearby body of water. Pour the dishwater into the hole, and cover it up well to hide the scent of food scraps and soap from curious critters. The dirt will help kick-start the process of breaking down the chemicals used to manufacture the soap. A water container like a camp bucket is useful for carrying water from a water source to your campsite.

USE NATURAL RESOURCES AS CLEANING SUPPLIES

Since you should use soap sparingly in the outdoors to keep wild spaces pristine, you can substitute naturally occurring abrasives for soap. Natural resources like sand, snow, or dirt can help loosen food stuck on the bottom or sides of cookware. Simply gather a handful of earth or snow, and use it like a sponge. Then dispose of it in the hole dug for the dishwater.

HEAT SOME DISHWASHING WATER

Washing dishes can seem like an even more unpleasant task in cold conditions, when fingers can go numb. If you have spare fuel, or a way to heat water over a campfire, warm up a pot of water specifically for washing and rinsing dishes.

CHOOSE YOUR STYLE OF WASHBASIN

If car camping, and you prefer a larger washbasin for cleaning dishes or you're camping in a big group, you may want to pack a bucket or storage container. Minimalist campers may opt to simply use their largest camping pot as a washbasin.

CLEAN UP FOOD SCRAPS

When you are finished washing dishes, strain any food debris from the dishwater and dispose of it wherever you are storing your garbage. Pour the dishwater over a rocky area well away from your campsite, or bury it in a hole.

DO DISHES AT HOME

For overnight camping trips where water is scarce, it can be easiest to transport the used dishes home and tackle them there.

PROPER FOOD STORAGE

Store food according to the rules and regulations specific to your camping area. If you keep animals from seeing or smelling your food, you may prevent them from chewing through your backpack or tent. Store your food properly, and when food is out, remain vigilant to keep adventurous creatures—especially those used to humans—from getting into your food supply. Mice and chipmunks are common offenders, but there are aerial thieves as well. Gray jays, also known as camp robbers, earned their name by dive-bombing the food supplies of unsuspecting campers.

It's the responsibility of campers to keep food out of reach of animals, not just because stolen food is a nuisance but for the health of the animals as well. Human food can cause animals to become sick, malnourished, or dependent on humans for food. Animals that become habituated to eating human food can also pose a safety threat, such as a bear that has grown accustomed to snacking on s'mores fixings or cookies left out on picnic tables or not carefully stored in bear-proof containers.

FOOD-STORAGE BASICS

Never leave food unattended, even for a few seconds. Mice, chipmunks, and jays can steal your goods with alarming speed. Before turning in for the night, make sure any scented items like sunscreen, lotion, or toothpaste are packed away with the food. Check your tent and backpack thoroughly for any crumbs or food wrappers, as these remnants can encourage an animal to chew through the fabric of your tent or backpack.

FRONTCOUNTRY FOOD STORAGE

Metal food lockers can be found at some campgrounds. When provided, these should be used to store any food, trash, or scented items, and be sure to latch the container properly so that it's secure from the dexterous paws of bears and raccoons.

If metal food lockers aren't provided, and if bear canisters aren't required, you should keep your food inside your cooler, stowed in your car. Read all food-storage rules for the particular campground before you leave home, so you know whether you should bring any specific food-storage tools, such as a bear-proof cooler or canister.

BACKCOUNTRY FOOD STORAGE

Read the rules and regulations before you go, or call a ranger station to find out how you should properly store your food at your backcountry campsite. When no regulations are posted, rent or purchase a lightweight bear canister or bear bag to bring along with you. Alternatively, bring enough lightweight rope or cord to suspend a bag of food from a tree or between two trees.

Bear canister or bear bag method

Certain wilderness areas require that bear canisters be carried into the backcountry. Some ranger stations rent out bear canisters, so check with the ranger station nearest the place where you'll be camping to see if you can pick one up on your way. Typically, you will need at least one bear canister per person, depending on the size of the bear canister and the length of the trip. Make sure all your food and scented items fit into your issued bear canisters before you leave the ranger station.

Bear canisters are effective against the prying paws of bears by usually featuring a locking system that must be opened with the thin edge of a coin or screwdriver. But the downside of canisters is that they are bulky and can add a lot of weight to pack into the backcountry.

Bear canister food storage

Despite their shortfalls, be sure to bring a bear canister if the area where you're camping requires you to carry one, as you could be fined by a ranger if you fail to do so.

Bear bags are a lightweight option when bear canisters are not required in bear country. The bear bags are made from a strong polyethylene material, which is tough for bears to tear open. You can also buy odor-proof plastic bags to store food in inside the bear bag, or an aluminum liner that can fit inside the bear bag, creating a barrier to keep a bear from smashing the bag's contents. The downside of bear bags is that, unlike bear canisters, they can still be carried away by a bear even if the bear can't get to the contents. So it's a good idea to hang the bag off the ground. Alternatively, you can bring a bear canister for your food and store your trash in a bear bag.

If you plan to buy a bear bag, make sure it's certified by the Interagency Grizzly Bear Committee when you know you'll be camping in bear country. When using a bear bag, cinch the drawstring according to the product's instructions.

Food-hanging method

When bears aren't as much of a threat where you're camping, you can opt to hang your food in a bag, suspending it from a stable tree branch or between two trees. Some backcountry campsites provide bear poles or metal cables specifically made to hang food.

If you know that poles or metal cables won't be available, pack a stuff sack large enough to hold all your food and trash, a couple

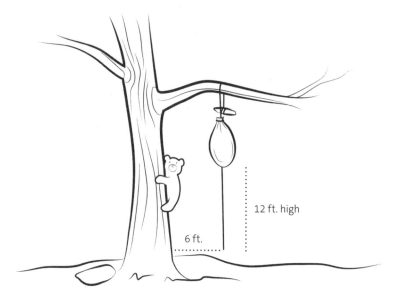

12 ft. high

6 ft.

of lightweight carabiners, and lightweight rope or cord that measures at least 40 feet in length. When deciding what food-storage method to use, consider whether you will be camping above tree line, where it may be hard to find trees with limbs that are high off the ground.

How to hang a food bag

The ideal site for hanging a bear bag is a minimum of 100 feet from your campsite (in grizzly country, consider placing your hang 300 feet from your camp to be safe). Once far enough from camp, locate a suitable tree. Sometimes a single tree will have the perfect branch for hanging your bag (12 feet up and 6 feet out from the trunk or nearest branch). In this case, you simply need to attach something weighted to the end of your rope or cord. A rock can work well, but you must be cautious when throwing a rock over tree branches, making sure to keep all group members at a safe distance. Have a spotter make sure no one (especially the thrower) gets hit by the flying rock. Another option is to use an old sock filled with gravel, small stones, or a single rock. A sock is easier to attach to the end of the rope. If you can locate a single tree branch to meet your needs, all you do is throw the rope over the branch (ensure that it's 12 feet up and 6 feet out), attach your bag to the rope with a carabiner, then hoist your bag to the desired height and tie it off on the nearest suitable anchor (rock, tree, etc.). In many areas finding the perfect tree for a single-branch hang is challenging. More often than not you'll have to do a two-tree hang, meaning you'll have to use two shorter branches on two different trees. This is most easily accomplished by throwing the weighted rope over one branch on one tree, then throwing the other end over one branch of another tree and attaching your bag to the center of the line. Have a helper pull on one end of the rope, while you pull on the other, raising the bag until it reaches 12 feet high and 6 feet out.

Learning how to hang a bear bag at the end of a long day, in the fading daylight, can be a frustrating experience. So make choosing a bear bag site and getting the ropes hung a priority when you first arrive at your campsite.

Camp fun should have a place, and an important one, in your plans for the trail. For the time being the camp is your home and it should never be allowed to become dull for want of a little gayety and wholesome amusement.

—Lina Beard and Adelia Belle Beard, *On the Trail: An Outdoor Book for Girls*, 1915

Chapter 6
Camp Activities

SPENDING TIME OUTDOORS AWAY FROM THE distractions of electronic entertainment is an opportunity to experience activities that invite more social interaction or quiet time. You may revel in the freedom to sit on a sunny rock and read or to lean up against a tree and journal. Or you may prefer to spend hours sitting at the picnic table, playing cards by lantern light. Perhaps you would like to participate in more active games like bocce ball, cornhole, or flashlight tag, or pursue activities that require no equipment, like watching birds and wildlife.

Organized fun can be a welcome distraction from bugs or bad weather. Playing games may be a necessary diversion if you find yourself trapped in a tent for hours, waiting out a rainstorm. On those stormy days, it's good to have a few card games at your disposal, or a book tucked into a tent pocket. Educational activities can also be a fun diversion, such as participating in the Junior Ranger program offered by the National Park Service, or learning how to identify the constellations. Whatever your interests or intentions for a particular camping trip, be open to starting new traditions, making up games, and swapping stories or singing songs.

GAMES

Certain games require that you pack equipment, while others you can play by using your own imagination or sense of humor. When planning any camping games, consider how much weight and extra bulk you can pack as well as the energy levels and ages of the members of the group. If frontcountry camping, you can bring along any board game that you would normally enjoy at home and play it during the day or by headlamp or lantern light at night. Just keep in mind that small, lightweight game pieces might blow away in the wind or get lost during travel. With some items of camping gear you can play nature-based games, like flashlight tag or scavenger hunt.

CARD GAMES FOR ADULTS

Hearts

Players: Three to seven.

Rank: Ace (high) to 2 (low). No trump suit in hearts.

Objective: To avoid winning tricks in any hand, which includes the queen of spades—the Black Maria. The player with the lowest score wins. An alternative goal is to win all 13 hearts and the Black Maria.

Setup: Shuffle the deck and select a dealer, who will deal the cards like so:
- *Four players:* Each player is dealt 13 cards.
- *Three players:* Remove the 2 of diamonds. Each player is dealt 17 cards.
- *Five players:* Remove the 2 of diamonds and the 2 of clubs. Deal each player 10 cards.
- *Six players:* Remove the 2 and 3 of diamonds and the 3 and 4 of clubs. Each player is dealt eight cards.
- *Seven players:* Remove the 2 and 3 of diamonds and the 3 of clubs. Deal each player seven cards.

Passing cards: Each player looks at their hand and then selects three cards to pass to another player. Before looking at an opponent's three cards, a player must first pass their three. The passing rotation proceeds as follows:

- *Four players:* The first hand is passed to the player on your left. The second hand is passed to the player on your right. The third hand is passed to the player across the table. The fourth hand is not passed. Continue this rotation until the end of the game.
- *More than four players:* The first hand is passed to the player on your left, and the second hand is passed to the player on your right. Continue this rotation until the end of the game.

Tricks: After the pass—the player holding the 2 of clubs plays that card to start the round, or trick. In a three-player game, since the 2 of clubs has been removed, the card that starts the trick is the 3 of clubs.

Each player follows suit. When a player does not have a card in a given suit, a card of a different suit in their hand must be discarded. However, if a player has no clubs during the first trick, the Black Maria or a heart cannot be played next. Whoever plays the highest card in the suit that is led wins the trick and keeps all the cards from that trick in a facedown stack next to them. The winner of the trick then begins the next trick. The Black Maria can lead at any time, but a heart cannot lead a trick until a heart or the Black Maria has been played in a previous trick.

Scoring: The game is played until a player reaches or goes over 100 points. Hearts are counted as 1 point each. The Black Maria is worth 13 points. At the end of each hand, tally the number of hearts each player has kept. If one player has kept all 13 hearts in addition to the Black Maria, the player can either choose to add 26 points to all the other players' scores or subtract 26 points from their own score. The player with the lowest total score wins the game.

Rummy

Players: Two to six.
Rank: K (high) to A (low). See "Ace either high or low" below for a common variant. When making a sequence, ace is always low and cannot be played above the king.

Objective: To be the first to play, or meld, all of your cards.

Setup: Shuffle the deck and select a dealer, who will deal the cards like so:
- *Two players:* 10 cards to each player.
- *Three or four players:* 7 cards to each player.
- *Five or six players:* 6 cards to each player.

After dealing, the dealer places the remaining stack in the middle of the table, which will serve as the draw pile. The dealer then turns over the top card in the stack and places it next to the draw pile faceup, which is the start of the discard pile.

Melds: A meld of cards can be played in groups (three or four of a kind) or sequences (three or more consecutive cards in the same suit).

How to play: On their turn, a player draws one card, which can either be from the top of the discard pile or the draw pile. The player can choose to play a meld of cards, and then must discard one card, adding it faceup to the top of the discard pile. The discarded card can be the card that was just drawn from the draw pile, but it cannot be the card that was pulled from the discard pile. If a player melds all their cards, they don't have to discard.

When one or more cards in a player's hand fit into a meld already laid on the table, a player can play that/those cards. This is called *laying off.* The player laying off the cards places them on the table in front of themselves. For example, if a player plays a meld that includes three 6s, the next player can lay off another 6 from their hand. And if a player plays a meld that includes a sequence, such as 5-6-7 of diamonds, the next player can play the 4 or 8 of diamonds (or both), or the 8 and 9 of diamonds, for example. When a player plays the last card in their hand, they "go out," after which, the round is scored. Once the draw pile has been exhausted, all the cards in the discard pile are shuffled and restacked to form a new draw pile.

Scoring: All the remaining cards in the other players' hands are counted toward the score of the winner of the hand. Aces are worth 1 point. Number cards are worth their face value. Face cards are worth 10 points. Going rummy means that a player plays all of their cards in a single play, in their first play of the hand. When scoring, all points are then doubled for that hand. The first player to reach 150 points wins.

CARD GAMES FOR KIDS

Spoons

Players: Three to thirteen.

Objective: To be the first player to have all four of the cards in your hand be of the same rank (e.g., four queens). The other objective is to claim a spoon before they're all snatched up.

Setup: Setup requires a standard 52-card deck and enough spoons to equal the number of players minus one. For example, if six people are playing, five spoons are needed. Players sit in a circle. Before the start of the game, place all the spoons in the center of the circle, close enough so that every player can reach them. Select a dealer. The dealer shuffles the deck and deals four cards to each player, then places the remaining stack of cards facedown in front of the person to their left.

How to play: To begin play, the person to the left of the dealer draws one card from the stack, looks at it, and either places it facedown in front of the person to their left, or places it in their own hand. A player can only have four cards in their hand at a time, so if you decide to keep a card that you draw, you must discard one card from your hand. The game continues like this, with each player placing discarded cards facedown in front of the player to their left. Players continue simultaneously drawing cards and discarding until someone collects four cards of the same rank, at which point, that person will try—as quietly as possible—to grab a spoon from the middle of the circle. As soon as any other player sees a player doing this, they can also grab a spoon for themselves. The last player to do this (when the spoons run out) is out of the game. Another round is played, with one spoon removed. Rounds are played until two cowinners remain.

Go Fish

Players: Three to six.

Objective: To gather the most groups of four cards of the same rank.

Setup: Select a dealer, who then deals five cards to each player. The rest of the stack is then placed facedown to form a draw pile.

How to play: The person on the dealer's left goes first. On your turn, you ask any other player if they have a specific card rank (from a rank that you already have in your hand). For example, "Do you have any 4s?" If the person you asked has any 4s in their hand, they must give them all to you. If you successfully obtain cards, you can then go again, asking any player for any rank that you already have in your hand. If the player you ask does not have any cards in the rank you requested, they say, "Go fish," and you must then draw the top card from the draw pile. If you draw a card that's in the rank you just asked for, you can show it to the other players and take another turn. When your turn is over, the person who said "Go fish" is the next person to play. Once you collect four cards in the same rank, you must show the set to the other players and place them facedown in front of yourself. The game ends when either the draw pile is exhausted or someone has no cards left in their hand. The person with the most sets of four wins the game.

DICE GAMES

Farkle

Also known as Hot Dice, Zilch, and Zonk, Farkle is a game with simple rules that requires very little equipment. Whatever you decide to name the game, all that is required are six six-sided dice and at least two players. While camping, it can be helpful to also use a flat-bottomed bowl in which to roll the dice, so they don't scatter all over the ground.

A person is randomly selected to start and rolls all six dice. If the person rolls at least one 1 or 5, they can roll again, but must first select either the 1 or the 5 (or both) to score, removing them from the next roll. After making the selection, the person must then gather up all the dice still in play and roll again. Each roll, the player must select which dice to add to their score and then pick up and roll the remaining dice, risking losing all their points if they roll a Farkle. The player continues rolling until they decide they are happy with the points accumulated so far or they Farkle, meaning that none of the dice rolled are worth any points or a 1 or a 5 hasn't been rolled. When this happens, the players say, "Farkle," and all the dice get passed to the next person to roll. At the beginning of the game, each player gets into the game by trying to roll a score of 500. Once a player has done so, that player is entitled to play any unrolled die left by the player ahead of them, adding to the score the previous player achieved. Sometimes a player can be kept out of the entire scoring process by failing to score that initial 500 points. When scoring, 1s and 5s can be scored separate from other combinations like triplets or straights. If you Farkle three times in a row, you lose 1,000 points. On any given round, if a player who is in the game decides to keep the accumulated points and pass the dice to the next person, the next player can decide to roll any remaining unscored dice and continue adding on to the points scored by the previous player.

Scoring:
- Single 5 = 50
- Single 1 = 100
- Three 1s = 300
- Three 2s = 200
- Three 3s = 300
- Three 4s = 400
- Three 5s = 500
- Three 6s = 600
- Four of any number = 1,000
- Five of any number = 2,000
- Six of any number = 3,000
- 1–6 straight (1, 2, 3, 4, 5, 6) = 1,500
- Three pairs = 1,500
- Four of any number with a pair = 1,500
- Two triplets = 2,500

Once a player reaches 10,000 or more points, each person gets to roll one more time to try to get above that person's score. The highest score wins.

Fork Over the Chocolate

A hilarious game, Fork Over the Chocolate is best played after several nights camping, when food tastes better than ever and chocolate cravings are running rampant. The required equipment includes a bar of good quality chocolate, a pair of dice, a knife, a fork, a plate, a pair of large gloves (such as winter or work gloves), a hat, and a pair of sunglasses. Other clothing items can be added to the mix as well.

The game can be played at a picnic table or in a circle on the ground. To start, the first person rolls both dice, then passes the dice to the next person. If someone rolls doubles, then that person must put on each item of clothing or accessory: the gloves, the hat, the sunglasses, and any other piece of clothing that is part of the required dress code. Once all the items are being worn, the person is allowed to start cutting into the chocolate, using the fork and knife. Only sawing motions are allowed. Breaking the chocolate by stabbing the knife into it is against the rules. Only a square of chocolate can be sawed off at a time. If the person successfully saws off a piece, they can try to pick it up and eat it with the large gloves. Meanwhile, the other participants continue to roll the dice until the next lucky person rolls doubles. As soon a double is rolled, the person with the chocolate must remove all the designated clothing and accessories and hand them over to the person who has rolled the next double. The game ends once everyone has had a turn eating the chocolate, or when the laughs start to die down. The remaining chocolate can then be divided up for all to enjoy.

ACTIVE GAMES

Cornhole

Certain outfitted campgrounds provide cornhole boards, but if not, you will need to bring your own, plus eight cornhole bags. Four of the bags should be one color, and the other four a different color. Cornhole boards take up a lot of room, so if space is an issue or you're backcountry camping, leave cornhole at home.

To play, place the boards 27 feet apart. The game is played with two teams of two. Team partners stand at opposite cornhole boards, facing each other. All eight cornhole bags start on one

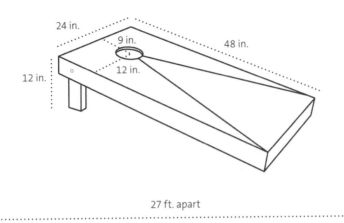

24 in.
9 in.
48 in.
12 in.
12 in.
12 in.

27 ft. apart

board. A player from one team goes first by throwing a bag of their team's color, aiming for the hole in the opposite board. The player on the other team then throws one of their bags, also aiming for the hole in the opposite board. The two players take turns throwing one bag until all the bags are at the opposite end; then the players at that end score the points and gather up the bags. The player on the team who got the most points that round throws first on the next round. The team that gets to 21 points first wins.

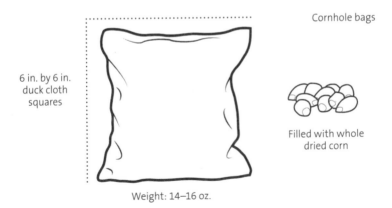

Cornhole bags

6 in. by 6 in.
duck cloth
squares

Filled with whole
dried corn

Weight: 14–16 oz.

Scoring:

- If a bag hits the ground first and then bounces up onto the board, the bag is removed from the board and is not counted.
- 3 points: Bag that lands in or falls into the hole.
- 1 point: Bag that lands anywhere on the board's surface (and stays on).

- 0 points: Bag that lands on the ground, or is hanging off the board and touching the ground, or is touching another bag that is touching the ground.
- All the points are added up and the difference in the two scores is added to the winning team's points. For example, if one bag from each team lands on the board, and one bag from one team lands in the hole, the two board bags cancel each other out and the team with the bag in the hole is awarded three points. If the teams get the same number of points in each round, neither team is awarded points and the team who won the last round starts first in the new round.

Bocce ball

The only equipment required for bocce is a bocce ball set. A classic bocce ball set is heavy, and should only be used when frontcountry camping. Lightweight backpacking bocce ball sets can be purchased at some outdoor gear stores. Many variations of bocce exist, and a fairly lax version is described below.

To play, divide people up into two teams of one, two, or four people, and then divide the eight bocce balls evenly between the teams. In most bocce sets, the *jack* is the smallest ball. Randomly select which team goes first. Designate a line behind which each person throwing must stand. One player from the team going first throws the jack somewhere into the designated area (try to stay off fragile wild areas, and stick to rocky, sandy, or gravelly ground). You can play by setting boundaries, or just roam freely. The player who threw the jack then throws one of their bocce balls out into the designated area, trying to make it land as close to the jack as possible. A player from the next team throws one of their bocce balls, again aiming so that the ball lands next to the jack. Once one player from each team has thrown a bocce ball, everyone then throws a second ball (alternating players on each team). If there are eight players, each player throws only one ball. If there are four players, each throws two balls; if there are two players, each throws four balls plus the jack is thrown by the first player.

After all the bocce balls have been thrown, the points are added up. Whichever team has the bocce ball closest to the jack gets the points—one point for a ball not touching the jack, and two points if the ball is touching the jack. For example, if one team has one ball closest to the jack, they get one point. If they have the two closest balls to the jack, they get two points. The team that wins the round throws first for the next round. Whichever team reaches 12 points first wins.

Flashlight tag

A good game for children to play, flashlight tag requires at least three players, one flashlight, and a space where children are safe to run around at night. This game can also be played at dusk.

Like the classic game of tag, someone is randomly selected to be *it*, or the person who chases the other players around. The person who is *it* carries the flashlight and counts to a set number (between 30 and 100), depending on how far away the other players will be hiding. While the *it* person counts, the others run and hide behind objects such as trees, bushes, or rocks. Once the *it* player is finished counting, they will investigate hiding places with the flashlight. If you're illuminated, you're *it*, and the game starts over.

Scavenger hunt

An effective strategy for keeping children occupied, a scavenger hunt can also be tailored to suit all ages. Some versions of outdoor scavenger hunts include lists of objects that participants must collect. However, this kind of activity is counter to Leave No Trace Seven Principles. For example, gathering rocks, bugs, or plants may disrupt fragile ecosystems or disturb wildlife. An alternate version only requires taking pictures. Begin by writing a list of poses, places, and activities that each team must photograph in a specified amount of time and within a certain designated boundary. For example, items on the list might include:

- Photo of a waterfall
- Photo of the team spelling out CAMP with their bodies
- Photo of a spider
- Photo or video of a teammate eating a triple-decker stack of marshmallows
- Photo of the whole team hugging a tree

Be creative with the photo prompts. More points can be given for more difficult photos or photos that picture the whole team. A scavenger hunt can be run by having each individual competing against the other participants, or by dividing the group into even teams of two or more people. The coordinator then distributes the list of required photos to each team. The teams then go off in search of their photo opportunities and return to camp before time runs out. Back at camp, the teams can share their photos and add up their points. The team with the highest score wins.

GROUP CIRCLE GAMES

Mafia

A variant of Mafia is Werewolf, which features a different story line and other characters—but the rules for both are essentially the same. A deck of playing cards is all you need. One suit represents the mafia members—diamonds, for example. In another suit—not the mafia suit—the king represents the doctor and the queen represents the detective. All the other cards that are not the mafia, doctor, or detective represent townspeople. From a regular deck of playing cards, pull out all the necessary cards to play the game, which should equal the number of people playing. Divide the number of players by three, and that's the number of mafia members—or diamond cards—that should be shuffled into the playing deck.

One person is designated as the narrator (it helps if the narrator is already familiar with the game) and acts as the facilitator. The narrator then hands out the cards randomly to the people playing. Once each player has looked at their card, the various roles should be kept secret and the cards should be given back to the narrator. The narrator will instruct everyone to "fall asleep," meaning that each player must close their eyes. Once every player's eyes are closed, the narrator will ask the mafia members to "wake up" and open their eyes. Trying not to make any noise, the mafia members must look around and make eye contact with every other member of the mafia, familiarizing themselves with the people on their team. The mafia members should then decide whom to kill by quietly agreeing on the same townsperson by nodding their heads when the narrator points to the right person. The narrator should keep quietly pointing to different members of the group until a consensus has been reached. Once the mafia members are in agreement, the narrator will ask them to go back to sleep, and after all the mafia members' eyes are closed, the narrator will instruct the detective to "wake up" and question the identity of someone by nodding when the narrator points to the person they think might be a mafia member. If the person the detective investigates is a mafia member, the narrator will nod their head, and if the person is not a member of the mafia, the narrator will shake their head no. The narrator will then instruct the detective to "go to sleep," and ask the doctor to "wake up." In the same fashion as the mafia and detective rounds, the narrator will point to random people in the group until the doctor nods their head. The selected person will then be saved from dying if the mafia had chosen to kill that person in that round. Finally, the narrator will tell the doctor to "go to sleep," and will then ask the entire group to "wake up" and open their eyes.

The narrator then has the task of making up a story about how the victim succumbed to their fate the previous night. The person killed is out of the game. If the detective investigated a member of the mafia, that mafia member is out of the game. If the doctor chose the person who was selected to be killed, that person can stay in the game. Each time a person is eliminated from the game, the narrator can reveal the identity of that person. After the narrator completes the story for that round, the townspeople begin an open discussion about who they think the members of the mafia are. Once a single person is nominated to reveal their identity, the group votes on whether that person is eliminated from the game. A unanimous vote in favor of the person being eliminated means that person must reveal their identity. If the vote is not unanimous, that person gets to stay in the game.

The game is over once all the mafia members have been eliminated, and then the townspeople win, or the only people left alive are mafia members and then the mafia wins.

Twenty Questions

A good game to boost morale or provide a distraction at the end of a long hike or car ride, Twenty Questions can be played with two people or more.

One person thinks of an object, person, or place, and after they've thought of one, the other players ask *yes* or *no* questions one by one. For example, a guesser could ask, "Is it a person?" And if the answer is yes, the next question might be "Is the person still living?" The guessers try to find out what the mystery person, place, or thing is in fewer than 20 questions.

Salad Bowl

A fresh twist on the classic game of charades, Salad Bowl is known by other names such as the Name Game, Fishbowl, or Celebrity. To play, the group splits up into two teams and each person on both teams writes down words onto 3–6 scraps of paper. The words can be the titles of books, movies, or television shows, or they can be the names of people or places. Players who want an extra challenge can permit a string of random words to be written down. All the paper scraps are folded up and thrown into the same bowl. A 45-second timer starts, so a player from one team draws a piece of paper from the bowl and describes whatever is written on it, using any words except those that are on the scrap of paper. Once that player's team correctly guesses the words, the person then selects another scrap of paper from the bowl and repeats the process, trying to get through as many scraps of paper as they can in 45 seconds. Once the timer goes off, the player collects all the correctly guessed pieces of paper and puts them in a pile for their team. A player from the other team goes next and the 45-second timer starts over. The game continues until the bowl is empty. Both teams then count up their scraps of paper and record the number. All the paper scraps are then put back into the bowl.

For the second round, the process continues with the same scraps of paper, except this time, the standing player can only say one word as a clue (without using any of the words that are written down on the scrap paper). So for example, if the paper scrap says, "Abraham Lincoln," the one-word clue could be "president." Once the person gives the one-word clue, they must wait until their team guesses the scrap paper word(s) correctly. So it's important to give some thought to the one-word clue before speaking. The same process continues until the bowl is empty. The teams then tally up their scrap papers and put them back in the bowl.

The third round is played like charades, with the standing player acting out the words written on the scrap papers. One version of the game requires the person to act out the words while underneath a blanket. Hilarity often ensues. The game is over once the bowl is empty. The teams then total up their points from all three rounds, and the team with the most points wins.

WILDLIFE WATCHING

No equipment is needed to spend time outdoors observing wildlife, except perhaps a pair of binoculars if you want to get an up-close view, or a guide if you want to identify the different birds and animals you see. A few simple tricks will help you spot wildlife and react safely when animals are near.

enjoyable way to pass the time. Some outdoor writing prompts include:

- Tell a story from the perspective of something you see in the woods—it can be a rock, tree, beetle, or even a stream.
- Write about your first camping experience.
- Describe an experience you had in nature and why it was meaningful to you.
- Sit in the woods and describe everything you see around you, from the ground to the sky.
- Describe your favorite place in the natural world and why it has had such an impact on you.

WHITTLING

Whittling can be used as a meditative activity or to fashion something useful, such as chopsticks (see page 84) or tent stakes. Softwoods, such as pine, are ideal to start with.

The act of whittling is simple, but some precautions should be taken to minimize the risk of injury. To open a pocketknife, pull the blade out from the handle so that the tip of the blade faces away from you. When working a stick with a knife, run the blade away from you along the grain, pressing down firmly against the wood, which should shave off a piece of the stick. Always make sure your knife is sharp, and sharpen it if you feel it becoming harder to whittle.

STORYTELLING

Telling ghost stories is a classic go-to campfire activity that will leave everyone jumpy and anxious, but also beg-ging for the next story. You can read a favorite tale from a book collec-

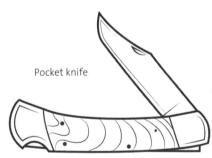

Pocket knife

tion of scary stories or retell a story that you might have heard on a previous camping trip. See page 209 for a list of scary story collections.

STARGAZING

In the wilderness, without the light pollution from city centers, the night sky takes on a whole new dimension. Stars shine with more definition, and constellations are easier to spot. Stargazing is best enjoyed by lying on a blanket or a sleeping pad and staring up at the sky on a clear night. For a truly mesmerizing experience, camping trips can even be planned to coincide with meteor showers.

There are 88 constellations, which are groups of stars named after the shapes or mythological images they resemble. Constellations can help you sort the twinkling dots scattered across the night sky. If you're a newcomer to amateur astronomy, eager to begin exploring the night sky, you'll have to overcome one of astronomy's biggest hurdles—learning to identify the constellations. But with a little practice, you'll be able to acquaint yourself with some of the major formations that astronomers have named.

North circumpolar constellations

Circumpolar constellations are star formations that never rise or set with the seasons, meaning they appear to remain in fixed locations in the night sky, regardless of your latitude. We begin in the northern sky, realm of those always-visible star groups known as the north circumpolar constellations. The most prominent figure is the Big Dipper (note: the Big Dipper is not a constellation). These bright stars—four forming the bowl, three more tracing out the handle—create one of the most recognizable patterns in the night sky, an ideal guide for locating surrounding constellations.

As any good Boy or Girl Scout will attest, you can find Polaris, the North Star, by tracing a line between the stars Dubhe and Merak at the end of the bowl of the Big Dipper and extending it about five times the distance between them. When astronomical newcomers see this celebrated star for the first time, they are astonished that it isn't much brighter than the stars in the Big Dipper.

Polaris is the brightest star in Ursa Minor, the Little Bear, which contains the Little Dipper. Like its big brother, the Little Dipper is made up of seven stars—four in the bowl, and three in the handle. Because four of its stars are dim, the Little Dipper is hard to see in light-polluted skies.

If you trace a line from the bowl of the Big Dipper past the North Star and continue it an equal distance beyond, you'll arrive at an eye-catching group of stars that form a distinct letter M or W. This is Cassiopeia, Queen of Ethiopia.

Summer

Summer is a season of mixed blessings for astronomers. The nights are warm but short and often hazy. The summer sky is a veritable gallery of cosmic masterpieces. The Milky Way arches high across the sky, which is richer than its winter counterpart because we now look toward the heart of our galaxy. Dominating the evening sky are three first-magnitude stars forming the Summer Triangle. Vega is the brightest of the three and is located in a nifty little constellation called Lyra the Lyre.

Our second Summer Triangle star, Deneb, is the tail of Cygnus the Swan. Deneb and four other bright stars of the Swan form an asterism called the Northern Cross, which is immersed in the Milky Way. Deneb is at the top of the cross, the star Albireo is at the base. Albireo is a double star famous for its rich colors of golden yellow and sapphire blue. The star pair can be split with binoculars, but the colors can be seen only through a telescope.

Farther south on the Milky Way is the bright star Altair and its parent constellation, Aquila the Eagle. If you follow the Milky Way from Aquila toward the southern horizon, you should find a group of stars that looks like a teapot. This asterism is part of Sagittarius the Archer. This constellation marks the location of our galaxy's center. The area teems with deep-sky treasures—especially bright nebulae and star clusters. To the right of the teapot is the ruddy first-magnitude star Antares, the "heart" of Scorpius the Scorpion. Like the winter star Betelgeuse, Antares is a red supergiant star in the last stages of its life. A fishhook-shaped row of stars trailing down and to the left of Antares forms the Scorpion's tail and stinger, while an upright row of three stars to Antares's right marks the location of its claws.

Autumn

As the nights begin to lengthen and a chill pervades the air, the summer Milky Way exits center stage (although the Summer Triangle remains visible in the west until early winter). Following the Summer Triangle is one of the night sky's prettiest constellations—Delphinus the Dolphin. Four stars, arranged like a diamond, form the Dolphin's head, while a fifth creates the tail. You can imagine a dolphin leaping out of the water as you gaze at this constellation.

In its wake is a rather barren expanse of sky whose most prominent feature is the Great Square of Pegasus the Winged Horse.

Alpheratz is at the top left corner of the Great Square. From here, two rows of stars branch out and up. This is the constellation Andromeda the Princess. And yes, it is home to the great Andromeda Galaxy. At a distance of 2.7 million light-years from Earth, it's the most remote object readily visible to the naked eye. Through binoculars, however, you'll see an elliptical glow (the galaxy's bright nucleus), which appears larger in small telescopes.

Winter

If the winter sky seems more alive with stars, it's no illusion. Besides the obvious facts that the air is clear and dry then, we're looking at a star-rich region that defines one of the spiral arms of our Milky Way Galaxy. Of the 21 brightest stars in the entire night sky (so-called first-magnitude stars), 7 are in this area.

On a winter evening, the sky is home to what most astronomers agree is the grandest of all constellations—Orion the Hunter. A rectangle of bright stars—which includes, at opposite corners, first-magnitude Betelgeuse and Rigel—is bisected by a diagonal row of three bright stars (the belt). Beneath the belt hangs a row of three stars—Orion's sword. Don't be fooled by their uninspiring naked-eye appearance; the middle star in the sword isn't a star at all.

It's the Orion Nebula—one of the grandest telescopic showpieces the night sky has to offer. In binoculars, it appears as a fuzzy patch of light. When you gaze at this wondrous glowing cloud, you view creation itself, for within this luminous glow stars are being born.

Orion is the focal point of a stunning gathering of bright stars and constellations. The belt points down and to the left of a brilliant white star: Sirius, the brightest star in the night sky, leader of the constellation Canis Major the Great Dog. Sirius always dazzles, but the star especially captivates when positioned near the horizon. During winter, atmospheric refraction causes Sirius to sparkle in a rainbow of colors—a beautiful sight through binoculars or a small telescope.

Return to Orion's belt and continue up and to the right, and you arrive at a V-shaped group of stars called the Hyades. This is the head of Taurus the Bull. The reddish-orange first-magnitude star at the upper left end of the V is Aldebaran—the eye of the Bull. Each end of the V extends outward to a star that forms one of the Bull's horns. Continuing past the Hyades, you'll see a little cluster of stars—one of the loveliest naked-eye sights in the night sky. This is the Seven Sisters, or Pleiades. Six are visible to the unaided eye under average sky conditions; binoculars reveal the seventh star, plus dozens more.

The uppermost horn of Taurus is part of a pentagon of stars that includes the bright golden-yellow star Capella. This pentagon is the constellation Auriga the Charioteer. Auriga lies above Orion and is overhead on a midwinter evening. The fact that these five stars represent a man on a chariot carrying a goat (Capella) attests to the vivid imagination of its ancient discoverers. The little triangle of stars beneath Capella represents the goat's three kids.

Orion's heavenly court includes Gemini the Twins. From Orion, extend a line upward from Rigel through Betelgeuse to this neat rectangular constellation, which contains the bright stars Pollux and Castor. Midway and slightly left of a line between Sirius and the stars Pollux and Castor is the first-magnitude star Procyon. Procyon forms an equilateral triangle with Betelgeuse and Sirius. It's about all you'll see of Canis Minor the Little Dog.

Spring

As the days lengthen and the weather warms, Orion and his wintry retinue progress slowly into the western sky. Leo the Lion now assumes center stage high in the south. Leo's most notice-able feature is an asterism (a grouping of stars) that reminds observers of a sickle or a backward question mark. The period on the question mark is the first-magnitude star Regulus. To the left of the Sickle are three stars that form a right triangle. We see the Lion from the side; the Sickle outlines his head, and the triangle, his hindquarters. Viewed with a little imagination, Leo definitely sports a feline profile.

During spring, the Big Dipper appears nearly overhead from mid-northern latitudes. If you follow the handle of the Dipper away from the bowl, you'll "arc to Arcturus," a golden-yellow first-magnitude star in the constellation Boötes the Herdsman. The constellation itself is shaped like a huge kite, with Arcturus at its base. Continuing the arc, you'll "sprint to Spica." This blue-white first-magnitude star is in Virgo, which is a huge, sprawling constellation.

If you look below and to the right of Spica, you'll spot a neat little group of four bright stars that resembles the outline of a sail. This is the constellation Corvus the Crow. It's impressive how stately this little constellation looks, perched above the treetops to the south on a clear spring evening.

Summer

Autumn

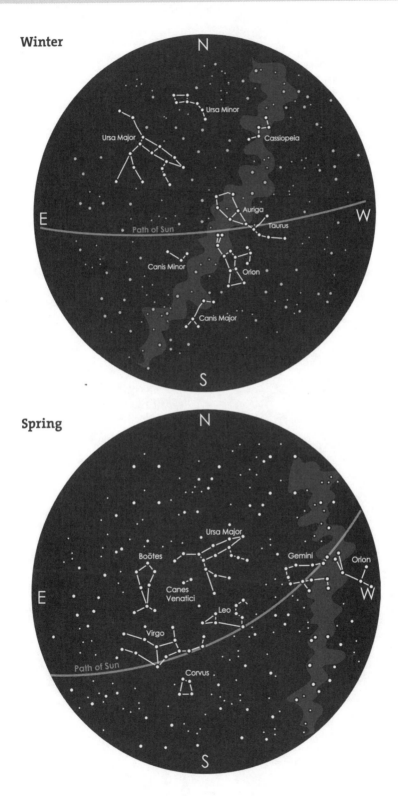

Winter

Spring

Avoid as much as possible asking another member of the party to do your work, or to wait upon you: it is surprising how easily you can make yourself disliked by asking a few trifling favors of one who is tired and hungry.

—John M. Gould, *How to Camp Out*, 1877

Chapter 7

Camping Etiquette

WILDERNESS ETIQUETTE CONSISTS OF generally accepted codes of conduct that dictate good behavior in the outdoors. While some etiquette is enforced—like observing fire regula-tions—other principles should be followed out of a sense of responsibility to protect the environment and to limit disturbing the outdoor experience of other campers. For example, playing your favorite music over a Bluetooth speaker in your campsite—even quietly—can carry across a lake so that campers on the opposite shore hear every lyric. Not everyone shares the same taste in music, nor do they necessarily go to the woods to hear music, so it's best to simply enjoy the sounds of nature so that others may enjoy them too. Remember your voice carries much farther than you realize near bodies of water, so avoid shouting or talking loudly, and insist that children use their quiet voices too.

Keep in mind that wilderness etiquette is constantly evolving to adapt to modern camping behaviors and updated regulations, so it's good practice to look up the most current Leave No Trace Seven Principles every few years. Similarly, not all codes of conduct within the US are universally accepted across the globe, so do your research on wilderness etiquette specific to any country you plan to visit.

While certain etiquette principles apply to all modes of camping, some only apply specifically to frontcountry or to backcountry camping, so when planning for any trip be sure to brush up on the particular conventions for the type of camping trip you're planning.

STANDARD CAMPING ETIQUETTE

FOLLOW THE RULES

Read and respect the rules of each campground and natural area. Obey regulations that restrict the use of firearms and fireworks, smoking, or driving motorized vehicles. Rules and regulations are set in place for a reason—follow them and you will ensure that you and your camp neighbors not only enjoy your time but also help preserve wild spaces for future campers.

REVIEW FIRE REGULATIONS

For safety and general regard for other campers, you should check whether campfires are allowed where you're going. Call the campground or ranger station ahead of your departure date. Always bring a camp stove as backup.

DON'T UPROOT, TRAMPLE, OR DAMAGE LIVING FLORA

When gathering firewood, only collect dead twigs or downed branches. Do not saw or break off branches from living trees or shrubs. Avoid trampling ground-cover plants as this can contribute to erosion and soil degradation, and make the soil inhospitable for future plant life. Don't uproot or pick plants and flowers, even during wild-flower season.

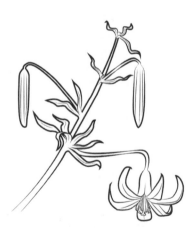

Tiger lily (*Lilium columbianum*)

BE POLITE, LATE ARRIVALS AND EARLY RISERS

If you arrive at a campground or backcountry campsite after dark, speak softly and avoid pointing flashlights, headlamps, or car headlights in the direction of other people's campsites. Use a car's lowlights when headlights are a necessary light source for tasks such as setting up a tent upon arrival. Early risers should behave with the same respect for other campers and limit the amount of noise they make in the morning.

USE BIODEGRADABLE SOAP

If used in small quantities, biodegradable soap has a much lower impact on the environment than mass-market soaps. Do not use any soap near bodies of water, as it can disturb water quality and harm flora and fauna. Do not wash dishes in a river, lake, or stream. Instead, carry water away from shore, add biodegradable soap, and clean and rinse utensils, cups, plates, and pans. Then dig a hole 200 feet away from any nearby water sources and dispose of the soapy water in the hole, covering it enough to hide any scents.

BE RESPECTFUL WHEN SMOKING OR DRINKING

Use cigarettes far away from other campers, as the smoke can waft into your neighbors' campsites. Never throw a lit cigarette on the ground. If you must smoke in the woods, along trails, or in a campground, it's a good practice to fieldstrip the cigarette butt when you are done. That means: extinguish the cigarette, roll it between your fingers to scatter the remaining tobacco on the ground, and place the paper and filter in your pocket for disposal in your garbage bag.

When consuming alcohol, be mindful of noise and behavior in your group so as to not disrupt the outdoor experience for other campers. Make sure to pack out your empty bottles and cans. No one likes to find broken glass or litter in a campsite.

USE TOILETRIES SPARINGLY

Using cosmetics like shampoo, conditioner, face wash, and lotion can leave chemicals behind in the wilderness that don't biodegrade. Instead, consider abstaining from using these products while camping. Some campgrounds have shower facilities where these kinds of products are fine to use.

When brushing your teeth, use the toothpaste spray method rather than spitting out a glob of toothpaste than can attract wildlife. Locate an area away from your campsite and water bodies where you can spray the toothpaste onto the ground, without hitting someone else's campsite or another camper. This method disperses the toothpaste enough so that wildlife doesn't damage ground flora while trying to eat it or become sick from eating too much.

SWIM WITH CAUTION

Before swimming in lakes and streams, consider how much DEET or sunscreen you have on your skin that will wash off into the water. Even body oil can have an adverse effect on the water quality. Consider all the other wildlife and campers who will be drinking the water downstream before you swim or bathe. If you do need to wash off, carry water away from shore and take a sponge bath with a small amount of biodegradable soap or no soap at all, and dig a hole where you can dispose of the wastewater.

CLEAN UP AFTER YOURSELF

Make sure trash makes it into trash receptacles and toilet paper goes into the toilet. Properly pack up and store food immediately after every meal. Help keep camping areas pristine so that future campers can enjoy them too. If you encounter litter in a restroom, do your part and place wastepaper into the proper receptacles. If it's a bigger mess than you can deal with, or if it has been vandalized, report it to the ranger or camp host.

LEAVE TECH AT HOME

Give nature a fair chance to entertain you by leaving entertainment electronics like video-game players, iPads, and laptops at home. Use smartphones for emergency purposes only, and turn any Wi-Fi devices to airplane mode so you won't be as tempted to use entertainment applications. Consider packing a camera so you won't have to open your phone to take photographs, and therefore won't be as inclined to check email or catch up on news or social media. Work on consciously shifting your focus to being in a different place and enjoying the natural sights, scents, and sounds of the outdoors. Tune out technology and tune in nature.

DON'T CUT THROUGH CAMPSITES

Respect other campers' personal space and avoid cutting through campsites unless someone has pitched a tent right along a main path of travel. Find a way around a campsite that doesn't cause you to trample flora or disturb wildlife.

DON'T BLARE MUSIC

Just like respecting other campers' personal space, you should also respect other people's camping experience by not playing your own music at your campsite or while participating in an outdoor activity like hiking. If you want to play music while camping—whether it's live music like strumming a guitar or playing music from a radio or Bluetooth speaker—check in first with all the other surrounding campers. If they don't mind, then you should still limit the volume and stop playing music by the posted quiet hours of the campground, or use headphones.

REDUCE LIGHT POLLUTION AND GLARE

If car or RV camping, turn off your headlights and RV awning light before you go to bed. When using headlamps around other people, use the red-light setting, as this helps keep your eyes and other people's eyes adjusted to the dark and isn't as harsh when accidentally pointed directly into someone else's face.

As a general rule, limit the amount of artificial light you use while camping, as this reduces light pollution and makes it easier to view and appreciate a starlit sky.

SET UP HAMMOCKS RESPONSIBLY

Never tie up a hammock between two trees that bend or bow from a weighted hammock. Use living, wide-trunked, sturdy trees so that you don't injure yourself or irreparably harm any plants. Don't string either end of the hammock more than five feet off the ground or over sharp objects like rocks or shrubs. Before climbing in, test the stability of the hammock by pressing your hands down into the hammock firmly. Then sit squarely in the hammock, testing its performance again, before swinging your arms and legs inside.

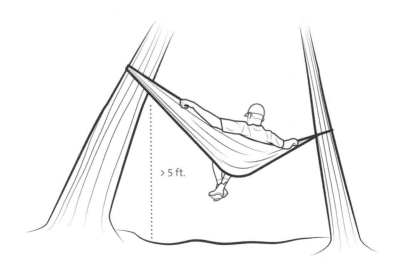

> 5 ft.

HELP WHEN NECESSARY

Offer emergency assistance to other campers. At the very least, notify the appropriate authorities, and keep the injured person safe and warm until other help arrives.

KEEP GROUPS SMALL

When organizing a camping trip, keep group size in mind, because larger groups are more difficult to manage and can produce potentially unsafe situations or disruptive experiences for other campers. An ideal group size is four to six people in the outdoors.

CHECK UNSOLICITED ADVICE OR REMARKS

Inevitably you will encounter campers who have more or less camping experience than you. It's never safe to assume the level of experience of any camper based on your limited observations. Sexism in the outdoors is widespread. Just ask any female camper or adventurer and she'll likely have a story about men making comments like, "You're pretty strong for a girl," "I'll carry that for you," or "You're doing that wrong." According to studies by the Outdoor Foundation, women make up nearly half the people who participate in outdoor activities. It would be irrational to assume the majority of these women do not have the same outdoor skills as their male counterparts. Similarly, other factors such as race, age, and disabilities never warrant assumptions about skill level or wilderness competency.

When interacting with other campers, the best approach is to be friendly and to avoid asking questions or making remarks that imply judgment or authority. For example, asking, "Where are you headed?" is a less presumptive question than "You know that there are only two hours until sunset, right?" Questions that are framed to presume a person's abilities or motivations not only have the potential to offend but also perpetuate an outdoor culture of posturing and elitism rather than one of acceptance and inclusivity. However, there are times when questions about skill level are warranted. When a person's safety is at risk or when a person looks like they may accidentally harm another person, then a question or comment might be necessary. For example, if you see someone paddling around in a canoe while thunderclouds are forming, you can kindly call out, "Hey! Did you hear that a lightning storm is predicted to hit this afternoon?" If the person says, "Yes," then they likely understand the situation. If the person seems confused by the question, you can explain that it would be safest to get off the water until the storm passes. Similarly, if you witness someone who may potentially harm an animal, water source, or plant, you can provide friendly information about the repercussions of a person's actions, such as, "Did you know that feeding animals can lead them to suffer health problems?" or "Hey, I saw that you were washing dishes in the lake using soap. I just learned that even biodegradable soap can have adverse effects on water quality. Did you know that?" or "Hi, I noticed that you were cutting branches off live trees to use as firewood. We have some extra firewood. Would you like some?" These kinds of questions can lead to longer conversations—rather than lectures—about safety, environmental stewardship, and camping etiquette.

When all else fails, approach people with kindness and curiosity. When interacting with strangers in the outdoors, a good option is always a friendly "Hi! Have a nice day!"

LEAVE SOUVENIRS BEHIND

If you come across a cultural or historic site, do not collect objects like arrowheads, pottery, woven baskets, or mining equipment. Leave everything as you find it, including natural souvenirs like stones, flowers, petrified wood, feathers, bones, and sticks. Inform members of your group that it is illegal to remove artifacts and to pick flowers and plants in most national and state parks.

Arrowhead

RESPECT WILDLIFE

Keep pets on a leash when outdoors, so they don't disturb or kill wildlife. Never feed or touch wild animals. Human food can negatively impact the health of wild animals and can cause them to become dependent on humans for food. Even if animals are tame enough to approach you, do not hold out your hand with food. Keep a safe and respectful distance between you and any wildlife, especially nesting birds, mothers protecting their young, or animals that are behaving strangely. Report any aggressive animals to the nearest ranger station.

DO NOT ROLL ROCKS

Never throw or roll rocks off the edge of cliffs or down steep slopes, as the consequences can be extremely dangerous or even deadly. Even when no humans are standing in the potential path of a rolling rock, the disturbance to the environment can alter the landscape or cause harm to wildlife.

LEAVE DRONES AT HOME

A drone is a small unmanned aircraft. It can capture beautiful shots of outdoor scenery from an aerial view. The problem with this device is the interruption it causes when you are trying to enjoy the quiet and technology-free peace that nature offers. While flying, a drone makes a sound like a huge housefly, a loud buzzing noise that is a nuisance in the outdoors. Not only that, but the flying object can be an eyesore when it obstructs scenic views. In addition to the aesthetic and auditory intrusions that drones cause, they can also disturb wildlife like nesting birds or mother animals who are trying to protect their young. Given these drawbacks, drones should be left at home. Certain areas like national parks prohibit drones, and people who are caught using them will be issued a hefty fine.

FRONTCOUNTRY-SPECIFIC ETIQUETTE

STORE AND DISPOSE OF TRASH AND RECYCLING PROPERLY

Dispose of trash and recycling at designated receptacles. Take loads of trash and recycling to the labeled bins throughout your trip so that you don't accumulate so much waste that it attracts wildlife to your campsite. Temporarily store any trash or recycling wherever you store your food, but in separate bags. If no receptacles are available at the campground, dispose of trash and recycling when you return home.

DON'T BRING YOUR OWN FIREWOOD

To limit the spread of foreign species, do not bring firewood from home. Introducing non-native bacteria and insects can disrupt ecosystems by causing the spread of invasive species. Many campgrounds sell split firewood and kindling for a small fee. If firewood is not for sale, check to find out if you can gather downed branches or dead twigs.

DON'T BRING GENERATORS

Check campground rules to see whether RV generators are allowed. Even if generators are permitted, decide whether they are necessary, since they cause quite a bit of noise and can disrupt the outdoor experience for other campers.

WASH DISHES AT YOUR CAMPSITE OR AT A DESIGNATED WASHING STATION

Do not wash dishes in a bathroom facility or sink that isn't specifically designated as a dishwashing site, as food can clog up the drain and leave a mess. See page 187 for proper campsite washing protocol.

DON'T BURN TRASH

Be sensitive to other campers and don't burn plastics or other synthetic materials that will produce a bad odor or release harmful chemicals into the air.

TREAT THE CAMPGROUND FACILITIES RESPECTFULLY

Clean up after yourself in communal spaces like restrooms, kitchens, firepits, and dishwashing stations. Flush the toilet after you're done using it. Do not wash dishes in bathroom sinks or showers. Limit the amount of time you spend in campground showers, to limit water use and so that other people can take a turn. If storing perishable food in a shared kitchen refrigerator, label your food items with your name and the date. That way, if you forget to take food home with you, the campground staff will know when to throw it away. Use campfire best practices in communal firepits. Don't leave food remnants in the sink at dishwashing stations.

BACKCOUNTRY-SPECIFIC ETIQUETTE

PACK IT IN; PACK IT OUT

Any trash or recycling that you accumulate while in the back-country should be stored with your food, but double-bagged in a separate bag. Do not bury any trash or recycling, as these can take years to biodegrade in fragile wild environments.

DON'T DIG TENT TRENCHES

Digging trenches around your tent to redirect rainwater runoff can irreparably damage a campsite and create dangerous obstacles for future campers. If digging trenches is an absolute necessity, make sure to cover them back up before you leave.

SOCIAL MEDIA BEST PRACTICES

Hashtags invite thousands of people to view a single photo of a scenic camping area on social media in a matter of seconds, and geotagging enables anyone who desires to to find the exact location. National and state parks have observed an increase in the number of visitors to locations that are the most frequently posted on social media. This kind of wide-ranging advertising can motivate more people to visit an outdoor destination than the natural area can accommodate. Growing foot traffic comes with consequences like soil erosion, increasing quantities of litter, more people putting themselves in dangerous outdoor situations or not following regulations, and worsening water quality. For example, a geotagged photograph of a campfire on the shore of a pristine alpine lake might tempt others to re-create this idyllic scene in the exact spot, regardless of fire regulations. A photograph of a hand feeding a chipmunk in a national park might lead people to think that feeding animals in that park is a common and accepted practice.

When deciding whether to post, consider a few best practices to reduce any potential negative impacts on the natural beauty or ecosystem of a special outdoor location. You can also use social media to spread tips about conservation and low-impact practices. For example, when posting a photo of a tent with a lake in the background, use the caption to remind people to camp at least 200 feet from a body of water. Think first before geotagging or listing the name of the location. Assess whether the area can accommodate more campers. If the area you want to tag is a private business or someone's property, ask if they want any social media promotion. Some scenic areas and campgrounds post a hashtag or social media handle on the bulletin board for visitors to tag in their photos, to help increase the number of visitors or to help spread awareness about a protected area.

Consider leaving certain places secret by not posting photos of them. Tell friends and family who visit the area not to post about the location on social media either so that the places you love most can remain pristine for years to come.

CAMPING INTERNATIONALLY

As a general rule, Leave No Trace Seven Principles should be adhered to no matter where you go camping, whether camping high in the Alps or deep in an Ecuadorian jungle. And you should do diligent research before any camping trip abroad to learn about unique best practices specific to the place you'll be visiting.

CHECK LAWS AND REGULATIONS
While the idea of international camping is a romantic notion, some countries may have laws that restrict where you camp, or whether you camp at all. Learn local driving laws and understand how they're different from the driving rules you're familiar with. Research the specific food-storage regulations, and make sure you bring the appropriate gear (e.g., bear canister).

INVEST IN A GOOD MAP
Research the best maps for your travel destinations. Some maps may not be written in English, so be prepared to ask for help with the translation.

RESEARCH CAMPING OPTIONS
In some parts of the world, camping is strictly prohibited outside of designated campgrounds. Research ahead of time whether that's the case where you'll be traveling. In extreme regions of the world, such as the jungle or arctic, a guide service might be a smart investment, as they'll be able to make educated decisions about weather, wildlife, and hazards in that area.

In some countries, certain individuals advertise their property for camping. Home-rental websites and applications now allow you to look up these places and book campsites months in advance of your trip.

ASK FOR HELP
Ask around to see if anyone you know has camped in a particular location abroad and query them about risks, cultural considerations, and best places to camp.

While visiting your destination country, ask locals for recommendations, tips, and help with directions.

RESEARCH THE LOCAL RISKS

Learn what unfamiliar animals, insects, and plants pose risks. For example, in Australia, branches may fall on your tent repeatedly if you camp under a gum tree. In Svalbard, an island located halfway between Norway and the North Pole, an accidental encounter with a polar bear might end in stolen food or worse. When camping in Costa Rica, it's advisable to sleep elevated off the ground in a hammock to avoid scorpion stings.

PLAN FOR LOCAL WEATHER

Look up the typical weather for the season in which you'll be camping and prepare accordingly. In some countries, it's more difficult to find technical clothing or specialized gear, so pack like you won't be able to source gear after arriving.

RESPECT CULTURAL NORMS

To avoid unintentionally offending locals or attracting unwanted attention in the country you're visiting, look up whether you should adhere to any cultural norms during your stay. For example, in some cultures, immodest dress is seen as disrespect-ful. In most countries, it is common courtesy to ask permission before taking a photo of someone, and in others, someone's faith might prohibit you from taking any photos at all.

COMMUNICATE EFFECTIVELY

When trying to communicate with someone who speaks a different language, especially in an emergency situation, speak slowly and clearly. You don't need to talk more loudly to get your point across. If the person still doesn't seem to understand what you're saying, try rephrasing or using different vocabulary words. If that doesn't work, you can always use hand motions, or write or draw your intended message. It might be useful to load a language translator onto your smartphone for use in such situations.

Before you leave on an international trip, learn some key phrases that can be used to help you react calmly in emergency situations.

BE PREPARED TO CHANGE YOUR MEAL PLAN

Unless you plan to take all the food for your camping trip with you on the airplane, expect to modify your meal plan according to the local foods available at markets and grocery stores. You will also not be able to bring fresh foods like apples, bananas, or oranges through customs. Research the local cuisine, and have some fun experimenting with new fruits, vegetables, and grains.

PACK A LIQUID-FUEL CAMP STOVE

Liquid fuel is often easier to find abroad than propane or isobutane canisters. And it's likely you will not be allowed to transport filled propane or isobutane canisters on an airplane. So if you choose to purchase liquid fuel, avoid filling the stove canister with pumped fuel at a gas station. Additives in gasoline can cause blockages in the stove that might cause it to fail.

If you wish your children to
    think deep thoughts . . .
take them to the woods
    and hills,
and give them the freedom
    of the meadows.

—Richard Jefferies

Chapter 8
Camping with Kids

C AMPING WITH CHILDREN IS ALL ABOUT making memories to last a lifetime. This kind of camping can feel formidable, so approach it like an opportunity to spend time with kids in the outdoors—a place where you can watch them grow and gain an appreciation for the natural world. Without the distraction of screens and other electronics, you may find more time to have conversations, tell stories and jokes, and listen to your children. Or better yet, think of it as a way to start new family traditions or pass along old ones.

Have your child adjust to the outdoors gradually, and take precautions to ensure that they stay safe. The trick is to create enough of a controlled environment that you can keep your child out of harm's way, while still allowing enough freedom for them explore, learn, and master the art of camping.

CAMP AT HOME FIRST
Before heading off into the wilderness, run a practice test by setting up the tent in your backyard and cooking over a camp stove. Is your tent big enough to fit everyone? Does your child sleep well? A camping test run will let children get used to the idea of sleeping in bags on pads rather than in their own beds, and will help you plan the gear and activity list for an actual camping trip.

DON'T UNDERESTIMATE THE POWER OF FOOD

For most children, one of the fun parts of camping is getting to eat special foods like s'mores, campfire griddle pancakes, hot cocoa, and novelty snacks like jerky, fruit leather, trail mix, and the occasional candy bar. So don't forget that food can be used as a powerful motivator and reward. Bring more snacks than you think you'll need, because children have relentless appetites in the outdoors. Be sure to pack convenient no-prep snack options like granola bars and trail mix. Set expectations about mealtimes so that children know when they will be able to eat next, and be sure to monitor their energy levels throughout the day so

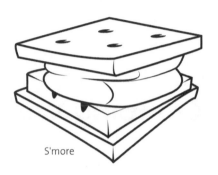

S'more

you can detect when someone might need a snack. For example, a particularly grumpy child might just be a hungry child. Strike a good balance of healthy food and treats. Teach good habits like sharing food, waiting your turn to load up your plate, and not selecting only the chocolate morsels in a bag of trail mix.

SET REASONABLE GOALS

If you're planning a hike during your camping trip, be aware of the endurance level of each child, which will vary by age, ability, and experience. A three-mile hike might seem doable to your own child who has walked that far before. But to your child's friend, it might be the first hike they've ever done. With every activity, increase the distance and level of difficulty over time.

SET REASONABLE RESPONSIBILITIES

Empower children to be competent campers by giving them simple tasks to help out, such as letting them organize the kitchen utensils, asking them to select a good spot to store shoes before going into the tent, or having them collect small dead twigs for kindling.

REDUCE FEAR WITH LIGHTING

The outdoors at night might feel scary to children who aren't used to that level of darkness. Give each child their own light source such as a flashlight or a headlamp, and make sure they keep it in the same place so they can always find it when they need it. Alternatively, they can each wear a headlamp like a necklace, so they'll always have it handy. Teach children how to use light sources so they don't shine them in other people's eyes. Invest in solar-powered string lights to hang from a tree for some added sparkle and light at night, or place a lantern on a picnic table for extra illumination.

ENTERTAIN WITH OUTDOOR-FRIENDLY ACTIVITIES

Leave screens and electronics at home. Instead, bring along books, board games, coloring and activity books, art sets, and sports equipment. Activities like these will help children stave off boredom when faced with days without electronics. If you have to hunker down in a tent to wait out a storm, tell stories to pass the time. Sing songs around the campfire, and facilitate camp games like scavenger hunt, cornhole, bocce ball, Frisbee, and flashlight tag. Keep kids moving so that they use up all their energy and are tuckered out by the time night rolls around.

PACK THE RIGHT CLOTHES

Pack clothes for children that are comfortable, not too nice to get dirty, and appropriate for the weather. Remember to bring layering systems so that items can be put on or taken off as the temperature fluctuates. Don't forget accessories like gloves, hats, sunglasses, and wool socks.

SET CHILDREN UP FOR SLEEP SUCCESS

Select a sleeping bag that has the right temperature rating and is the right size for your child. The rating should be lower than the lowest-possible temperature likely to occur while the child is camping. Make sure the sleeping bag doesn't have a lot of extra room, as large air pockets can reduce a sleeping bag's insulating properties. If you buy a larger sleeping bag so that your child can grow into it, you can add insulation by stuffing warm clothes into the extra room at the bottom of the bag. Use a sleeping pad for some added comfort and insulation. A foam pad is a lightweight and inexpensive option for a child.

PACK SECURITY ITEMS

Ask your children which security items they want to bring along on a camping trip, such as a stuffed animal, blanket, or toy. It's best if these items are also dirt-friendly or washable. If backcountry camping, limit the weight and number of items they bring.

SCHEDULE NAP TIMES

Children might think a change of scenery means nap times are canceled. It's likely this will not be the case. With all the outdoor stimuli, children may need naps in nature more than usual. Stick to their regular nap schedule, and if they have trouble getting to sleep, you can try strapping them into their car seat and going on a drive (if car camping). If a child is trying to nap in a tent, set up a battery-powered fan to create some white noise and reduce any other noises coming from nearby campsites.

APPLY SUNSCREEN AND INSECT REPELLENT

Even on cloudy days, make sure children wear sunscreen. Keep kids from getting bug-bitten by applying insect repellent. Reapply both sunscreen and bug spray throughout the day as necessary, especially if kids go for a swim or sweat a lot from activity.

SET FIRE-SAFETY RULES

Educate children about how to behave around campfires, and teach the stop-drop-and-roll safety procedure in case someone catches clothing on fire. When everyone is gathered around a campfire, instruct little ones to sit a safe distance from the open flames and to not engage in activities like roasting marshmallows unless supervised by an adult. You can also draw a line in the ground around the fire and tell children not to step beyond it. Crawling toddlers should be kept in a portable playpen or carrier while fires are aflame.

DON'T FRET ABOUT DIRT

While camping, it's inevitable that kids will get their clothes, hair, and skin dirty. Pack wet wipes for an easy way to clean dirt off children's skin. Pack an extra change of clothes in case one set becomes unwearable. Don't forget to bring a mild hand sanitizer for children to use before mealtimes.

SET PLANT-SAFETY GUIDELINES

As a general rule, children should not eat any wild plants. Touching certain plants can cause rashes, fever, or nausea, and eating the wrong species can lead to illness or death. Set hard rules about plant safety, and show children which plants they should avoid eating or touching at all costs, such as poison oak, poison ivy, poison sumac, foxglove, lilies of the valley, nettles, or deadly nightshade.

ESTABLISH CAMPSITE AND CAMPGROUND BOUNDARIES

While children should be encouraged to explore the outdoors on their own terms, set some boundaries for how far away they can wander, when they should return (make sure they're carrying a timepiece), and what activities they can do while they're gone (e.g., play sports with other campers, hike, bicycle, or participate in a scavenger hunt). Teach children not to cut through other people's campsites and to stay on designated paths.

SET GUIDELINES FOR ETIQUETTE AROUND OTHER CAMPERS

Set a time when quiet hours begin so that children aren't up too late, and because some kids have a hard time controlling the volume of their voices. Teach children to practice safe behavior around strangers and what they should do if approached by someone they don't recognize. When playing with other children at a campground, kids should follow the same standards for sharing, playing fair, and being polite that they would practice at home or at school.

REVIEW EMERGENCY PLANS

Teach children that if they get lost, they should practice the "hug a tree" method, meaning they should stay put next to the nearest tree until someone they know finds them. If they have a whistle with them, they should blow it if they get lost—three whistle blows every few minutes until someone finds them. Go over other emergency plans, such as what they should do during a lightning storm, the steps they should take if you get injured and you're the only adult in the group, how they can stay calm if they have asthma and need their inhaler or they suffer a snakebite or bee sting.

LET CHILDREN HELP PACK

Give kids the opportunity to plan appropriately for the predicted weather and planned activities. Ask questions like, "Since it might rain one day, what should you pack?" or "We might go on a hike during hot weather, so what kind of clothes do you want to pack?" Give older kids a list of personal items they can pack and double-check that they've packed everything on the list *before* you leave home. Give children their own duffel bag to store their toys, clothes, and personal gear. If you have more than one child, make sure the duffel bags are different colors. Tell children to pack all their personal items back into the bag at the end of each day. Having a go-to place to store their own stuff will help keep the campsite tidy and reduce the amount you have to clean up after the kids.

SET REASONABLE EXPECTATIONS FOR YOURSELF

The first few camping trips with children might require patience and constant surveillance, so be prepared to give yourself some slack when trips aren't as carefree and rejuvenating as you

Camping tips by age range

Ages three and under

Small children shouldn't sleep in their own sleeping bag, as they might squirm out in the middle of the night. Instead, dress them in fleece or long underwear and place a warm, soft blanket over them and a foam sleeping pad underneath them. For babies, consider packing a travel high chair or stroller, or even a travel playpen for a familiar place to sleep and to prevent them from crawling off while you're tending to a camping task like cooking or building a campfire. Invest in mesh netting for bug protection, or string up a tarp for some extra shade.

When a child is 12 months or younger, before applying insect repellents and sunscreen read the product label first for application instructions and the recommended age. Don't allow young children to apply their own bug repellent.

When hiking, you can carry a small child in a front or back child-carrier pack. But be sure to take breaks so they can get out and explore on their own. Apply sunscreen and help them dress appropriately for the weather, which might include sunglasses or sun hats. Stop frequently for snacks and sipping on water, in addition to rest breaks, especially if the child is walking on their own. Throughout the trip, check that your child is warm enough by feeling their hands and feet, which should feel warm. If the skin on their hands or feet feels cold, check the temperature of their neck and chest, and add more layers if these places also feel cold.

Ages four and five

Give children within this age range small responsibilities, like filling up water bottles at the campground spigot, helping to set up the tent, or organizing their toys, books, and clothes. At the beginning of the trip, gift them with their first piece of gear, such as a headlamp or magnifying glass, as this will empower them to learn new skills and will boost their camping confidence.

Ages 6 to 10

This age range is prime time for teaching children camping and safety skills, such as tying knots, bandaging a minor wound, reading a map, lighting a stove, building a campfire, and learning how to dress appropriately for the weather.

With each new year, gradually extend the length of hikes that you might take and the difficulty of the activities (such as how much weight they must carry in their own backpack). Pack more snack food than you think you'll need, and remind children throughout each day of a camping trip to drink water.

Appropriate gear gifts for this age might include a pocketknife or binoculars.

Ages 11 to 13

Younger teens might challenge you to go outside your comfort zone, because they are just as capable at doing the same activities as adults. They have more strength, endurance, and can master skills like setting up tents, tying knots, building campfires, and navigating. During the trip, allow teens the freedom to explore on their own and teach them new skills like how to find constellations or identify native plants. Give them bigger responsibilities like planning a meal, doing dishes, or monitoring smaller children. Before leaving home, give them a list of personal gear items that they are responsible for packing themselves. After they've packed, go through their packed gear with them to make sure they haven't forgotten anything.

hoped. Have a plan set in place in case of emergency, bad weather, or if children are having so little fun that they just want to go home. When something goes awry, tell kids to think of it as an adventure. On the next trip, you can try a different season and location, and pack different foods and activities.

For if there is anything a dog does love better than its own soul it is to hike with its master, and every normal boy and girl, and every normal man and woman, loves the company of a good dog. When they do not love it the fault is not with the dog but with them; there is something wrong with them that the outdoor world alone will cure.

—Dan Beard, *The Book of Camp-Lore and Woodcraft*, 1920

Chapter 9

Camping with Pets

BRINGING PETS ALONG ON A CAMPING TRIP IS an understandable impulse. Pets usually benefit from the exercise and excitement that comes from being in nature, and they usually make good campmates. However, allowing a pet to roam freely may disturb wildlife and put your pet at risk. Dogs can pick up the scent of potential prey and wander off—sometimes never to be found again. They can also be attacked by larger predators like cougars or bears. Training feline pets to become "adventure cats" is gaining popularity, but cats are territorial by nature and being displaced—if only for a weekend—can cause unnecessary stress. Though possible and enjoyable, proper precautions and training should be taken before attempting to camp with cats.

Keep in mind that bringing a pet along on a camping trip can limit the activities you do and where you are allowed to camp. Your anxiety might be higher as a result of needing to stay constantly vigilant, but you will also likely have more fun. Ultimately, it's your responsibility to look after your pet's health and safety, and to make sure that your pet doesn't bother other campers or harm the natural world. Follow the pet restrictions and rules wherever you camp, so your actions do not give camping area managers any reason to prohibit pets entirely.

BEFORE YOU GO

CHECK LOCATIONS WHERE PETS ARE ALLOWED

Not all camping destinations and hiking trails permit pets. Check before you go to know whether your dog is allowed to camp and hike with you. For example, pets are allowed in all US national forests, but are required to remain on a leash no longer than six feet. Most national parks do not allow camping with pets in the backcountry, although certain designated trails or campgrounds are pet-friendly. BLM land offers many millions of acres of off-leash roaming space for pet owners and their four-legged companions. Some campgrounds will charge an extra fee for pets.

ASSESS YOUR PET'S HEALTH AND TEMPERAMENT

Does your pet have any special needs or dietary requirements? Is your pet physically capable of tagging along during your planned activities? Does your pet occasionally become aggressive around children or other dogs, or bark nonstop if under stress? Each animal has its own temperament, and no one knows better than you how your pet behaves in unfamiliar surroundings or among strangers. Exercise caution and good etiquette when deciding whether to bring your pet so you don't put your pet or others in harm's way. If you're not sure, err on the safe side and leave your pet at home.

HOW MUCH CAN YOUR PET PARTICIPATE?

Certain activities like kayaking or cycling are not a good fit for bringing your pet along. Assess the amount of time you'll be spending doing activities that may require leaving your pet in the car or tent for too long and adjust your plans accordingly.

GET UP TO DATE ON VACCINATIONS

Protect your pet against disease that can be transmitted by fleas, ticks, and other wildlife. Make sure your pet is current on all their vaccinations and ask your vet whether your pet needs any vaccination specific to the area where you'll be camping.

INVEST IN COLLARS AND ID

If venturing into the outdoors with your pet—especially if your pet will be off leash for any part of the trip—make sure you invest in a collar and ID tag. Make sure the collar or harness fits well and doesn't slip off easily. Consider going one step further and take your pet to the vet to be microchipped and registered, a process that will list your pet's ID number in a database. That way, if your pet loses its collar, someone will be able to look up your contact information and reunite you with your lost animal.

TRAIN YOUR PET

In case your pet gets off its leash or harness, make sure they respond to a specific command to come back to you. Train your pet not to jump up on strangers. Dogs should be taught not to bark at strangers and to "stay" when told to do so. Train your pet to stay calm in a tent. Do an overnight camping test run in the backyard with your pet. Sleep in your tent, and see how your pet handles the close quarters. You may also consider training your pet to wear a pack made to carry its food or water, and other care items. The packs are designed to fit an animal like a harness with saddlebags. The saddlebags are appropriately sized for the size of the harness and dog. The packs may be purchased at pet stores and outdoor outfitters.

WHAT TO BRING

FOOD AND WATER

Calculate how much food you should bring, plus an extra day's worth, and store the food in a resealable plastic bag. If you're planning to have your pet join you in any high-exertion activities, bring more food than normal, in case your pet needs additional calories. Pack a food bowl along with a portable drinking bowl that you can refill with

Pets with a saddlebag can hold their own food and water

fresh water throughout your trip. Lightweight, collapsible bowls are a good option when backcountry camping. If water will be scarce at your camping destination, bring enough water for your pet to last the length of your stay, plus an extra day's worth.

MEDICATION

Remember to pack any special dietary food or daily medication that your pet might need, plus any special medication-administering tools. For example, if you normally need to convince your dog to eat a pill by hiding the pill in a piece of cheese, remember to pack cheese for this purpose as well.

FIRST-AID KIT

Pets can suffer injuries too, so either augment your group first-aid kit to include pet-specific items or pack a separate first-aid kit for your pet that includes normal first-aid equipment like gauze, adhesive tape, tweezers, and antiseptic wipes, along with pet-specific items like a self-cling bandage (which sticks to itself but not fur), a muzzle (to prevent biting wounds), and a pet first-aid book.

LEASH

Pack a leash and a collar (or a harness) to keep your pet from wandering into other people's campsites or farther up a trail than you'd like. You can also pack a longer leash that can be tied to a tree or staked down to let your pet explore your campsite without going beyond its boundaries. Be sure to pack a stake in case the camping area prohibits tying a pet tether to a tree. If your pet is prone to getting tangled up, or you're worried that a person might trip over the long leash or line, you can opt to bring a portable pet pen. Lightweight, foldable pens are available at some pet or outdoor gear stores, and are a handy way to keep your pet from straying too far at camp.

LIGHTS

Consider investing in lights that your pet can wear when it's dark. This will help you spot your pet if it runs off into the night.

WASTE BAGS

You must pick up and pack out pet waste even in the wilderness. Pet waste can contaminate water sources and at the very least—when left on a trail or near a campsite—be an unpleasant surprise for other campers. Bring enough waste disposal bags to last the length of your camping trip.

If you plan to camp with your cat, pack a small litter box that can be placed inside your tent. If you have a long car ride to your destination, make sure your cat can access the litter box while the car is in motion. Lightweight and collapsible reusable litter boxes can be purchased at some pet stores.

TOWELS

Place a towel on the seat of your car for the ride to and from your camping destination. This will make car cleanup easier after you return home, since you need only throw any used towels in the wash. A towel is also a handy item when your pet decides to splash around in puddles or water bodies. Lightweight backpacking towels are ideal for backcountry camping, as they pack down small and dry quickly.

CARRIER

Some pets are fine hanging out in the rear of a vehicle with a hatchback, or even in the back or front seats of a car. But if your pet is particularly mobile while you're driving a vehicle, consider packing a carrier that gives them room to lie down comfortably for the whole ride. Some pets even prefer to sleep in their carriers at night, so consider using it at your campsite as well.

BED AND BLANKET

While some pets are perfectly content to curl up on the ground or in the back of a car, others are more likely to settle down and relax if you bring along a comfortable bed or blanket. Providing them with their own bed may also serve as a deterrent from them wanting to climb into your sleeping bag with you when nighttime falls. As a sometimes more comfortable alternative, portable cots can also be purchased for older pets with joint issues.

WARM JACKET

Although descended from their wild ancestors, domesticated dogs and cats still get cold. That's why it's important to pack a warm layer for your pet. An array of styles, materials, and sizes are available at most pet stores.

COOLING JACKET

While camping in particularly hot conditions, it might be necessary to invest in a cooling vest for your pet so they don't overheat.

A cooling vest is made of mesh that cools off your pet as moisture evaporates from the material. However, when facing a weather forecast with extremely high temperatures, it might be best to leave your pet at home for their safety.

PET GEAR CHECKLIST

- Collar
- Leash
- Long leash or line
- Water bowl
- Food dish
- Medication
- First-aid kit
- Lights (optional)
- Waste bags
- Towels
- Bed and blanket
- Food-storage container
- Pet pen (optional)
- Warm jacket (optional)
- Cooling jacket (optional)
- Favorite toy
- Tie-out

WHILE CAMPING

PREVENTING CAR SICKNESS

When driving to and from your camping destination, the constant movement of your vehicle might cause your pet to become carsick. Signs of motion sickness include:

- Vocalizing distress
- Restlessness
- Frequent urination or bowel movements
- Trembling
- Panting
- Excessive drooling
- Licking lips
- Vomiting

To help prevent pet car sickness, you can talk to your veterinarian about medications that might help limit symptoms.

However, motion sickness can be prevented in some pets by getting them used to spending time in their carrier in the car. Set the carrier somewhere in your house and leave the carrier door open so your pet can become accustomed to the small space. Next, have your pet spend some time in the carrier in the car (with the carrier's door facing toward the front) while the engine isn't running. Try this a few times, and after your pet seems to calm down, turn on the car's engine and leave it running, allowing your pet to get used to the noise and vibrations. Eventually, you can try driving your pet around on shorter trips, gradually increasing the length as they become more comfortable. Keep the air-conditioning on (if it's hot), and bring treats and toys for your pet to keep them entertained and relaxed. Stop the car frequently to take breaks, and allow your pet to get some air, urinate, and stretch out.

VEHICLE SAFETY

Never leave your pet in a car for too long. If you must leave a pet inside a car for any amount of time, park in the shade and crack a couple of windows before locking up. A car can heat up quickly in hot weather or if left in the sun. On a hot day, a pet left in a car can succumb to heatstroke in a matter of minutes.

FOOD STORAGE

Store pet food where you store your own food. If your pet doesn't finish all their food during a mealtime, pack away leftover food so it doesn't attract critters.

WASTE MANAGEMENT

Pick up after your pet every time. Bring the appropriate number of waste bags for the length of your trip and bring them along on every activity. If you happen to forget waste bags on any outing, bury waste far away from trails or other frequently traveled areas and bodies of water.

KEEP YOUR PET ON A LEASH

Check the specific leash policy for the location where you'll be camping, and follow the rules about restricted areas. While it can seem unfair to restrict your pet from running free, leash regulations should be followed to prevent pets from harming or disturbing wildlife, running through other people's campsites, or trampling fragile natural areas.

ETIQUETTE AROUND PACK ANIMALS

Some areas permit the use of pack animals, like horses, mules, and alpacas. When pack animals come near, hold on tight to your pet's collar or harness. Hold your pet's throat to prevent barking, as sudden noises can startle pack animals.

MONITOR BEHAVIOR

If you know your dog can be aggressive toward people or other dogs, don't take it on trails or to other frequently traveled areas. Don't let it jump up on people, especially children. Keep dogs on a tight leash as some people have a fear of them. Only allow someone to pet your dog if they ask and your dog behaves predictably around strangers. Watch pets around other people's campsites so they don't steal or beg for other people's food.

WATER ETIQUETTE

Avoid letting your pet drink from or play in water sources that are used by people replenishing their water supply. Pick a spot down-stream from campers, or fill up the pet's personal water dish.

CO-SLEEPING

Many outdoor recreation areas require that pets sleep in your tent or car at night. Although you may wake up to a somewhat smellier sleeping area filled with fur, sharing your tent or car quarters with your pet will keep them—and wildlife—safe.

STAY VIGILANT

Make sure your pet is supervised at all times so it doesn't eat poisonous plants, chase other animals, get too close to the campfire, or track mud into your tent. Unless it's bedtime, your pet should be under constant watch so it stays out of harm's way and doesn't disturb others.

TICK REMOVAL

Throughout your trip, and after you return home, you should check your pet for ticks. Feel along your pet's body, starting at the head and working toward the tail, being sure not to miss the legs and belly. Press your fingertips against the skin to feel for any bumps. Note whether your pet is excessively scratching or licking an area, as this might indicate where a tick has latched on. If you find a tick, follow these steps:

1. Put on protective gloves.
4. Ask a campmate to hold your pet and keep it calm.
5. Grab onto the tick's head with a pair of sharp tweezers, as close to the skin as possible.
6. Pull the tick out in a straight, steady motion.
7. Once the tick has been removed, examine the area for any remnants of the tick's head. If you find anything, take your pet in to see the vet.
8. Disinfect the bite site with an antiseptic wipe.
9. Reward your pet with a treat.
10. Keep an eye on your pet for any signs of inflammation, swelling, or disease, such as fever, loss of appetite, swollen lymph nodes, or fatigue. If your pet shows any symptoms, take your pet to the vet immediately.

A possible mosquito or gnat
in the mountains is no more
irritating than the objectionable
personality that is sure to be
forced upon you every hour at
the summer hotel.

—Grace Gallatin Seton-Thompson, *A
Woman Tenderfoot*, 1900

Chapter 10
Camp Safety

KNOWING HOW TO RESPOND IN AN EMERGENCY situation is an essential camping skill. If you're lucky, you won't ever have to put emergency-response expertise to use. But accidents happen—especially while outdoors. A number of unpredictable variables in nature can stack the odds against you when it comes to safety; you may encounter territorial animals, avalanches, poisonous plants, wildfires, or aggressive snakes, and you may need to deal with the more predictable minor nuisances like blisters, biting insects, and sunburns. Without proper caution and treatment, these minor conditions can lead to more serious issues like infection, severe allergic reactions, and heat exhaustion. Be prepared and take preventive steps to reduce the risk of injury and illness.

At the very least, take a basic first-aid and CPR class if you plan to do any activities in the outdoors. Depending on where you're camping, it might take hours to get to the nearest hospital for emergency medical care. That's why it's so important to learn how to respond calmly in stressful situations. Reacting rationally in an emergency helps ensure that an injured person receives the right care in time—and safely. Consider taking a more rigorous course like a Wilderness First Responder class. The curriculum covers a range of wilderness-specific emergency-response skills that could make the difference between survival and death in some scenarios.

FIRST-AID KIT

No matter how long you'll be camping or what activity you're planning in the outdoors, always carry a first-aid kit. You can buy kits prepackaged from outdoor gear supply stores or you can create your own, using the below checklist. Learn how to use each of the items before you leave home.

FIRST-AID CHECKLIST

Basic
◊   Waterproof container to hold supplies
◊   Hand sanitizer
◊   First-aid manual
◊   Antiseptic wipes or ointment
◊   Triple antibiotic ointment
◊   Nonadhesive sterile pads
◊   Gauze pads (pack different sizes)
◊   Compound tincture of benzoin
◊   Medical adhesive tape
◊   Adhesive bandages (pack different sizes and shapes)
◊   Butterfly bandages
◊   Moleskin pads
◊   Sharp tweezers
◊   Safety pins
◊   Hydrocortisone cream
◊   Insect sting relief ointment
◊   Duct tape

Medications
◊   Prescription medications
◊   Pain/anti-inflammatory medicine such as ibuprofen
◊   Antihistamine
◊   Throat lozenges
◊   Anti-diarrhea medication
◊   Aspirin (in case of a heart attack)
◊   Antacid tablets
◊   Poison oak/ivy treatment

Additional items
◊   EpiPen
◊   Aloe vera
◊   Eye drops

◊   Oral rehydration salts
◊   SAM Splints of various sizes
◊   Triangular cravat bandage

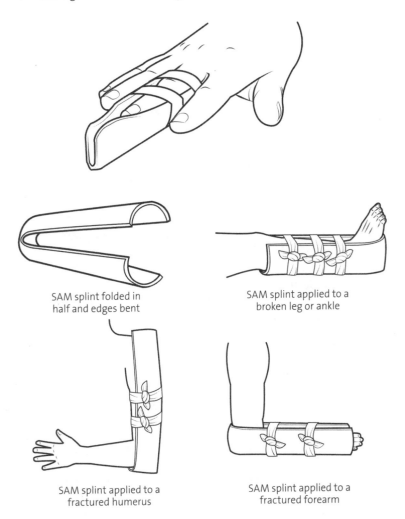

SAM splint folded in
half and edges bent

SAM splint applied to a
broken leg or ankle

SAM splint applied to a
fractured humerus

SAM splint applied to a
fractured forearm

◊   Blunt-tip scissors (for cutting off clothing)
◊   Oral thermometer
◊   Irrigation syringe (for cleaning dirt and debris from wounds)
◊   Non-latex gloves
◊   CPR mask
◊   Notepad and pencil

WILDERNESS HAZARDS AND PREVENTION

BLISTERS

Moisture, pressure, friction, and heat are the three most common causes of blisters, so if you take steps to limit these three factors, you'll reduce the chances of forming a blister.

To limit the amount of moisture that can build up inside your shoes, take breaks when hiking and air out your shoes and socks, or change into a fresh pair of socks. Don't wear cotton socks, as they retain moisture.

Make sure your shoes and socks fit well and there are no parts that rub against localized spots on your feet or ankles. Even repeated friction from a wrinkle in a sock can be enough to cause a blister. When hiking, you can reduce friction by wearing thin liner socks under your regular hiking socks. Break in your shoes or boots before any camping trip, and bring a backup pair of shoes in case you don't have time to break in new shoes.

Address any hot spots immediately to prevent full-blown blisters from forming. You can cover these areas with moleskin, tape, or a padded bandage after drying off the area first.

Prevent blistering from too much sun exposure by protecting your skin with sunscreen and clothing.

If a blister becomes infected, seek medical attention quickly. Pay attention to any of the following symptoms of infection:

- Persistent pain
- Pus development
- Redness or inflammation

Blister first aid: If a blister develops, cut a circle with a hole the size of the blister from a piece of Molefoam. Place the Molefoam over the skin with the hole centered over the blister. Then cover the area with tape or moleskin. You can also protect the blister by adhering a special blister bandage that contains gels for cooling or pads for cushioning. Avoid popping or draining a blister, allowing it to heal on its own first. However, if it becomes too painful to ignore, you can release the fluid with a needle. First, gently wash the blister and the surrounding area with soap and water. Sterilize a needle with an alcohol wipe or a match flame. If using heat to sterilize the needle, make sure it cools down before it comes in contact with the blister. At the edge of the blister, insert and withdraw the needle and then press down on the blister to release the fluid. Apply antibiotic ointment and cover the blister with a bandage, or alternatively, cut a hole in a piece of Molefoam the size of the wound and tape that over. If a first-aid kit isn't handy, makeshift bandages can be made of duct tape or medical tape.

POISONOUS PLANTS

Wild foraging is appealing, especially while camping in a place where berries, mushrooms, and other edible plants are abundant. When it comes to eating wild food, the old adage *better safe than sorry* is a wise admonition. The consequences of eating the wrong species can be dire.

Poison oak (*Toxicodendron diversilobum*)

When identified correctly, wild foods like mushrooms and berries are tasty and nutritious. However, eating poisonous species can lead to stomach cramps, seizures, heart complications, halluci- nations, and even death. Exercise extreme caution when forest foraging, and if you do sample any unfamil- iar foods harvested from the woods, be sure you get the OK from a wild food expert first.

Poison ivy (*Toxicodendron radicans*)

Some plants don't need to be consumed to transmit their poison. Coming into contact with plants like stinging nettles, poison oak, poison sumac, and poison ivy can cause severe contact dermatitis. Any skin that brushes up against the underside of nettle leaves can start to show signs of a

Poison sumac (*Toxicodendron vernix*)

rash. But skin-to-leaf contact isn't necessary for plants like poison oak, poison sumac, or poison ivy to transfer their noxious oils. The oils on the leaves can rub off onto clothing, which, if it comes into contact with skin, can have the same rash-causing effect. Learn to identify the poisonous plants in the areas where you plan to camp. Never burn the branches of poison oak, poison sumac, or poison ivy, as the toxic oils end up

Stinging nettle (*Urtica dioica*)

in the smoke, which if inhaled, can cause serious respiratory issues. Urgent medical attention is required if you inhale smoke emitted from burning poison oak, poison sumac, or poison ivy.

Poisonous plant ingestion treatment: Seek medical attention immediately if any of the following symptoms occur after ingesting a plant:

- Vomiting
- Seizures
- Nausea
- Shortness of breath

If possible, note the physical characteristics of the plant so you can describe it to your doctor.

Poisonous plant topical treatment: Clean the area with soap and water, and apply a cold compress. Rub an over-the-counter corticosteroid cream onto the area, and take an oral over-the-counter antihistamine to reduce inflammation, swelling, and itching.

MOSQUITOES

Bites from mosquitoes are not only itchy but can cause diseases like Zika, West Nile virus, malaria, dengue, and yellow fever. Depending on where you're camping in the world, the types of diseases transmitted by mosquitoes will vary. Some vaccines and medications are available to help prevent certain types of mosquito-borne diseases, so check in with your doctor before traveling overseas.

Camping by any body of water (river, lake, stream, bog) means bugs will likely be a nuisance. Bring bug spray with more than 23.8 percent DEET to protect against itching bites, along with mosquito- and tick-borne infections. DEET can reduce sunscreen's effectiveness, so apply sunscreen to your skin 20 minutes before using bug repellent. Check the product's label to know how frequently you should reapply, and be sure to reapply after swimming or strenuous activity. If pregnant or breastfeeding, check to make sure the repellent you're using is pregnancy-registered. For added protection against bugs, you can invest in permethrin-treated, loose-fitting, light-colored clothing or buy a permethrin spray and apply it to your camping clothes. You can also use permethrin spray on your camp chair, hat, tent, and sleeping bag. Consider buying and wearing a hat with built-in bug netting to cover your face and neck if you expect bugs to be out in force.

Other mosquito-prevention products can be used in addition to bug repellent, such as mosquito netting, mesh face shields, and allethrin devices. A lightweight option for bug proofing an area, this device must be screwed into an isobutane canister, and then it slowly burns an allethrin-soaked pad to create a zone protected from mosquitoes. When there is no wind, an allethrin device creates a protective 15-foot-diameter shield against mosquitoes.

Take preventive measures during peak mosquito hours, such as dawn and dusk, or near bodies of still water like ponds or swamps. However, different species of mosquitoes across the globe exhibit varying patterns for the time of day they more frequently bite, so do your mosquito-behavior research for the specific location you plan to visit.

Mosquito bite first aid: To control itching and reduce inflammation, apply an over-the-counter corticosteroid cream to the bite areas.

TICKS

Ticks are not only blood-sucking nuisances but also carriers of disease; they should be removed

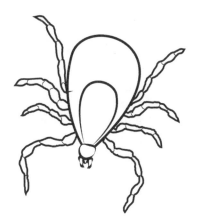

immediately if found on you, your child, or your pet. Most tick bites don't irritate the skin or itch, but they can cause allergic reactions or transfer tick-borne diseases like Lyme and spotted fever.

While camping in areas where ticks are known to be present, wear long pants tucked into socks and long-sleeved shirts tucked into the waistband of your pants. Ticks can be spotted more easily on light-colored clothing. For added protection, apply DEET or Picaridin repellent to exposed skin and treat your camping clothes with permethrin. Reapply repellent and permethrin as frequently as the product's label recommends.

Throughout a camping trip, check children and dogs frequently for ticks. Places on the body where ticks are most commonly found are the armpits, backs of knees, groin, behind ears, back of head, and neck.

Before crawling into your tent or sleeping bag, remove all clothing and carefully search your body and clothing for ticks.

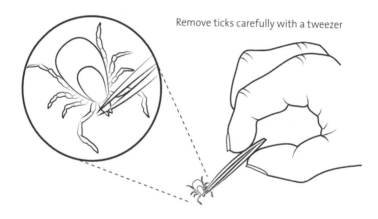

Remove ticks carefully with a tweezer

After returning home, wash and dry all clothes on hot cycles to kill any stowaway ticks.

To remove a tick that has latched itself onto your skin, use a pair of fine tweezers or surgical forceps to gently pull the tick out of its bite site. A tick's mouth is made of hooks that can dig into the skin and point backward like the type of blades that puncture a tire if you drive over them the wrong way. These hooks embed themselves in the skin, so it takes a firm and smooth upward pulling motion to detach the tick from your skin. Position the tips of the forceps or tweezers close to the skin, around the tick's mouth—don't squeeze the body—and pull up firmly. Don't worry if part of the tick's mouth stays embedded under your skin—it's most important to remove the body, as that's the part of the tick that can transmit disease. The mouth will eventually work itself out like a sliver.

After removing a tick, visit your doctor if you experience any of the following symptoms within days, weeks, or months of a camping trip:

- Fever
- Fatigue
- Muscle or joint pain
- Muscle weakness
- Tender lymph nodes
- Headache or migraine
- Rash
- Redness or swelling of the bite site
- Unsteadiness
- Visual disturbances
- Trouble breathing

If bitten by a tick: After removing the tick, clean the area with rubbing alcohol, watch for any of the above symptoms, and visit your doctor. If possible, note the color and physical characteristics of the tick so you can describe it to your physician.

INSECT STINGS

Avoid sniffing or looking at flowers from close range. Watch where you step—especially if barefoot—so as to not stumble upon a bee, yellow jacket, or hornet's nest. To prevent stings from insects like yellow jackets and wasps, avoid leaving food or sweet beverages out.

In case of allergic reaction: Apply a cold compress or ice pack to the afflicted area, and take an oral antihistamine if swelling occurs. In severe cases, you may need to seek medical care immediately or inject epinephrine on the spot.

INSECT AND SPIDER BITES

For mosquitoes, see page 256 for protective measures against bites. Avoid walking into an anthill or stepping in the path of red-headed ants.

Spiders tend to keep to themselves unless disturbed. To avoid startling a spider, use caution and consider wearing gloves when handling or collecting firewood. Shake out shoes and turn gloves,

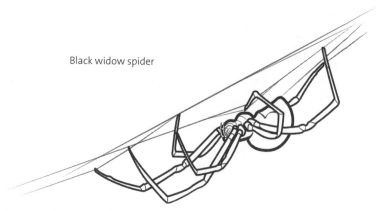

Black widow spider

hats, and sleeping bags inside out to check for spider inhabitants before using them.

Treating a spider bite: If possible, take note of the spider's color and physical characteristics. Clean the wound with soap and water, and apply a cool compress to the site to reduce inflammation and pain. Elevate the bite area if it's located on an arm or leg. Take oral over-the-counter antihistamines or pain relievers. Check the area for signs of infection.

SNAKES

Not all snakes pose a threat to humans, but it can be alarming to find any snake—even a harmless one—in your campsite. Take a few precautions to reduce the chance of encountering a snake.

Keep camping gear off the ground, and set your campsite up away from logs that snakes might hide under. Before leaving your campsite for the day, zip up your tent and shake it gently when you return so that any visitors sleeping underneath can slither away. Check your tent for any holes.

While hiking, watch where you step. Don't listen to music using headphones, which can prevent you from hearing a snake's alarm signal in time to react.

Most importantly, leave snakes alone. Provoking snakes by prodding them with sticks or throwing rocks in their direction is one of the most common reasons why people get bitten.

If bitten by a snake: Some snakebites are *dry bites*, which means the snake doesn't actually release any venom. Though still painful, dry bites usually don't cause many symptoms beyond redness and swelling in the wounded area. Because you can't know whether a snake has released venom, proceed as if it has and remain calm. Back away until you're out of the snake's range, but try to note the color and shape of the snake so you can describe it to a doctor. Remove any tight clothing or jewelry in case swelling occurs. If necessary, reposition your body so that the snakebite is below your heart and, if possible, rest until help arrives or you are transported to a medical facility. Cover the wound, but don't flush it with water as any

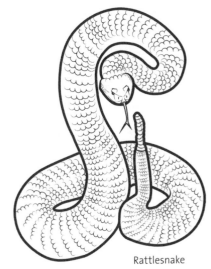

Rattlesnake

leftover venom can help identify the species of snake.

If you are bitten by a snake outside of cell range, take a few minutes to calm down and consider your evacuation route and the last time you remember having cell service. If you have a pen and timepiece handy, circle the bite area and note the time. Continue circling the area if it increases in size—every 30 minutes—and jot down the corresponding times along with any symptoms you're experiencing. Walk slowly until you get to cell service and can access emergency medical help. Never do any of the following:

- Cut the wound or try to suck out the venom.
- Apply ice or a tourniquet.
- Drink alcohol or caffeine, as these stimulants can increase the rate at which your body absorbs the venom.
- Capture the snake.

Within 15–30 minutes, symptoms from venomous snakebites can include:

- Bruising
- Severe pain
- Swelling
- Nausea or stomach pain
- Bleeding at the site
- Dizziness
- Blurry vision
- Difficulty breathing or swallowing
- Confusion

- Paralysis or coma
- Headache
- Stinging, tingling, or burning feeling on the skin
- Weakness
- Irregular heartbeat
- Anxiety

Some people can suffer from a severe allergic reaction if bitten by a poisonous snake. Symptoms can occur in a couple of minutes and include:
- Itching of the eyes, lips, ears, throat, or mouth
- Feeling flushed
- Weakness
- Shortness of breath
- Difficulty speaking or swallowing
- Stomach cramps
- Nausea
- Losing consciousness

In case of a severe allergic reaction: Inject epinephrine, and if that's not possible, seek medical attention immediately.

BURNS

Two of the most common types of burns people suffer while camping are sunburns and campfire or stove burns. Sunburns can be prevented by wearing sun-protection clothing such as long layers (long-sleeved shirts and long pants) and a sun hat, and by applying sunscreen to any exposed skin.

Prevent burns from open flames by exercising caution while cooking or starting or tending a campfire. Use pot holders or oven mitts to handle hot pots and pans. Light camp stoves with caution. Let an area air out before lighting a stove if the fuel canister or tank leaks gas for longer than a few seconds. See page 128 for campfire-safety protocol.

Burn first aid: If someone's clothing catches fire, first extinguish the flame, then remove any burned clothing—unless clothing has burned to the skin, in which case you should cut or tear the clothing around the burn site. Remove any jewelry or tight clothing. Burns are classified by degree, so before treating a burn, assess the level of burn.
- *First-degree burn:* When the burn is superficial, and there is only minor pain, redness, or blistering, you can reduce

inflammation and pain by holding the burn under or immersing it in cool—not cold—water. You can also use a cold compress. Take an over-the-counter pain reliever until the pain subsides. Monitor the wound for symptoms, and visit your doctor if you experience increased pain, infection, swelling, fever, or oozing from the site.

- *Second-degree burn:* When the burn has penetrated the first two layers of skin, immerse the site in cool water or apply a cold compress (not ice). Don't pop any blisters that develop. Dress the site with a loose, nonstick bandage, and secure it over the wound with tape. Visit the doctor if pain or swelling increases, or there are signs of infection.

- *Third-degree burn:* Burns that penetrate past the first two layers of skin, have a diameter longer than three inches, or that are dry, leathery, black, white, or brown are third-degree burns, and emergency help should be requested immediately. These serious burns should not be soaked in cool water, but instead covered loosely with a nonstick bandage. These same steps should be taken for any burns to the face, hands, feet, major joint, or groin. If the burned person isn't also suffering from a head, neck, or leg injury, lay the person in a comfortable, flat position (though a person with a facial burn should sit), and cover them loosely with a blanket or warm coat. Elevate the burn wound above the heart, and the feet should be 12 inches off the ground. Monitor the person's breathing and pulse for signs of shock. Do not place a pillow underneath the head of someone who suffers from a burn on their neck.

HEAT EXHAUSTION

Your body can overheat if exposed to high temperatures, especially when the climate is humid or while doing a strenuous activity. If left untreated, heat exhaustion can lead to heatstroke, which can be deadly. Heat exhaustion is preventable if you stay hydrated and give your body the opportunity to cool itself down in hot conditions.

Protect yourself from the sun, and drink plenty of fluids with electrolytes. Being sunburned or dehydrated can limit your body's ability to sweat or regulate its temperature. Reduce your alcohol intake during high temperatures, as alcohol can make you feel hotter. Don't sit around in a tent or parked car on a hot day, since enclosed spaces can be many degrees hotter than the outside temperature.

Loose-fitting, lightweight clothing will help keep your body cool on hot days. Give your body time to adjust to hot weather by limiting the amount of physical exertion during the first part of any hot-weather camping trip and limiting activities during the middle of the day, when the temperature can be warmest.

If you know that certain medications or medical conditions can affect your body's ability to regulate its temperature, use caution when camping and take extra precautions to stay hydrated, limit physical exertion, and keep out of the sun.

How to treat heat exhaustion: Move the affected person into the shade or a cool place, and have them remove any heavy or tight clothing. They should lie down with their legs and feet elevated. Fan the person to cool them down, or apply a cool cloth or sponge to their skin. The overheated person should drink cool water and avoid alcoholic beverages or anything with caffeine. Monitor the person closely for any signs that their condition is worsening, such as confusion, fainting, seizures, or if the person is unable to drink fluids.

HYPOTHERMIA

Hypothermia is a condition that causes your body's core temperature to drop to such a dangerously low level that it can cause damage to your vital organs, or death. Dress in warm layers to trap heat around your body, and to protect your skin from the cooling effects of rain, snow, and wind, or to prevent your skin from coming into direct contact with cold surfaces. A layering system enables you to take clothes off or put clothes on as your body's temperature or the weather fluctuates. Don't wear so many layers during exercise that you sweat a lot, as this extra moisture can cause your core body temperature to drop. Wear a moisture-wicking inner layer to keep your skin dry. Never wear any cotton layers in cold weather. An insulating midlayer (fleece, wool, down, or synthetic down) should be worn over the first layer, and an additional breathable outer protective layer should be worn to act as a shield against the elements and to prevent sweating. Cover your feet with wool socks and waterproof shoes. Use a scarf to warm your neck. Wear mittens or gloves to protect your hands and a hat to minimize heat loss from your head.

Calories will help your body stay warm, so fuel up on foods. Remember to drink plenty of water, as being dehydrated increases your risk of becoming hypothermic. Cold conditions can make you feel less thirsty, so it's especially important to monitor your fluid intake.

Watch for early warnings of hypothermia, which include

- shivering;
- feeling cold; and
- the *umbles*, which is a catchall term that includes grumbling, stumbling, bumbling, and mumbling.

Treating hypothermia: When you notice any of the above early symptoms, try to raise your core body temperature immediately. Move your body, and if possible, move to a warmer location or, at the very least, try to find a protected location out of the wind, rain, or snow. Drink warm fluids and eat carbohydrates for some quick energy. If available, put on more layers. Monitor yourself and others in your group for any of the following symptoms:

- Numb hands or feet
- Shallow breathing
- Shivering
- Drowsiness or confusion
- Loss of consciousness

To treat hypothermia, restore warmth to the body slowly. Get to a warmer place, and remove any wet clothing. Don't apply hot-water bottles or warmers directly to the skin; instead, wrap something around warm items first. Cover the hypothermic person in blankets or other warm layers. Have the person drink fluids, but avoid caffeine or alcohol. Monitor their symptoms in case their condition worsens.

FROSTBITE

When skin or underlying tissue is exposed to harsh cold, it becomes more susceptible to frostbite, a condition that can damage extremities to the point of causing permanent injury or necessitating amputation. In cold temperatures, your body works to keep its core temperature warm, which slows the blood flow to your extremities, causing the skin and tissue in those areas to grow colder. The most common places where frostbite manifests are ears, nose, toes, and fingers. Prevention strategies are the same as those for avoiding hypothermia, so be sure to layer up, drink fluids and eat food, and keep your core temperature warm. Wear mittens or gloves, though mittens will keep your fingers warmer. Consider a protective layer for your face if the conditions are extremely harsh. Watch for the following symptoms:

- Numbness
- Throbbing
- Burning, tingling, or stinging sensations
- Red, yellowish-gray, or white exposed skin
- Exposed skin that feels waxy or firm

Treating frostbite: If you notice any of the above symptoms, warm your body immediately. Warm cold cheeks or your nose with warm hands, or if your hands are cold, place them underneath your armpits. Flap your arms and stomp your feet to generate blood flow to these areas. Drink fluids, eat food, and add more layers. Do not place the affected areas in hot water, as this can cause damage. You can instead soak the affected area in warm water, or place a warm cloth over the area.

ALTITUDE SICKNESS

Mountain or altitude sickness can affect anyone of any age or fitness level, but your risk increases when you move to a higher elevation quickly or when you don't give your body time to acclimate to the thinner air. At high altitudes less oxygen is available, so your lungs and heart have to work harder to help your blood cells carry oxygen throughout your body. People who live at higher elevations are more used to this lack of oxygen, as their bodies can adjust over time. People who live at lower elevations who travel to high-altitude places need time to acclimate to the change in barometric pressure. When your body has trouble adjusting to high elevation, three forms of altitude sickness can occur:

Acute mountain sickness (AMS)

The mildest form of altitude sickness, AMS includes symptoms such as dizziness, headache, nausea, and muscle aches.

High altitude pulmonary edema (HAPE)

When the body can't get enough oxygen, your lungs can fill up with fluid, which further inhibits your blood's ability to deliver oxygen throughout your body. If left untreated, HAPE can lead to health complications, and in some cases, death.

High altitude cerebral edema (HACE)

Usually occurring when you stay at high elevation for more than a week, this a serious condition that causes fluid to build up in the brain. HACE can be a life-threatening condition if medical attention is not sought immediately.

If camping or participating in activities at high elevation, monitor yourself and others in your group for any of the following symptoms:
- Fatigue
- Loss of appetite
- Pins and needles
- Headache
- Dizziness
- Vomiting
- Shortness of breath
- Trouble sleeping

Mild forms of these symptoms may mean that you just need to spend more time acclimating. But if symptoms worsen or don't improve within a couple of days, head to an elevation lower than 4,000 feet as soon as possible. Seek medical attention immediately if you or a member of your group experiences any of the following symptoms:
- Continuing shortness of breath or panting, even when resting
- Ongoing fatigue
- Tightening in the chest
- Trouble walking or loss of coordination
- Severe headache that isn't relieved by taking over-the-counter medications
- Coughing up pink froth
- Disorientation or confusion
- Fever
- Numbness
- Coma

Help prevent altitude sickness by acclimating to the elevation gradually. Spend at least a full day anywhere above 4,000 feet to allow your body time to adjust to the change in oxygen levels. When above 10,000 feet, let your body adjust for at least 1–3 days, and after that increase the elevation in 1,000-feet-per-day increments. With every 3,000 feet gained, rest for at least a day at that height afterward. If possible, come back down in elevation to sleep. Wear sunscreen, stay hydrated, and eat lots of carbohydrates. Limit your alcohol and tobacco intake. Monitor yourself and others for any signs of altitude sickness so that you can react quickly in case someone needs to get down to a lower elevation immediately. If you know you'll be camping at altitudes above

10,000 feet, ask your doctor for a prescription for Diamox, a medication that helps reduce the symptoms of altitude sickness.

Treating altitude sickness: The most effective way to treat altitude sickness is to hike to a lower elevation, ideally below 4,000 feet. If symptoms become severe, seek emergency medical attention right away.

ALLERGIC REACTIONS

People can be allergic to a number of things in the wilderness, including insect stings or bites, snakebites, sunscreen, poisonous plants, pollen, or contact with parasites in a freshwater lake. Take some precautions to prevent an allergic reaction to known triggering allergens so as to prevent anaphylactic shock.

Sunscreen

Contact dermatitis can occur within a few hours of applying non-hypoallergenic sunscreens. If you have sensitive skin or have experienced this kind of reaction to sunscreen, invest in brands that are hypoallergenic, or consider applying zinc oxide or titanium dioxide instead.

In case of allergic reaction: Apply a topical corticosteroid cream to the irritated area or rash. See your doctor if symptoms don't ease up or if they continue to worsen.

Poisonous plants

Poison oak, poison ivy, and poison sumac can not only cause contact dermatitis—which manifests as an itchy rash—but in some cases can trigger a more serious allergic reaction. Most people are allergic to these poisonous plants to some degree, and symptoms can appear 1–6 days after coming into contact with the toxic oil. Learn to identify these plants and wear long pants, long-sleeved shirts, and closed-toe shoes to cover up exposed skin to protect against any accidental contact. If your clothes come into contact with the leaves, avoid touching the fabric until it can be washed. Be on the lookout for these poisonous plants, and if you are exposed, watch out for any of the following symptoms, which necessitate seeking medical help:

- Fever
- Headache
- Nausea
- Trouble breathing or swallowing

- Rash that covers more than 25 percent of your body
- Swelling of the face or around the eyes
- Rash on your face, eyes, lips, or genitals
- Difficulty breathing

In case of rash: Wash the area with soap and lukewarm water, and if the rash doesn't go away, apply an over-the-counter topical corticosteroid cream or calamine lotion. Wash your whole body in lukewarm water and any clothes that might have also come into contact with the plants. Avoid scratching, as this can lead to infection. To reduce itchiness, you can take an oral antihistamine pill or apply a cold compress to the irritated area. Take notice of anything that has touched the rash, like fingernails or hands, as the poisonous oils can transfer.

In case of serious allergic reaction: Seek medical attention immediately. Reducing or relieving symptoms may require taking an oral steroid or other medical treatment.

GASTROINTESTINAL PAIN

While camping, purify your water every time before drinking it. Take precautions to avoid accidental ingestion of potentially contaminated water. Don't rinse vegetables in untreated water and then eat them uncooked. If you go swimming, avoid letting water into your mouth. Consuming untreated water can lead to a range of illnesses, but most commonly causes gastrointestinal distress and diarrhea. The symptoms for most waterborne illnesses will present themselves after you return home, but if you do suffer from such an affliction while camping, take some measures to minimize discomfort and to reduce the chances of worsening your condition.

Gastrointestinal cramping and illnesses can also be caused by eating spoiled food, so be sure to check the state of food first before consuming it, especially if it has been unrefrigerated for more than three hours.

Treating gastrointestinal issues: Drink lots of fluids and replenish electrolytes, as loose bowels can lead to severe dehydration. Avoid consuming alcohol, caffeine, spices, fruits, or hard cheeses.

SPRAINED ANKLE

When backpacking, wear sturdy boots with ankle protection, as the weight of a backpack can put a lot of strain on ankles. You can help prevent sprains by gently rolling your feet in a circular motion and stretching before any activity. Watch where you put your feet while hiking or participating in any outdoor activities, especially in wet conditions, as surfaces can be slick. Exercise caution when hiking through snow, as your foot can sink much deeper than you anticipate. Around camp, try not to trip over guylines or tent stakes. Stay hydrated and eat enough calories to prevent fatigue, as you are more likely to get injured when tired. Injuries are also more likely to happen when you're rushing to get somewhere, so avoid putting yourself in a situation where you have to hurry to get to your destination. If you or a member of your group twists an ankle, assess the severity of the injury by making note of any of the following symptoms:

- Loss of range of motion
- Tenderness
- Pain
- Swelling
- Inability to bear weight
- Discoloration

Treating a sprained ankle: If a twisted ankle causes severe pain and starts swelling immediately, the foot should be immobilized and you should seek medical attention quickly, as these might be signs of a fracture or more serious sprain. If the foot can still bear some weight, you just might need to "RICE" the ankle. RICE stands for rest, ice, compression, and elevation. Rest as long as possible to allow the injury time to heal. If possible, ice the injury. Wrap the ice in cloth first, and apply it for 20–40 minutes every 2–4 hours for up to 48 hours. If ice isn't available, you can soak the ankle in the nearest cold water source. You can also soak a bandanna in cold water and wrap it around the ankle. Compress

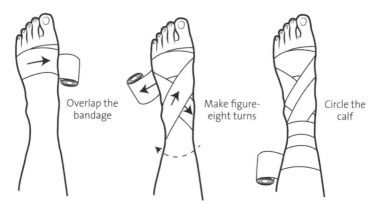

Overlap the bandage

Make figure-eight turns

Circle the calf

the injury by wrapping an elastic bandage around the ankle. This will help reduce swelling. Don't wrap the bandage so tightly that it constricts blood flow or forces too much pressure onto the injury. Finally, elevate the ankle while you rest.

BROKEN BONE

Preventing serious injuries like a broken limb is often a matter of exercising care while hiking or doing any other strenuous activity. Before attempting any outdoor activity, make sure you are well fed and hydrated, as you're more likely to injure yourself when exhausted. Always use a light source at night, and avoid doing any activities after dark. Don't take shortcuts or go off trail, as accidents can happen when navigating uncharted terrain. Wear all the appropriate safety gear for any activity you might participate in, such as a helmet for mountain biking or rock climbing, or trekking poles for hiking if you tend to need extra support.

Treating a broken bone: Some signs that a bone might be broken include:
- Rapid bruising or swelling
- Grating feeling when the injured body part moves or is touched
- Change in length or shape of the injured body part (e.g., one arm appearing shorter than the other)
- Bone sticking out of the skin

If the injury is bleeding, clean the wound and apply direct pressure with a sterile bandage or piece of gauze. To check to make sure there is no damage to blood vessels, you can pinch one of the person's fingernails or toenails below the injury site. When you let go, the nail should become pink again within a couple of seconds. If it takes longer to regain the normal color, this could mean blood vessels have been damaged. Signs of an injured nerve include lost feeling in the extremities below the injury. Blood vessel or nerve damage requires immediate care, and the person should be evacuated immediately.

If you rule out blood vessel or nerve damage, you can immobilize the injury with a makeshift splint. There's little risk in splinting a potentially broken body part, even if the injury is more minor. Remove any jewelry, and cut away clothing to get to the site of the injury if moving clothing will cause pain. If a broken limb is notably misshapen, and you have experience in this area, you can try pulling gently down on the injured limb while the person holds it steady. However, all pulling should cease immediately if the pain increases substantially. Pulling the limb back into place will help to splint it in a normal position.

Pad the splint with gauze or clothing, and tie it around the injury in a way that will immobilize any joints near the fractured area. Carry a splint in your first-aid kit for emergencies. If you don't have one, a splint can be fashioned out of something long and rigid like a tent pole, hiking pole, or sturdy stick. Place the rigid frames of the splint on either side of the injury. Splint an arm up against the person's chest in a relaxed bent angle. Splint a broken leg up against the uninjured leg. It's a good idea to practice putting the splint on the person's uninjured side before attempting to fashion it around the injury, as this will limit the amount of any pain accidentally inflicted. After the splint is set, make sure that any swelling inside the splint isn't cutting off circulation, and monitor the injury every hour for blood vessel or nerve complications. To reduce pain, the person can take an over-the-counter pain reliever. Determine whether self-evacuation is possible. If not, call or send someone for help.

SHOCK

A person can go into shock after sustaining a variety of injuries or after experiencing significant bodily stress. Shock is a serious condition that can be life-threatening if not tended to immediately. Preventing a person from going into shock while treating an injury or illness should be the primary concern. Know what types of injuries are the most shock inducing, and learn what signs to look for that indicate a person may be slipping into shock. The types of conditions that most commonly cause shock include:

- Dehydration
- Severe allergic reaction
- Severe trauma
- Blood loss
- Severe head trauma
- Severe infection
- Severe burn
- Heart failure

If a person is suffering from any of the above, be vigilant about watching for signs of shock, which include:

- Sweaty skin
- Rapid breath
- Blue-looking skin

- Vomiting
- Dizziness
- Fainting
- Nausea
- Pale or cold skin
- Disorientation
- Thirst
- Weak or rapid pulse
- Agitation
- Significant blood loss
- Unconsciousness

Treating shock: If the person is conscious and is able, have them lie down on a flat surface with their legs elevated just until the legs are positioned above the heart. If the person is unconscious, carefully lay them on their side (meanwhile protecting the spine and head). This will help prevent choking on fluids like vomit or blood. If the person is already experiencing shock, don't move them. Remove any wet clothing, and cover them instead with warm blankets, jackets, or sleeping bags. Have the person drink water, or water mixed with electrolytes (adding a small amount of salt and sugar to the water will also work). Allow the person to rest for at least 24 hours, unless the person's condition worsens. It may be necessary to initiate an emergency evacuation.

LIGHTNING

Know what to do if lightning strikes
If flashes of lightning are visible from where you're camping, take some precautions to minimize your risk. The best way to prevent being struck by lightning is to check the weather before your trip to be sure no lightning storms are predicted. Even if there is only a small chance of lightning, make other plans.

While camping, watch the skies for darkening clouds and large cumulonimbus clouds. These can be indicators of an approaching lightning storm. If lightning starts to strike in your area, estimate the distance between you and the lightning by counting the seconds between the flash of lightning and the roll of thunder. If the time is 30 seconds or less, seek shelter immediately.

Do not stand under trees or next to trees that are shorter than you. A stone shelter such as a cave is a safe shield against lightning. Just be sure no other occupants are living in the cave before climbing in. Breathing in the dust from rodent droppings (usually

Cumulonimbus clouds

found in places like caves) can lead to contracting hantavirus, so avoid kicking up dust while occupying any rock shelter. Do not seek safety inside small structures like open-air campground picnic shelters.

Take off your backpack if it's built with a metal frame and move at least 100 feet away from it. Put on a pair of rubber boots if you packed some, since rubber is a weak conductor.

If car camping, get inside your car, close the doors, and make sure all the windows are rolled up. Do not lean against the sides of the car or against the windows. Do not turn on the radio. If lightning strikes the car, the electricity will be conducted around the car's frame, but not through your body.

If you're staying at a campground with utilities, do not touch any electrical outlets or make a phone call using a landline. Avoid standing on or leaning against concrete walls or floors, as they often contain wire mesh that can conduct electricity.

If you are camping with a group of people, spread out. Maintain at least 50–100 feet between each person so that lightning cannot travel from one person to another if someone is struck.

If your hair stands on end or your skin tingles, immediately place your feet together and squat down with your head tucked into your chest or between your knees. Cover your ears with your hands, or place your hands flat against your knees and close your eyes. Do not lie on the ground, as the larger surface area offers lightning a bigger target.

Get out of or off any body of water. Being in or near water is extremely dangerous during a lightning storm.

Stay put for at least a half hour after a lightning storm passes.

If someone is struck by lightning: Wait long enough to make sure that the lightning has passed. Have the person lay down with their legs elevated above their heart, and monitor them for signs of shock. Look for any signs of other injuries such as burns, broken bones, or loss of hearing or eyesight. Check their pulse.

If the person is unconscious and breathing, perform CPR. If the person is unconscious and not breathing, perform mouth-to-mouth resuscitation first. Send for emergency medical help.

COUGARS

Cougar attacks are rare, but preventive measures can be taken to reduce your risk of becoming a cougar victim. Camp and hike in groups, rather than solo, and be extra cautious when camping with children, as cougars are more likely to prey upon smaller animals. When in cougar country, keep pets on leashes and consider turning back if you see any signs of a cougar, such as tracks. If you see a cub, don't approach it; its mother will be nearby and will protect the cub at all costs.

Cougar prints

Front

Rear

In case of a cougar attack: If you spot a cougar, stay calm and make yourself big. For example, if you're wearing a jacket, hold it up above your head. Bare your teeth and make loud, aggressive noises so the cougar sees you as an intimidation rather than prey. Don't run; back away slowly. If a cougar attacks, fight back and aim for the nose and eyes. If you are biking, keep your bike between you and the animal and use it as a weapon if necessary.

BEARS

North America is home to the black bear, the brown bear (which includes grizzlies), and the polar bear. Research if any species of bear inhabit the area in which you plan to camp, and learn about the behaviors of the particular local species so you can know how to avoid an encounter. Store food and garbage according to local regulations. Travel in groups rather than alone. Keep an eye out for signs that a bear may have recently passed through an area.

Grizzly bear   Black bear

For example, finding fresh scat signals that you need to be on the lookout for a bear and be ready with a plan for how you might react if you encounter one. Carry bear spray in case you do stumble across a bear at close range, and learn how to use the spray canister before you need it. Keep pets on leashes. Retreat from the area if you see a bear cub, as you don't want to run into the protective mother.

In case of a bear attack: If a bear approaches you or attacks, don't run. If you encounter a brown bear, you should back away slowly and keep your eyes on it. If a brown bear attacks and makes contact, play dead and do not try to defend yourself. If you think the bear is a black bear, you should make noise, throw things at it, and make yourself big. If a black bear attacks, try to fight back, aiming for the eyes and nose. If that doesn't work, play dead by clasping your hands behind your neck and lying on your stomach with your knees pulled in.

HOW TO HANDLE AN EMERGENCY SITUATION

KNOW WHEN TO CALL FOR AN EMERGENCY EVACUATION

In case of emergency—and you have cell service—call 911. Even if you don't think you have cell service, try anyway. However, knowing when a situation qualifies as an emergency is the tricky part. Search and rescue (SAR) groups advise people to assess whether a self-rescue is possible before calling for emergency assistance or evacuation. Depending on where you are when you or someone in your group gets injured, it could take a SAR team many hours to get to you (and sometimes longer to get back if they have to carry a person out on a litter), which means that sometimes it's in the injured person's best interest to attempt to get themselves back to civilization rather than waiting for an

Conscious choking

After checking the scene and the injured or ill person, have someone call 911 and get consent from the choking person.

1. Give five back blows. Bend the person forward at the waist, and give five back blows between the shoulder blades with the heel of one hand.
2. Give five abdominal thrusts. Place a fist with the thumb side against the middle of the person's abdomen, just above the navel. Cover your fist with your hand. Give five quick upward abdominal thrusts.
3. Continue care. Continue sets of five back blows and five abdominal thrusts until the object is forced out, the person can cough forcefully or breathe, or the person becomes unconscious.

If the person becomes unconscious, call 911 (even if you think there's no cell reception) if not already done, and give care for an unconscious choking adult, beginning with looking for an object.

Unconscious choking

1. Tilt the head and give rescue breaths.
2. If the chest still does not rise, give 30 chest compressions.
3. Look for and remove object if seen.
4. Give rescue breaths.

If breaths do not make the chest rise, repeat steps 2 and 4. If the chest clearly rises, check for breathing.

emergency team. Depending on the injury, it might be enough to administer basic first aid or prescribe some rest. Assess what the best course of action should be considering the location, type of injury, number of people in the group, and the weather.

KEEP YOURSELF SAFE

Before entering a scene after someone has sustained an injury, first check to make sure that the area is safe to enter. For example, if someone in your group wades into a river and gets dragged downstream from the force of the water, it's not wise to jump in after the person, as you might get pulled along too. Likewise, if a person trips and tumbles off the trail and down a hill, make sure that you can get to them safely before going to them. Look for potential hazards like tree limbs that might fall, any thin ice that might crack, or avalanche danger.

ASSESS THE SCENE

Before helping an injured person, take note of the various factors that might be at play. See if you can determine what happened. Count the number of people who might be injured. Quickly assess whether the injuries sustained might be life-threatening so that you can prioritize care. Find out how many nearby people are available to help, and assign tasks depending on how many people can offer assistance.

TAKE ACTION

Once you have determined that you can safely enter the situation and you can compose yourself calmly, take the following actions when administering emergency help:

When the injured person is conscious

1. Obtain the person's consent by describing what you think the injury is and how you plan to help, and asking permission to provide care. Introduce yourself and describe your level of first-aid or Wilderness First Responder training.

2. If other able people are nearby and willing to offer help, tell one person—by pointing at and speaking to them directly—to run and get a first-aid kit. Tell another person to get warm clothes, blankets, or sleeping bags to cover the injured person to keep them warm. Send a pair of people to run for additional emergency help if you don't have a way to call 911 and the person is in need of specialized emergency care.

3. Determine how alert the person is by asking the following orienting questions:
   - What's your name?
   - Can you tell me where you are?
   - What day is it?

4. If you might be exposed to any bodily fluids, put on gloves.

5. Check the person's pulse by placing your index and middle fingers on the side of their neck, just to the side of their windpipe. Alternatively, place the same two fingers on the thumb side of their wrist, over the radial artery, which is located between the bone and tendon. Once you feel a pulse, count the number of beats in 15 seconds and multiply this number by four. The average normal range for a resting heart rate is between 60–100 beats per minute.

6. Ask the six SAMPLE questions, and tell a bystander to record the answers:
    o   **S**igns and symptoms: What symptoms are you experiencing? (Take note of any signs of illness or injury, such as sweating, bleeding, pale skin, etc.)
    o   **A**llergies: What allergies do you have? Have you ever had an allergic reaction to a medication?
    o   **M**edications: What prescription medications are you taking? What are the possible side effects of taking that medication?
    o   **P**ast medical history: Have you ever experienced this injury/illness before? Have you had any surgeries or do you have any medical conditions that might be contributing to your current state?
    o   **L**ast oral intake: When was the last time you drank any fluids? When was the last time you ate something?
    o   **E**vents leading up to the injury or illness: What happened? What do you think caused the injury/illness?

7. Systematically scan the person from head to toe. Start at the head and neck and move down from there:
    o   *Head:* Look for any cuts, bruising, or bleeding. Take note of the color of the person's skin and whether they're sweating. Look in their ears and nose for blood or other fluid. Check pupil size. Feel for any swelling, tenderness, or depressions. Listen to the person's breathing to determine if something is obstructing their airways. Is their breathing irregular, shallow, or wheezing?
    o   *Neck and shoulders:* Look for cuts, bruising, or bleeding. Check the person's pulse. Gently feel the neck for any tenderness or irregularity.

- o *Chest:* Note any trouble breathing or irregular chest movement. Look for any bruising, cuts, or bleeding. Gently feel for any tender spots.
- o *Abdomen and hips:* Look for distension or wounds. Feel for any tenderness.
- o *Extremities:* Look for cuts, bleeding, bruising, swelling, or deformity. Check for voluntary movement. Feel for range of motion in joints and any tenderness.

8. Take appropriate medical action according to your knowledge and level of training.

If the injured person is unresponsive

1. Speak loudly to get the person's attention. Shout their name if you know it.

2. If the person is an adult, tap their shoulder to get their attention. If the person is an infant, tap the bottom of their foot.

3. Check for any irregular breathing.

4. Check the person's pulse.

5. If the person is breathing:
   - Tell a bystander to call 911 or send for help.
   - Ask a bystander who knows the person the SAMPLE questions.
   - Conduct the head-to-toe check described above.

6. If the person is **not** breathing:
   - Tell a bystander to call 911 or send for help.
   - Conduct CPR, starting with chest compressions. Use an *automated external defibrillator* (AED) if one is available, and if you have been trained to use one.
   - Continue to do CPR until the person begins to breathe, until an AED is made available, or until a trained medical responder arrives.

How to perform CPR

Before giving CPR:

1. *Check the scene and the person.* Make sure the scene is safe, then tap the person on the shoulder and shout, "Are you OK?" to ensure that the person needs help.
2. *Call 911 for assistance* (even if you think there's no cell reception). If it's evident that the person needs help, call (or ask a bystander to call) 911, then send someone to get an AED. (If an AED is unavailable, or if there is no bystander to access it, stay with the victim, call 911, and begin administering assistance.)
3. *Open the airway.* With the person lying on their back, tilt the head back slightly to lift the chin.
4. *Check for breathing.* Listen carefully, for no more than 10 seconds, for sounds of breathing. (Occasional gasping sounds do not equate as breathing.) If there is no breathing, begin CPR.

Red Cross CPR steps:

Push hard; push fast. Place your hands, one on top of the other, in the middle of the chest. Use your body weight to help you administer compressions that are at least two inches deep and delivered at a rate of at least 100 compressions per minute.

Deliver rescue breaths. With the person's head tilted back slightly and the chin lifted, pinch the nose shut and place your mouth over the person's mouth to make a complete seal. Blow into the person's mouth to make their chest rise. Deliver two rescue breaths, then continue compressions.

Note: If the chest does not rise with the initial rescue breath, re-tilt the head before delivering the second breath. If the chest doesn't rise with the second breath, the person may be choking. After each subsequent set of 100 chest compressions, and before attempting breaths, look for an object and, if seen, remove it.

Continue CPR steps. Keep performing cycles of chest compressions and breathing until the person exhibits signs of life, such as breathing, an AED becomes available, or a trained medical responder arrives on scene.

Note: End the cycles if the scene becomes unsafe or you cannot continue performing CPR due to exhaustion.

PROTECT THE HEAD AND NECK

If you're unsure whether the person has sustained a neck or head injury, do not move them. Hold their head and spine stable if moving them is necessary to keep them safe.

DON'T PANIC

Whether you are helping an injured person or you happen to be the person who's injured, try to remain calm. For example, if someone in your group has broken their arm, and a bone is sticking out of the skin and the injured person hasn't noticed it yet, gently place a jacket over the injury and keep the person distracted and calm. Don't gasp in alarm. Drawing attention to the severity of an injury can cause a person to go into shock, which can be a serious condition. Tell the injured person to take deep breaths to help comfort them and keep them focused on something other than their injury. Keeping a level head will help you be able to assess the situation and think clearly about the actions that need to be taken.

ATTEMPTING A SELF-RESCUE

If you find yourself injured and alone, plan an exit strategy that gets you to the nearest help as quickly and safely as possible. Some safety tips include:

- Tend to any wounds prior to starting the journey to find help.
- If you happen to have something to write with and on, jot down the SAMPLE notes (see page 279) about your injury and keep these notes on your person. In the event that someone finds you unconscious, they will be better able to assist you if they have some context for your injury and reason for your unconscious state.
- Assess your situation. Note the amount of gear, food, and water you have available, and what you can carry. If you are physically able, pack enough food and water to last for several days. If you cannot carry much gear, it may be better to stay put and wait for help to find you.
- Be sure to stop and rest in the shade when you feel tired. Maintain a hiking pace that is sustainable. Slow and steady will still keep you moving forward, whereas rushing can tire you out to the point of exhaustion.
- Take half-hour breaks in the shade to eat food since it can be difficult for an ill or injured body to digest food. If you are still tired after a half hour, rest for another half hour.
- Drink plenty of water.

- Stop and address small problems before they become bigger problems. For example, if you notice that your sprained ankle is swelling quite a bit, stop and rest. If a stream is nearby, soak the injured ankle in the cold water to reduce swelling.
- Avoid hiking during the heat of the day, which is usually between 10:00 a.m. and 4:00 p.m. Find a shady spot to rest until the temperature cools down.
- Avoid hiking at night.
- Stay calm. Panicking can cause a stress response in the body that can tire you out even more.

When one has become accustomed to out of door life, it is a difficult matter to settle down, even for a short time, within four walls.

—Dwight and Stella Woolf, *Tramping and Camping*, 1912

Chapter 11

Returning Home

BY THE END OF A CAMPING TRIP, YOU MIGHT BE exhausted, bug-bitten, sunburned, and covered in dirt and sweat. Your gear might be drenched and difficult to pack up. You might be in a hurry to get back to civilization and take your first shower in days. But the Leave No Trace Seven Principles still apply, even when you're about to head home. Take time to be a responsible camper and leave the campsite in good order. And when you arrive home, spend time cleaning, repairing, and organizing your gear so that it's ready for the next trip. After returning home from a camping trip, the short-term goal is often to shower, relax, and unwind, and leave the unpacking for the following day, or the following camping trip. But you'll be happier in the long run—and your gear will last longer—if you carry out a few cleanup chores immediately after getting home.

BEFORE LEAVING YOUR CAMPSITE

Leave the campsite in better condition than you found it so that the next campers will enjoy it as much as you did. Taking simple steps to clean up the campsite will help keep natural areas pristine and will ensure that everyone has a fair opportunity to enjoy the outdoors.

PUT THE FIRE OUT

It's your responsibility to make sure your fire is completely out so that there is no chance of it continuing to burn after you leave. See page 130 for step-by-step procedures for extinguishing a campfire.

If you have any extra firewood or kindling, leave it next to the fire ring for future campers. However, some places prohibit leaving firewood, so check the rules wherever you're camping, and if necessary, take it home with you or give it to another camping group instead.

PICK UP TRASH

If you're camping in a group, everyone should spread out and pick up any pieces of garbage they find. This includes any remnants in the campfire like newspaper, which might not have burned all the way.

PUT EVERYTHING BACK

If you moved benches, picnic tables, or other objects around during your stay, put them back where you found them when you arrived. Fill in and smooth over any trenches you dug or holes made by tent stakes. Wipe off any spills from picnic tables or benches. Pick up any bits of food that may have fallen to the ground.

CHECK OUT ON TIME

Some campgrounds set a specific time for checkout. Be sure you check out before the posted time so that the camp host has enough time to check your campsite and make sure it's ready for the next visitors. You shouldn't still be packing up when the next campers arrive. Checkout means that your campsite is clean, all your gear has been packed into your vehicle, and you have signed out or checked in with the camp host to let them know you're leaving.

AFTER RETURNING HOME

The first thing most people want to do upon returning home is shower. After camping in the wilderness, it can be hard to find the motivation to unpack, clean gear, wash clothes, and organize. However, following through on some simple tasks will improve the experience of packing and planning for your next camping trip. You're also more likely to remember the chores you need to do upon returning home rather than days, weeks, or months in the future when you might forget that you needed to clean your hydration bladder or pack more antibiotic ointment in your first-aid kit.

CLEAN GEAR

Most camping gear comes home dirty. Take some time to clean every item of gear to prolong its life, reduce mold and mildew, and make packing for your next trip easier. Clean any buildup from the inside of your hydration bladder (see page 77 for cleaning instructions). Rinse out and scrub the inside of any coolers. Wash dishes that may not have been thoroughly cleaned while camping, as any crumbs or food residue can mold or attract mice. Rinse out water bottles. Wipe off dirt from tent stakes.

WASH CLOTHES

This task might not seem like it needs explanation. However, some of the more technical items of camping clothing—like a down jacket or wool sweater—might have specific care instructions. Check the labels of all camping clothing before running it through regular washer and dryer cycles. Determine whether you should wash your rain gear or down garments or if you should wait a few more camping trips. See page 73 for general garment care instructions.

RE-WATERPROOF GEAR

Did the seams of your tent leak on this past camping trip? Did your rain jacket not seem as waterproof this time around? Did the inside of your boots get more soggy than usual? Buy the appropriate waterproofing supplies for the type of material you'll be waterproofing. Some products come in spray form. Others can be added to a load of wash. You can purchase a seam sealant to apply to the seams of your tent for some extra protection against the elements.

DRY OUT GEAR

If you camped through the rain and didn't have a chance to dry out gear before packing up, take the time to dry out wet gear. Remove any wet socks that might be rolled up inside shoes and air the shoes out in a dry area. Lay out or hang up your tent to dry. Turn your sleeping bag inside out and let it air-dry, or read the tag for proper drying instructions. Don't leave a sleeping bag out to dry in direct sunlight for too long, as the UV rays can damage nylon fabric.

DO REPAIRS

Set aside time to patch up a leaky tent, sleeping pad, down jacket, down sleeping bag, or hydration bladder. If your camp stove wasn't working properly on your trip, read the manual for cleaning instructions and troubleshooting information. Try to hammer out bent tent stakes until they're straight again. Replace a worn-out boot sole with a new one, and also replace any tattered laces.

REPLENISH GEAR

Make a list of any items that were used up or need to be refilled, restocked, or replenished before your next camping trip. Some of these items might include:

- Toilet paper
- Bug spray
- Sunscreen
- First-aid items
- Biodegradable soap
- Batteries
- Fuel
- Matches
- Fire starters
- Resealable plastic bags
- Trash bags
- Foil

KEEP GEAR ORGANIZED

Invest in some large plastic storage bins to keep gear dry and out of the way in between camping trips. Label the bins so you can easily find what you're looking for when packing for your next camping trip. Make sure all gear is dry and clean before packing it away. Avoid storing gear in a place that gets a lot of direct sunlight. Invest in a set of camping-only cookware. Instead of using your normal utensils, pots, pans, and knives from your home kitchen supply, accumulate a set of utensils and cookware that you use only while camping. Store in a mess kit, bag, or plastic storage container. That way, you'll already have all your camp cooking gear packed.

REMOVE BATTERIES

When you get home, remove any batteries from gadgets like headlamps, flashlights, or portable fans, radios, or GPS devices, and store batteries in a resealable plastic bag with the rest of your camping gear. This will help prevent corrosion in between camping trips.

MAKE A SHOPPING LIST

Before you forget, make a list of gear you want or need to buy before your next camping trip. Do you need to replace tent stakes or get a warmer jacket? Did you decide that the sleeping pad you bought just isn't comfortable enough? If you were envious of your friend's ultralight hammock or rechargeable headlamp on this past trip, add them to a gear wish list and check wish list items off as you save enough money to purchase them. Update your gear-packing checklist with any new items that you want to remember to bring on trips.

START PLANNING THE NEXT TRIP

Once you've planned your first successful camping trip, you're likely to catch the camping bug. It's a special kind of satisfaction that can be found in nature. For solo campers, the result is often restorative. For groups, the shared experience can deepen bonds. With a little practice and planning ahead, you can make camping a regular part of your life.

Over time, camping preparedness will become second nature and you'll adopt the camping style that works best for you, your lifestyle, and your budget. Hopefully this book has taught you that camping doesn't require advanced wilderness survival skills or high-tech gear in order to stay safe and comfortable, or to have fun. Once you have mastered the simple art of camping, help someone else learn how to camp. Share your traditions and favorite camping locations. Teach wilderness skills and responsible environmental stewardship. Sleeping under the stars is something that should be experienced by everyone, and camping provides a gateway accessible to all.

Glossary

AED: An acronym for automated external defibrillator, an AED is a portable electronic device used for correcting an irregular heartbeat that could be life-threatening. If a person is suffering from cardiac arrhythmia, applying an AED device will send an electric signal that can reestablish a normal, safe heart rate. An AED class should be taken before attempting to use one to help save someone's life.

Backcountry: A remote wilderness area that might provide limited road access, and even then, the roads might be unpaved. Often, access to the backcountry requires human-powered transportation such as hiking, biking, or paddling. Campsites are usually barebones and without facilities or amenities, and water needs to be packed in or filtered from a natural water source.

Backwater: Similar to backcountry, backwater refers to a remote wilderness area that is accessed via a watercraft, such as a canoe, a kayak, or a raft. Sometimes, boats with motors are not permitted beyond certain boundaries in backwater regions.

Bandit camping: A term used interchangeably with free camping, bandit camping refers to camping for free in an area not developed for camping.

Biodegradable soap: Soap containing ingredients that break down over time. Though better for the environment than non-biodegradable versions, soap made specifically for camping should be used with water transported and disposed away from any natural body of water.

Bivy: Short for bivouac, a bivy sack is a waterproof shelter often smaller than a standard tent. It's an alternative that weighs less than most tent models.

Boondocking: Another term for free camping, boondocking refers to camping in the boondocks, or a remote area, without paying a nightly fee.

Cathole: Sometimes referred to as a pighole, a cathole is a small hole dug to bury human waste so that no trace remains. A cathole can also be used to dispose of wastewater from washing dishes or taking a sponge bath.

Compound tincture of benzoin: Used in first-aid care, compound tincture of benzoin is an antiseptic solution, and is also used to stop bleeding from wounds like cuts and blisters. It is included in many preassembled first-aid kits and should be applied according to the instructions listed on the product, or according to the standard procedure taught in a first-aid class.

CPR: An acronym for cardiopulmonary resuscitation, CPR is a medical procedure that can be applied to a person who is not breathing or who does not have a pulse. CPR involves manually applying chest compressions to the unconscious person's chest, and should only be administered by someone trained in CPR. Classes are offered where a person can become certified in CPR competency.

Cumulonimbus cloud: Cumulonimbus is a cloud formation that should be paid attention to in the wilderness, as it can sometimes signal an oncoming thunderstorm. Cumulonimbus clouds are often dark, towering formations and should serve as a warning to seek appropriate shelter from lightning.

Declination: In compass reading, declination is the angle between true north and magnetic north. When the angle is east of true north, the declination number is positive, and when the angle is west of true north, the declination number is listed as negative.

Dispersed camping: Another term used to describe free camping, dispersed camping means staying in an area for free, where there is no access to amenities like running water, firepits, or bathroom facilities.

Dry bag: A bag made of flexible waterproof material that folds in a way that creates a watertight seal. Dry bags are used for keeping gear dry during kayaking, canoeing, and rafting trips. They can also be used to line the inside of a bike pannier to make it waterproof.

Dry camping: A term used to describe a style of RV camping when there is no access to hookups. This often means that the campsite does not provide electricity, water, or sewer connections for RVs.

Footprint: Another term for a ground cloth, a footprint is a piece of fabric that is placed underneath a tent to protect the bottom of the tent from abrasions and other damage. An ideal footprint size is the same as the area of the bottom of the tent that it will be used under.

Free camping: Although a self-explanatory term, free camping is a widely accepted and legal form of camping where permitted. Leave No Trace Seven Principles must be strictly adhered to, but free camping allows people to camp in undeveloped campsites for free.

Frontcountry: Wild areas that are road-accessible and often provide more amenities and facilities than backcountry areas. The campsites in frontcountry campgrounds are also often more developed.

Glamping: A term that combines glamour and camping and reflects a more luxurious style of camping, often in special structures like yurts or platform cabin tents with comfortable beds and bedding and other amenities.

GPS: An acronym for global positioning system, GPS is usually used to refer to GPS navigation devices, or handheld receivers that use satellites to calculate the geographic coordinates of your exact location. You can also use GPS devices to log waypoints along a route or to call or send text messages when you're located outside of cell-phone reception.

Ground cloth: A piece of durable fabric that can be used as a footprint underneath a tent, or to provide a barrier between you and the ground if you're sleeping without the cover of a tent.

Guyline: A rope or cord used to hold an object in position or stable against the elements, such as a rain tarp, tent, or rainfly.

Guyout loop: Loops that are used to attach guylines. Many tents, rainflies, and tarps are manufactured with built-in guyout loops or holes.

Hydration bladder: A plastic reservoir used to carry water. It usually has a long hose that can be used to drink the water conveniently from the bladder, without removing the bladder from a backpack first.

Litter: A stretcher used to carry an injured person from an accident site to safety. Litters are usually carried in by search-and-rescue operations.

Magnetic north: The position of a compass needle pointing north, which is determined by the pull of the earth's magnetic field.

Molefoam: A protective adhesive foam bandage that provides cushioning for blisters after they form.

Moleskin: A soft adhesive bandage that can be used as a preventive against blisters, and can also be used as a protective barrier after a blister has formed.

Multi-tool: A pocket-size device that includes a range of basic tools, including items such as a knife, scissors, can opener, screwdriver, or pliers.

Mylar: A type of polyester resin used in the manufacturing of heat-resistant gear.

O-ring: A gasket built into the design of many liquid-fuel-canister camp stoves to help regulate the pressure of the fuel.

Pannier: A type of bag or basket typically used to store gear, which is secured to a bike rack during a bikepacking or bike touring trip. Some companies manufacture waterproof panniers that function like dry bags.

Parachute cord: A lightweight but durable nylon rope that can be used to fashion guylines for tents, rainflies, and rain tarps. Parachute cord can also be used to hang food bags or to string up temporary clotheslines.

Portage: The process of carrying a watercraft over land. Portaging is sometimes necessary when canoeing or kayaking from lake to lake when there is no outlet, or when bypassing dangerous rapids on rafting trips.

Put-in: An area designated for launching rafts, kayaks, and canoes.

R-value: A rating that lists a material's insulating power. The higher the R-value, the more a material will retain heat and insulate effectively.

Space blanket: A sheet designed to retain maximum heat. A space blanket is often made of material that reflects body heat back toward the person wearing the blanket. A space blanket is sometimes included in preassembled first-aid or survival kits.

SPOT device: A type of GPS device that uses satellites to send text messages when you're located out of cell-phone range. In emergencies, a SPOT device can be used to send a person's location to the closest search-and-rescue or emergency service for help.

Switchback: A sharp turn in a path or trail, usually at 180 degrees, that ascends or descends a hill at a lower angle than just straight up or down the most direct route.

Thru-hiking: Also spelled *through-hiking*, thru-hiking refers to end-to-end journeys along one of the three longest trails in the US, which include the Pacific Crest Trail, Appalachian Trail, and Continental Divide Trail.

Trowel: A lightweight handheld shovel used to dig catholes.

True north: The northernmost point on the earth, according to the earth's axis rather than the magnetic poles.

Tyvek: A high-density synthetic fabric made of polyethylene fibers first used as a weatherproof house wrap and also suitable for use as an inexpensive ground cloth.

Ultralight: A style of gear that weighs very little. Ultralight can also refer to a style of backcountry camping that necessitates packing only minimal gear or gear that has been manufactured to weigh much less than the other product models on the market.

Vestibule: A small chamber built into tent designs that allows room to store gear. In larger deluxe tents, vestibules can also serve as additional rooms within the tent.

Waypoint: A geographic coordinate that can be logged on a GPS device. Waypoints are most useful when they mark significant natural features such as a lake or trail junction.

Wild camping: A term for free camping that is used in countries outside of the US, especially in Europe.

Wilderness First Responder: A person who has been certified in Wilderness First Responder (WFR) training. WFR courses teach skill sets that allow a person to respond competently and safely in an emergency situation in remote locations, or out of range of immediate professional medical attention.

Resources

Adventure Cats

An online resource that provides information about camping with cats.

www.adventurecats.org

American Red Cross

Resource for basic first-aid and CPR training.

www.redcross.org

Dirty Gourmet

Backpacking recipe blog.

www.dirtygourmet.com

Fresh Off the Grid

Online camp cooking resource.

www.freshoffthegrid.com

Junior Ranger Program

A program managed by NPS that allows children to learn more about wilderness and the national parks.

www.nps.gov/kids/jrrangers.cfm

Leave No Trace Seven Principles

Center for Outdoor Ethics and go-to reference for the most current Leave No Trace Seven Principles.

www.lnt.org

National Park Service (NPS)

The federal government agency that manages all the national parks and runs the national parks Junior Ranger program.

www.nps.gov

National Outdoor Leadership School

An outdoor education school that offers outdoor skills classes and Wilderness First Responder courses.

www.nols.edu

REI Co-Op Journal

REI-managed blog that includes information about gear and other camping tips.

www.rei.com/blog

Reserve America

An online campsite reservation tool.

www.reserveamerica.com

Smartphone camping apps

Camp and Tent: Resource for finding tent-friendly campgrounds where RVs are not allowed.

Camping List: Handy tool for making sure you've packed all the items on your camping checklist.

Chimani: The go-to informational guide to national parks in the United States.

Coleman - Get Outdoors: Camping comfort recipes, campsite recommendations, and gear endorsements.

First Aid: Features best first-aid protocols for emergency situations.

GoSky Watch: Star identification guide.

Knot Guide: Reference guide for knot-tying skills.

MyNature Animal Tracks: Reference guide for animal track identification.

REI National Park Guide & Maps: Trail data and hike descriptions of national parks and other outdoor recreation areas.

Star Walk 2: Star identification guide.

Survival Guide: Survival skills information and resources.

PlantSnap: Tree identification reference guide.

Bibliography

50 Campfires. "25 Uses for Duct Tape on Your Next Camping Trip." Accessed April 6, 2018. http://50campfires .com/25-uses-for-duct-tape-on-your-next-camping-trip/.

American Red Cross. "First Aid Steps." Accessed May 10, 2018. https:// www.redcross.org/take-a-class/first-aid/performing-first-aid /first-aid-steps.

Arnold, Daniel. *Early Days in the Range of Light: Encounters with Legendary Mountaineers*. Berkeley: Counterpoint Press, 2009.

Baggaley, Kate. "What to Do If You Break Your Leg in the Middle of Nowhere." *Popular Science*. Posted July 20, 2017. Accessed May 8, 2018. https://www.popsci.com/break-bone-in-wilderness -first-aid-how-to.

Barrows, Eva. "5 Steps to Telling Campfire Stories." *KOA Blog*. Accessed May 22, 2018. https://koa.com/blog/campfire-stories/.

Bento, Matt. "How to Choose the Best Fleece Jacket." *OutdoorGearLab*. Last updated October 23, 2018. Accessed April 6, 2018. https://www .outdoorgearlab.com/topics/clothing-mens/best-fleece-jacket /buying-advice.

BookYourSite.com. "9 Camping Etiquette Principles All Campers Should Know." The Road Map. Posted February 23, 2017. Accessed May 8, 2018. http://roadmap.bookyoursite.com/camping-etiquette/.

Cook, Stacey. "12 Tips for Camping in the Rain." *REI Co-Op Journal*. Accessed May 14, 2018. https://www.rei.com/blog /camp/12-tips-camping-rain.

Costello, Tom, and Elisha Fieldstadt. "Flying Drones at National Parks Can Result in Penalties, Fines." *NBC News*. Posted December 26, 2015 Accessed May 29, 2018. https://www.nbcnews.com/news/us-news /flying-drones-national-parks-can-result-penalties-fines-n486206.

Craigin, Harry. *A Boy's Workshop*. Boston: D. Lothrop & Co., 1884.

Curtis, Rick. *The Backpacker's Field Manual: A Comprehensive Guide to Mastering Backcountry Skills*. New York: Three Rivers Press, 1998.

Dell'Amore, Christine, and Todd Wilkinson. "How to Not Get Attacked by a Bear." *National Geographic*. Posted September 16, 2015. Accessed May 10, 2018. https://news.nationalgeographic .com/2015/09/150916-bears-attacks-animals-science-north -america-grizzlies/.

Fresh Off the Grid. "How to Find Free Camping in the US & Canada." Posted December 17, 2017. Accessed May 18, 2018. https://www .freshoffthegrid.com/how-to-find-free-camping-usa-canada/.

Garrett, Penney. "How to Choose the Best Camping Stove." *OutdoorGearLab*. Last updated May 3, 2018. Accessed April 4, 2018. https://www.outdoorgearlab.com/topics/camping-and-hiking /best-camping-stove/buying-advice.

Hagemeier, Heidi. "Camping with Dogs: How to Navigate Rules and Regulations." *REI Co-Op Journal*. Posted August 21, 2015. Accessed October 30, 2018. https://www.rei.com/blog/camp /camping-with-dogs-how-to-navigate-rules-and-regulations.

Health Direct. "Snake Bites." Council of Australian Governments. Last reviewed September 2017. Accessed April 26, 2018. https://www .healthdirect.gov.au/snake-bites.

Henkes, Beth, and Tod Schimelpfenig. "Blister Prevention and Care." *REI*. Posted April 25, 2018. https://www.rei.com/learn/expert -advice/blister-prevention-care.html.

Hinnant, Kristin. "The Ultimate Guide to Camping with Kids." *Hike It Baby*. Posted March 23, 2018. Accessed May 1, 2018. https://hikeit baby.com/blog/the-ultimate-guide-to-camping-with-kids/.

Hiskey, Daven. "Does Drinking Alcohol Really Keep You Warm When It's Cold Out?" *Mental Floss*. Posted January 9, 2013. Accessed May 16, 2018. http://mentalfloss.com/article/32256/does -drinking-alcohol-really-keep-you-warm-when-its-cold-out.

Johnson, Elaine. "How to Use a Camping Stove." *Sunset*. Accessed May 17, 2018. https://www.sunset.com/food-wine/techniques/camp-stove.

Krichko, Kade. "Stoves 101: How Much Fuel Should I Carry?" *The Summit

Register, MSR. Accessed May 24, 2018. https://thesummitregister
.com/stoves-101-how-much-fuel-should-i-carry/.

Kwak-Hefferan, Elisabeth. "100 Essential Skills Every Backpacker Should
Know." *Backpacker*. Posted May 9, 2018: https://www.backpacker
.com/skills/100-pro-level-hiking-skills-everyone-should-know.

Lanza, Michael. "How to Gear Up and Get Your Kids Started Camping
and Backpacking." *REI Co-Op Journal*. Accessed May 1, 2018. https://
www.rei.com/blog/camp/kids-camping-gear-how-to-get-started.

Larsen, Leia. "Bridging the Adventure Gap: Minorities in Outdoor
Adventure." *Standard-Examiner*. Posted October 16, 2014. Accessed
May 29, 2018. http://www.standard.net/Recreation/2014/10/16
/bridging-the-adventure-gap-mi.

Mayo Clinic. "Heat Exhaustion: First Aid." Mayo Foundation for Medical
Education and Research. Posted May 1, 2018. Accessed May 4, 2018.
https://www.mayoclinic.org/first-aid/first-aid-heat-exhaustion
/basics/art-20056651.

Mayo Clinic. "Snakebites: First Aid." Mayo Foundation for Medical
Education and Research. Posted March 9, 2018. Accessed April 26,
2018. https://www.mayoclinic.org/first-aid/first-aid-snake-bites
/basics/art-20056681.

McIntosh-Tolle, Lindsay. "How to Adjust the Declination on a Compass."
REI. Accessed April 18, 2018. https://www.rei.com/learn
/expert-advice/compass-declination.html.

McIntosh-Tolle, Lindsay. "How to Use a Compass." *REI*. Accessed
April 18, 2018. https://www.rei.com/learn/expert-advice
/navigation-basics.html.

McKay, Brett and Kate. "How to Roast the Perfect Marshmallow."
The Art of Manliness. Last updated July 25, 2016. Accessed May 25,
2018. https://www.artofmanliness.com/articles/how-to-roast-the
-perfect-marshmallow/.

More, Daniel. "Allergic Reactions at the Campground." *VeryWell Health*.
Posted May 2, 2018. Accessed May 4, 2018. https://www.verywell
health.com/camping-allergies-82630.

Mother, Den. "How Do I Survive a Forest Fire?" *Backpacker*. Posted June 8,
2016. Accessed May 7, 2018. https://www.backpacker.com/survival
/den-mother-forest-fire.

Murray, Lindsey. "7 Tips Every Camper Should Know about Campfire
Cooking." *Real Simple*. Accessed May 10, 2018. https://www.real
simple.com/food-recipes/cooking-tips-techniques/campfire-cooking.

National Park Service. "Camping with Kids." Last updated May 25, 2018. Accessed May 31, 2018. https://www.nps.gov/subjects/camping/camping-with-kids.htm.

NOLS. "What to Do When You Sprain Your Ankle in the Wilderness." *NOLS Blog.* Posted August 21, 2015. Accessed May 7, 2018. https://blog.nols.edu/2015/08/21/what-to-do-when-you-sprain-your-ankle-in-the-wilderness-video.

Nordqvist, Christian. "What's to Know about Altitude Sickness?" *Medical News Today.* Last updated January 30, 2018. Accessed May 4, 2018. https://www.medicalnewstoday.com/articles/179819.php.

NSW Government. "Mosquitoes Are a Health Hazard Fact Sheet." Last updated January 17, 2017. Accessed April 27, 2018. http://www.health.nsw.gov.au/infectious/factsheets/pages/mosquito.aspx.

NSW Government. "Tick Alert." Revised March 2013. Accessed April 27, 2018. http://www.health.nsw.gov.au/environment/Publications/tick_alert_brochure.pdf.

The Outdoor Foundation. "Outdoor Participation Report, 2016." https://outdoorindustry.org/wp-content/uploads/2016/09/2016-Outdoor-Recreation-Participation-Report_FINAL.pdf.

Pet MD. "How to Remove Ticks on Dogs and Cats." Accessed May 4, 2018. https://www.petmd.com/dog/parasites/how-to-remove-a-tick-from-dog-cat.

Peterson, Doug. "Tips for Camping with Kids." *REI.* Accessed May 1, 2018. https://www.rei.com/learn/expert-advice/camping-kids.html

Pietrangelo, Ann. "Poison Oak Rash: Pictures and Remedies." *Healthline.* Posted July 12, 2017. Accessed May 5, 2018. https://www.healthline.com/health/outdoor-health/poison-oak-pictures-remedies.

REI. "Food Storage and Handling for Campers and Backpackers." Accessed May 11, 2018. https://www.rei.com/learn/expert-advice/food-handling-storage.html.

REI. "How to Choose a Backpack." Accessed June 27, 2018. https://www.rei.com/learn/expert-advice/backpack.html.

REI. "How to Choose a Backpacking Stove." Accessed April 2018. https://www.rei.com/learn/expert-advice/backpacking-stove.html.

REI. "How to Clean a Hydration Bladder." Accessed April 17, 2018. https://www.rei.com/learn/expert-advice/how-to-clean-a-hydration-bladder.html.

REI. "Meal Planning for Backpacking." Accessed May 8, 2018. https://www.rei.com/learn/expert-advice/planning-menu.html.

REI. "Tips for Canoe and Kayak Camping." Accessed May 2, 2018. https://www.rei.com/learn/expert-advice/camping-basics.html.

Quirós, Gabriela. "How a Tick Digs Its Hooks into You." *NPR* (National Public Radio). Posted March 20, 2018. Accessed April 27, 2018. https://www.npr.org/sections/goatsandsoda/2018/03/20/594922001/watch-how-a-tick-digs-its-hooks-into-you.

Schneider, Hans. "15 Tips for Winter Camping." *The Clymb* (blog). Accessed May 9, 2018. http://blog.theclymb.com/tips/15-tips-for-winter-camping/.

Setzer, Adam. "Tarp Tips: Quick Shelter for Rain, Wind, or Saving Weight." *REI Co-Op Journal*. Accessed May 11, 2018. https://www.rei.com/blog/camp/tarp-tips-quick-shelter-for-rain-wind-or-saving-weight.

Siler, Wes. "How to Make Camping in Scorching Hot Weather Enjoyable." *Outside*. Posted June 26, 2017. Accessed May 3, 2018. https://www.outsideonline.com/2195431/how-survive-camping-scorching-hot-weather.

Solomon, Christopher. "Is Instagram Ruining the Great Outdoors?" *Outside*. Posted March 29, 2017. Accessed May 3, 2018. https://www.outsideonline.com/2160416/instagram-ruining-great-outdoors.

Stapleton, Valerie Loughney. "How to Choose Sleeping Pads." *REI*. Accessed April 5, 2018. https://www.rei.com/learn/expert-advice/sleeping-pads.html.

Stone, Lindsey, and Valerie Loughney Stapleton. "How to Wash a Sleeping Bag." *REI*. Accessed April 17, 2018. https://www.rei.com/learn/expert-advice/how-to-clean-a-sleeping-bag.html.

Thomann, Lauren. "10 Camping Ideas for Storing and Organizing Your Gear." *Life Storage Blog*. Posted August 9, 2017. Accessed May 11, 2018. https://www.lifestorage.com/blog/storage/camping-storage-tips/.

"Thunderstorms and Lightning." *Ready*, official website of the Department of Homeland Security. Accessed May 9, 2018. https://www.ready.gov/thunderstorms-lightning.

Tilton, Buck. "Backcountry Diarrhea: Treating the Runs." *Backpacker*. Posted September 30, 1997. Accessed May 7, 2018. https://www.backpacker.com/skills/backcountry-diarrhea-treating-the-runs.

Tkaczyk, Filip. "How to Read a Compass." *Alderleaf Wilderness College*. Accessed April 20, 2018. https://www.wildernesscollege.com/how-to-read-a-compass.html.

Trudeau, Aimee. "Camping Cleanup Tips." *Dirty Gourmet*. Posted September 6, 2012. Accessed May 14, 2018. https://www.dirtygourmet.com/camping-cleanup-tips/.

Turner, Amy. "Eco Hiking in Patagonia: Don't Forget Your Biodegradable Soap!" *Cascada Expediciones*. Posted April 4, 2013. Accessed May 23, 2018. https://www.cascada.travel/en/News /Eco-Hiking-Patagonia-Dont-Forget-Your-Biodegradable-Soap.

USDA Forest Service. "How to Put Out a Campfire." *Okanogan-Wenatchee National Forest*. Accessed May 16, 2018. https://www.fs.usda.gov /detail/okawen/alerts-notices/?cid=fsbdev3_053601.

USDA Forest Service. "If You Get Lost." Accessed November 16 2018. https://www.fs.fed.us/visit/know-before-you-go/if-you-get-lost.

Walker, Magee. "Avoid Cougar Attacks: 7 Things to Do If You Encounter a Big Cat." *The Clymb* (blog). Accessed May 9, 2018. http://blog .theclymb.com/tips/avoid-cougar-attacks/.

Weber, Johnathan, Scott F. Smith, and Michelle Salazar. "How to Choose Rainwear." *REI*. Accessed April 6, 2018. https://www.rei.com /learn/expert-advice/rainwear.html.

WebMD. "How to Prevent Frostbite." Accessed May 4, 2018. https:// www.webmd.com/first-aid/understanding-frostbite-prevention#1.

WebMD. "Hypothermia Treatment." Accessed May 4, 2018. https://www .webmd.com/first-aid/hypothermia-treatment.

WebMD. "Thermal Burns Treatment." Accessed April 24, 2018. https:// www.webmd.com/first-aid/thermal-heat-or-fire-burns -treatment#1.

Wellman, Andy. "How to Choose the Best Down Jacket." *OutdoorGearLab*. Last updated December 18, 2017. Accessed April 6, 2018. https:// www.outdoorgearlab.com/topics/clothing-mens/best-down -jacket/buying-advice.

WikiHow. "How to Make a Duct Tape Bowl." Accessed April 5, 2018. https://www.wikihow.com/Make-a-Duct-Tape-Bowl.

Wilderness Arena. "How to Prevent and Treat Shock in an Injured Person." Posted May 8, 2012. Accessed May 8, 2018. http:// wildernessarena.com/skills/first-aid-health-and-first-aid /preventing-and-treating-shock.

Williams, Chris. "Sexism in the Outdoors." *The Mountaineers Blog*. Posted July 15, 2015. Accessed May 30, 2018. https://www.mountaineers .org/blog/sexism-in-the-outdoors.

Woolman, Shiloh. "Allergies Can Turn Deadly for Some." *Wilderness Medical Associates International*. Accessed May 5, 2018. https:// www.wildmed.com/articles-resources/anaphylaxis-allergies -wilderness-medicine/.